FIVE-PLUS
TOOLS

FIVE-PLUS TOOLS

THE PAST, PRESENT, AND FUTURE OF BASEBALL

THROUGH THE EYES OF A SCOUT

DAVE PERKIN

SPORTS
PUBLISHING

Sports Publishing books may be purchased in bulk at special discounts for sales promotion, corporate gifts, fund-raising, or educational purposes. Special editions can also be created to specifications. For details, contact the Special Sales Department, Sports Publishing, 307 West 36th Street, 11th Floor, New York, NY 10018 or sportspubbooks@skyhorsepublishing.com.

Sports Publishing® is a registered trademark of Skyhorse Publishing, Inc.®, a Delaware corporation.

Visit our website at www.sportspubbooks.com

10 9 8 7 6 5 4 3 2 1

Library of Congress Cataloging-in-Publication Data is available on file.

Cover design by Richard Rossiter
Cover photos courtesy of AP Images

ISBN: 978-1-61321-652-1
Ebook ISBN: 978-1-61321-678-1

Printed in the United States of America

TO GABRIELA

Table of Contents

Preface

I N 2006, I was summoned for jury duty. In the early afternoon
of my first day of service, the clerk called my number and
instructed me to report to a courtroom down the hall.

Unlike most jurors, the legal system does not intimidate me.
In 1984, I served as jury foreman in a murder case. Beginning in
1985, I spent fifteen years working in the legal profession, first as
a paralegal and later as a private investigator. In 2000, I entered
professional baseball and by 2006, I was a scout for the New York
Mets.

Some poor, unfortunate fool was on trial for possession of a
firearm. Considering who is allowed to own guns these days, I
was surprised the guy was on trial. Turns out he was allegedly
violating his parole. In my head, I flippantly reasoned that if the
defendant was mentally deranged but not on parole, he could
own all the rifles he wanted.

The jury selection process (known as voir dire) commenced.

I sat at attention in the jury box, turning my swivel chair to face the prosecuting attorney. Nattily attired and perfectly coiffed, the young lawyer approached me with grim seriousness, and earnest intent. The opening question was incisive:

"So, Mr. Perkin . . ." He paused for dramatic effect.

"If you are a baseball scout . . . does that mean you go out and watch games?"

Stunned, dumbfounded silence enveloped the courtroom.

The judge, who had been using the eraser end of a pencil to clean wax out of his right ear, whipped his head toward the prosecutor. All others in the court were quietly aghast, mouths open and eyes flared wide.

I chuckled slightly. My response was blunt, "Yes, that's the general idea."

Roars of laughter ensued. The prosecutor's face turned a deep, rich, ripe tomato red.

Knowing I couldn't top myself, my desire at that moment was to take a grand bow, tip a silk hat to the crowd, and tap dance out the back door. No such luck.

In a trial, each side has a predetermined set of peremptory challenges, meaning they can dismiss a jury candidate during voir dire without providing a reason to the court.

I was the first juror dismissed.

As the prosecuting attorney quickly realized, to his embarrassment, the obvious essence of scouting is watching baseball games. There is a bit more to it than that, but not much more. A great deal of misunderstanding exists regarding the scouting profession amongst the general public.

There shouldn't be, as it's ridiculously uncomplicated:

Watch players.
Write reports.
Conduct home visits.

Hope your club drafts a player you like.

If they do, try to sign him before the deadline.

Pray you can keep your job.

Do it all over again in the next draft cycle.

A quick primer: All thirty Major League Baseball teams have scouting departments. There are two sides to each scouting department: The professional side and the amateur side. Professional scouts cover players in the major and minor leagues, while amateur scouts cover high school, junior college, and college players in preparation for the annual amateur draft, which is held each June. The draft is 40 rounds long and is now held over a three-day period. That is a stark contrast to the NFL draft (seven rounds) and the NBA draft (two rounds).

An amateur area scout is assigned a specific geographic territory. His work is overseen by a cross checker (a.k.a. regional supervisor). All area scouts and cross checkers operate under the purview of the scouting director. Most of my experience is as a domestic area scout covering amateur players in Southern California and at national showcases.

This book is a collection of essays on scouting and baseball. The first section describes the basics of scouting amateur players in preparation for the annual June Draft. In the second section, I perform a sudden change of course to report on big leaguers I have encountered while also touching on selected classic moments in the game's history. The third section of this book concentrates on critical issues within the baseball industry.

My intent is not to glorify or destroy baseball and scouting or to revolutionize or reinvent either. I simply aim to illuminate a profession the general public knows precious little about.

Scouting should not be an arcane mystery. Still, scouts frequently receive naive questions from well-intentioned civilians.

My favorite question is: "If you sign a player for a multimillion-dollar bonus, do you get a commission?" Uh . . . no. If that were the case, scouts would try to convince the front office to sign a 29th round draftee for $5,000,000.

Another oft asked question is: "Do you scout little leaguers?" Understand that we are interested in a small percentage of college players and an even tinier percentage of high school players. Scouting little leaguers would not only be a personal embarrassment, but constitutes a waste of the organization's time and money.

I live in Southern California, and did so when I worked for the Mets. A playing partner once asked me on the golf course, "If you scout for the New York Mets, then why do you live in Southern California?" Unclear on the concept, was he.

Let me interject a word of warning. If you see a scout at a game, never, ever, ask him for his radar gun or stop watch readings. It's none of your business and is considered inappropriate etiquette.

If you want to know how hard a kid is throwing, get your own radar gun. Don't bother a scout when he is working. I realize it may not seem like work, but it is.

For all the goofy questions we get asked, scouts do occasionally get asked pertinent ones. My favorite is: "What do you look for?"

Now we're talkin'. Now we're gettin' somewhere.

My response to that question is always this:

Forget Hollywood.

All sports movies celebrate the underdog and chronicle his "against all odds" triumph. *Rudy, Seabiscuit, Hoosiers,* and *Cinderella Man* are popular examples.

The plots are familiar. It's about the little guy who is disrespected and disregarded. The kid no one gave a chance to. A scrapper. He's five foot nothin' and weighs 100 nothin'!

Born into poverty with a chip on his shoulder and a dime in his pocket. He battles the odds, beats the big guys at the buzzer and gets the girl to boot!

Forget the reel world and get back to the real world. I have this to say to any player I might scout who is long on heart but short on size and talent:

Get lost, pal.

The public is welcome to watch any film about an undertalented, overachieving, feisty scrapper. Give me the guy who beats him up.

A scene not included in *Cinderella Man* occurred in 1937, when Jim Braddock fought Joe Louis. In the 8th round, Louis knocked Braddock out cold. The impact of Louis's right fist on Braddock's jaw sent sweat from his brow flying 20 rows deep into the ringside seats.

The punch drove Braddock's lower teeth through his lower lip. Twenty-seven stitches were required. When Braddock left the hospital the next day, reporters asked him how it felt to get hit by Joe Louis. Braddock answered, "It's like getting stuck in the face with a broken light bulb."

I don't want a Cinderella Man like Jim Braddock. I want Joe Louis. To heck with Rudy what's-his-name, I want Jim Brown. Secretariat could run backwards wearing blinkers and a shadow roll and beat Seabiscuit by three lengths.

As a scout, I want athletes who are big and strong, throw hard, run fast, and can hit the ball out of sight.

Occasionally, the little guy, the underdog, will succeed in sports. Bully for him. But he is the rare exception to the overwhelming rule. I enjoy a heartwarming Hollywood story as much as anyone, but as a scout I deal in reality, not fantasy.

Unfortunately, this truth rarely infects baseball writers. Virtually every author who tackles the subject of baseball scouting writes flowery prose infused with whimsy and romanticism.

Stuff similar to this:

> Under a translucent sun-dappled azure sky, the wizened faces of the assembled scouts intently followed the action on the pristine diamond. Their deep, abiding love of the game is obvious but unspoken.
>
> Each sage observer, his gaze sharpened by years of experience, makes mental and written notes on every single movement and action of all players cavorting on the sparkling emerald green field.

Horseshit.

. . .

I'VE FALLEN ASLEEP at games. I'm certain every scout has, at least once in his career.

When scouting a high school player, 90 percent of a scout's time is spent hobnobbing and gossiping, talking on a cell phone or sneaking admiring peeks at attractive female fans in attendance.

We pay close attention when the one kid we have driven all this way to observe is hitting or pitching. When that kid is done for the day, we disappear—pronto. Vanish. Scouts rarely stay until the end of a game and almost no scout cares which team wins or loses. When we see what we need to see, we're gone. Bye-bye.

Writers can keep their romantic idealism. Professional baseball is a business first, second, and third. Fourth: it's a game.

The majority of scouts are outgoing, honorable, hard working, and conscientious gentlemen. Regrettably, the profession is sprinkled with back stabbers, social climbers, liars and butt kissers.

Now, don't get me wrong. All scouts truly love baseball and are deeply and sincerely thankful to avoid having a real job. Most scouts, myself included, wouldn't want to do anything else. However, a scout endures relatively low pay, long hours, incessant travel, and mind-numbing tedium. Not the idyllic dream job conjured up by many.

Don't delude yourself about baseball or scouting.

Professional baseball is a viciously political business. There are more double crosses and hidden agendas than in the story line of *The Godfather: Part II*. I've been the victim of baseball politics. All scouts have.

In a perfect description of scouting, a cross checker once said, "Scouting is a great job but a lousy profession."

The capriciousness of scouting is terrifying.

An owner can read one silly bestselling book and decide to fire his entire scouting staff and replace them with stat freaks.

A twenty-five-year-old Ivy League graduate who thinks a slider is a miniature hamburger can get a general manager's job and clean house. One intemperate phone call, one rash email, one unfounded rumor can put a scout out on the street.

Without warning, a scout can be replaced by the son-in-law of a suit in the front office. Quality scouts who work years for one ballclub can get replaced on a whim by the drinking buddy of the new scouting director.

One of the greatest scouts of all time served his organization with remarkable distinction for forty years. He was fired via a message left on his telephone answering machine. The scout had never met or spoken to the person who fired him.

There is no security, that's for sure. Most scouts' contracts are one year in duration, sometimes two. Every scout sweats out renewal time.

A supervisor of mine once told me, "Ain't nobody getting rich in this business." True.

The fabulous wealth in big league baseball is showered on players, not on scouts.

Most scouts begin as unpaid volunteers, formerly called "bird dogs." They're now given the corporate title of "associate." Next, a scout moves up to part-time. He's now under contract and is paid, but he typically receives only $1,000 a month, maximum. Some part-timers also get expenses. Whoopee!

A beginning full-time area scout is paid between $30,000 and $50,000 per year. Experience and/or a promotion to cross checker or regional supervisor may nudge the scout close to the $75,000–$100,000 range. Decent, but Alex Rodriguez makes more than that munching popcorn with Cameron Diaz at the Super Bowl.

By now, I'm certain you're thinking: *What keeps a scout coming back, year after year?*

Love of baseball and love of job are definite factors. A cynic may argue that many scouts don't know any other business and can't do anything else. That is true for only a tiny section of the scouting fraternity nowadays. The vast majority of scouts are smart, educated, multitalented men, many of whom could have their pick of higher paying jobs in other fields. I have my own theory as to why scouts perpetually return. Bear with me on this.

Talent evaluators judge prospects in five baseball skill areas, called "tools": hit, power, run, throw, and field. In their reports, scouts grade a player on a 20–80 scale. A score of 50 represents major league average in any one discipline. A grade significantly over 50 represents what scouts refer to as a "plus" tool.

All separate grades are added together and then divided by five to reach an "OFP" score—Overall Future Potential. It's an Orwellian sounding term, but the OFP grade is by far the most important judgment a scout renders.

Most prospects receive an OFP score under 50. Those who rate a mark from 50 to 60 are candidates to be selected in the early rounds of the draft. The rare, gifted players who are bestowed a score of 60–70 are commonly chosen in the first round.

Once in a generation, maybe once in a scout's lifetime, a prospect merits a 70–80 OFP grade. That baseball player does everything exceedingly well in an exceptionally difficult sport. Those are the Willie Mays, Hank Aaron, Mickey Mantle, and Joe DiMaggio types.

In life, we all search for love, happiness, contentment, fulfillment, financial security, and so on. It's the reason we get out of bed. Every morning we wake up to continue our quest, knowing full well our chances of ever achieving any or all of those goals to be heartbreakingly slim.

A baseball scout returns to the ballpark each new season for a less profound but parallel reason.

The amateur scout's life is a continuous search for a prospect he completely and fully realizes he will probably never find:

A player with "Five-Plus Tools."

Section One: Scouting

1

0–162

I N THE EARLY 1990s, I attended a baseball card and memorabilia show at the Convention Center in downtown Los Angeles.

I wandered throughout the packed convention hall, stopping at an IBM sponsored booth. The proprietor offered prizes to any and all who could answer a series of baseball trivia questions posed by a newfangled device called a Personal Computer.

I successfully breezed through two consecutive trivia games (five questions each) and, for my efforts, was awarded a golf ball imprinted with the company's colorful corporate logo. Why a golf ball was presented as a prize for winning a baseball trivia contest I have no clue. Two months later I drove the golf ball over the back fence of my local driving range.

As I slipped my prize into my pants pocket and walked on to examine other exhibits, a mid-30ish man engaged me in an impromptu conversation.

He was, he assured me, a baseball trivia expert. He proudly informed me that his area of expertise was the Babe Ruth-Lou Gehrig "Murderer's Row" New York Yankees of the 1920s and early '30s.

My new (and totally involuntary) friend puffed his chest out, lifted his chin, and proclaimed, "I've read eleven books on the subject."

"Really? Why, that's wonderful . . ." was my muted, distinctly non-enthusiastic response.

Privately, I concluded that instead of reading eleven Ruth-Gehrig books, a more intelligent use of this man's time would be to take a shower. Or give himself a shave. Perhaps get a job.

Often, in long-term relationships with friends, family, or romantic partners, we deliberately avoid discussing sensitive subjects, sometimes even for years. This not only prevents lingering bitterness, but permits us to avoid flying fists or whizzing dishes.

Since I had instantly recognized that my relationship with Mr. Ruth-Gehrig would be transient, I decided to lay a harsh reality on him. It's a viewpoint I held twenty-two years ago and one I hold just as strongly today.

Many baseball fans instantly and reflexively regard the 1927 New York Yankees as the greatest major league baseball team of all time. Well, I hate to burst your bubble, but the simple truth is this:

If a magical time machine existed which could transport the 1927 Yankees, as they were in their day, into modern major league baseball, *they would lose every single game.*

Nada. Nicht. Nuttin'. Zip. Zero. Bupkis. Today, the 1927 Yankees would get completely and totally destroyed in every single game they played.

Modern ballplayers are taller, bigger, stronger and faster than their counterparts of eighty-seven years ago. The modern player hits farther, throws harder, leaps higher and is substantially quicker and more athletic than ballplayers of the roaring '20s.

Baseball has the richest history and greatest lore of any American sport. The '27 Yankees were the finest team of their decade, rivaled only by the 1929 Philadelphia Athletics. As much as baseball fans revere the game's past, a reality must be acknowledged. The vast majority of pre–World War Two players would have absolutely no chance to compete in today's game.

Let's look at this issue from another perspective.

In 1927, the Heavyweight Champion of the World was Gene Tunney. Great fighter, superb boxer, whipped the tar out of Jack Dempsey twice. Tunney weighed 190 pounds. Today's top heavyweights weigh around 240 pounds. In a bout versus a modern heavyweight, Tunney would get—literally—killed.

How do you think the top basketball or football teams from 1927 would fare today against modern teams? Such a contest, I dare say, would be both an embarrassment and a frightening massacre.

I always snicker when watching a TV program or documentary film in which a baseball historian uses ancient statistics to disparage modern players. Using a professorial tone, the historian (invariably gray- or silver- haired) reflects on the marvels of the old-timers.

The rants classically follow this formula:

Starting pitchers today rarely throw more than 200 innings in a season and they almost never pitch a complete game! Why, in 1884, Old Hoss Radbourn won 59 games, pitched 678 innings, and completed 73 games! In 1903, Iron Man Joe McGinnity pitched 434 innings and completed 44 games! Today's pitchers are soft! They pale in comparison!

What needs to be taken into account is that the game played by Radbourn in 1884 and McGinnity in 1903 bears almost no resemblance to major league baseball today. Athletic talents and baseball skills of modern players are light years ahead of those possessed by ballplayers 100 years ago.

Below is a table that shows height, weight and age averages between the starting fielders of the 1927 Yankees, who went 110–44, and the 2013 Houston Astros, who went 51–111:

Team	Average Height	Average Weight	Average Age
1927 Yankees	72.25 in (6' ¼")	184.75 lb.	27.875 yrs.
2013 Astros	7.3.125 in (6' 1 ¾")	211.75 lb.	26.25 yrs.

Now while the Astros were a younger team, their fielders outweighed the Yankees by an average of 27 pounds, and while two Yankees weighed 200 pounds or more, six Astros fell into the same category. Also, the Yankees had six players who were six-foot or shorter, while the Astros only had one player who fell into that category. That means that 2013 Astros not only towered over the 1927 Yankees, but outweighed them by a substantial amount.

Ancient stats are, in my view, rendered irrelevant due to the overall weakness of the competition. The gaudy, fantastic numbers accumulated by old-timers reflects the inferiority, not the superiority, of Gilded Age and Progressive Era baseball.

Historians may find romance and charm in old-time stats and figures, but as comparative tools, those numbers are meaningless. Today's players are infinitely better than those of 85 to 130 years past.

All of this brings up a fascinating and, among baseball lovers, persistent question: Which great players of the past could play and be successful today?

This question can be answered but not by approaching it from the traditional angle. In keeping records, Major League Baseball considers 1900 to be the beginning of the "Modern Era." There are a lot of ridiculous things in baseball but this has to top the proverbial charts. I'm not sure how 1900 can be considered "modern" when airplane travel was non-existent, almost no one drove cars and much of the nation had no indoor plumbing.

Major League Baseball needs to adjust its record books. The Modern Era should begin in 1947, when the big leagues became integrated. Integration changed the game in myriad ways and the players involved were henceforth significantly more talented and athletic. In the best sense of the term, baseball became a different game.

A simple method can be used to understand the vast superiority of integrated post-1947 baseball over the segregated pre-1947 game. Pick any baseball season in the past ten years. Go to a baseball statistical website and view the top ten league leaders in the primary offensive categories: Home runs, batting average, RBI, hits, runs, etc. Or use saber stats if you prefer.

Next, eliminate from those lists all Black, Hispanic, and Asian players. The list still contains marvelous players, but obviously the overall quality of talent is greatly diminished by eliminating those three groups. For that principal reason, segregated pre-1947 baseball was clearly inferior.

Realize this: Babe Ruth never played a major league game with or against a Black, Hispanic, or Asian player.

Many additional reasons exist for the superiority of today's players, such as improved instruction, superior equipment quality, advanced fitness training, etc., but the primary factor is integration. Segregation rendered the pre-WWII product grossly inferior to the post war, integrated game.

Now back to our original question: Who could play today and who couldn't? I assert that most truly great pre-'47 players could play today. They would not be nearly as successful now as they were back then, but they would be productive.

Ty Cobb, Babe Ruth, Lou Gehrig, Walton Johnson, Lefty Grove, Jimmie Foxx, Hank Greenberg, Joe DiMaggio, Bob Feller, and Ted Williams would be stars in today's game.

My central contention is that fewer of their peers could play today. I'd say only about 20 percent of pre–World War II ballplayers could compete in modern major league baseball. Entire teams and the average pre-'47 big leaguer would fail miserably.

As we speed past 1947, the percentage of players who could make a modern roster increases. I'd say around 50 percent of ballplayers from the 1950s and 1960s could play today, with the percentages inching higher as we creep through the '70s, '80s, and '90s toward the present day.

Willie Mays and Mickey Mantle, along with Hank Aaron, Roberto Clemente, and Frank Robinson would be top-notch stars in this or any other era. Sandy Koufax was a left-handed pitcher who fired a 100 mph fastball mixed with a tremendous curve. I'd venture a guess and say he would find a roster spot in today's game.

In my opinion, the key conclusion to retain is that truly great players from one era would be stars at any other time. Those players would not post the same gaudy numbers as in their heyday, but they would be productive big leaguers.

The critical difference is that, as we travel further and further back into baseball's past, a rapidly diminishing number of players possessed the tools necessary to be competent big leaguers in baseball today.

One venerable baseball story has always infuriated me. Supposedly, a press box conversation in the 1950s focused on Ty Cobb. An old-time sportswriter was asked by a young whippersnapper, "What do you think Cobb would hit today?"

".350," was the veteran's response. "That's all?" replied the young reporter. "Cobb hit .400 three times and had a lifetime mark of .367!"

Dryly, the old man quipped, "You have to remember Cobb is seventy years old."

Now I hate to douse cold water on baseball history romanticists, but today, a twenty-five-year-old Cobb would be hard pressed to hit .310.

You don't need to read eleven books to figure that out.

2

The Basics of Scouting

IN EVALUATING POSITION players during games or showcases, scouts look for five elements:

1. Frame
   A player's build and body type.

2. Tools
   A scouting term which refers to a prospect's raw, basic physical ability. Tools are divided into five categories: run, hit, power, throw, and field.

3. Mechanics
   Indicates the youngster's understanding of the proper fundamentals of baseball and his ability to incorporate them into his game. It is vital to note that scouts prefer to see ballplayers whose mechanics are consistently correct, not occasionally correct.

4. Production
   A player's ability to perform well in actual game situations against quality competition. Every sport has witnessed numerous athletes who dazzle in showcase events or practices but flop in games. Such a player in baseball is

called a "two o'clock hitter," in reference to the time batting practice was taken in the days before night baseball
was introduced. Games commonly started at 3 p.m. in
those days.

5. Makeup
    Does not refer to blush or eyeliner.

> However, I did once see a high school pitcher throw a no-hitter
> while wearing pancake foundation and mascara. He pitched
> shortly after getting out of drama class. The makeup melted
> down his face as the game wore on, giving him an unintended
> Gothic look. This player is now in the minors.

Baseball scouts look for two types of makeup. First is how a player
conducts himself on the field; second is how a player conducts
himself off the field.

Frame

The first and most important element of scouting that the general public must understand is that Major League Baseball in
today's game is the province of big, strong, physical athletes.

Ditch the notion—still promoted by many baseball writers—
that scouts love the small, scrappy little battler who has a big
heart and strong desire but marginal ability. As I pointed out in
the preface to this book, the day those players flourished is long
gone and never to return.

True, there are several excellent undersized players currently in
the majors, such as Dustin Pedroia and Jose Altuve. Today's smaller
player carries one distinct advantage over his ancient counterparts:
they have tools. *Big* tools. Altuve's speed and hit and run tools are
all well above average, and Pedroia's fielding, hitting, and power
tools also grade out high on the scouting scale.

Scan the rosters (or watch the games) of any one of the thirty Major League ball clubs. At seven of the ten positions (P, C, 1B, 3B, LF, RF, DH), almost every single player is at or well above six feet tall and at or beyond 200 pounds.

Undersized players still have a (remote) chance to succeed at shortstop, second base, and center field, but even those opportunities are diminishing. Troy Tulowitzki and J. J. Hardy are big, strong shortstops. Today, we are seeing physical size in center fielders that we have never seen before: Mike Trout, Adam Jones, Carlos Gomez, and Matt Kemp, for example.

When did this trend start? I would pinpoint the late 50s and early 60s. In my video collection, I have kinescopes of the 1960 and 1961 World Series.

In the 1960 Series (Pirates vs. Yankees), I see vestiges of the old game of baseball mixed in with the new game. Representing the old game were smaller pitchers and players such as Bobby Shantz, Bobby Richardson, Yogi Berra, Dick Groat, Smokey Burgess, Rocky Nelson, Don Hoak, and Elroy Face. Few of those players would have any chance of playing today.

Yet, in that same Series, I see several players who represent the size and strength evident in the modern game: Mickey Mantle, Elston Howard, Bill Skowron, Tony Kubek, Dale Long, Vernon Law, and Roberto Clemente.

The 1961 Series (Reds vs. Yankees) provides similar examples. Smaller players like Whitey Ford, Berra, and Richardson are mixed in with big, strong modern style players like Joey Jay, Frank Robinson, Johnny Blanchard, Gordie Coleman, John Edwards, Jim Maloney, and Ralph Terry.

As I viewed portions of the old black and white broadcasts, it was as if I could see the game of baseball changing (slowly) right in front of my eyes. Crafty smaller players with limited raw tools were on display along with modern style players who possessed size, big tools, and powerful arms or bats.

Today, the debate is over, settled. The big guys won. Modern baseball is now a game of size and strength.

As a scout evaluates a prospect's frame, he asks himself this question: Is the player a big, strong, physical athlete, or does he "project" to become one? A projectable player (usually in high school) is one with an athletic build who is tall and lanky. This type of build (particularly if he has broad shoulders) indicates a prospect will be able to add positive weight (muscle) as he matures.

Let's take two hypothetical examples. A scout goes to a high school game. One starting pitcher is a mature framed 5'10" 200 pound righty throwing 90 mph. The other is a 6'4" 160 pound righty with a pipe cleaner build topping out at 88.

So the question is: Who is the pro prospect?

The answer is the skinny kid by a million miles. He is a prospect who should add positive weight in the near future. That muscle should enable him to throw much harder five to seven years down the line. This youngster is a single digit round draft prospect.

The shorter kid has reached his ceiling and will probably not throw harder in the future. Scouts will either draft him very late or simply allow the kid to go to college.

Of course, there are exceptions. Due to the scarcity of left-handed pitching, frame is irrelevant when scouting left-handed pitching prospects. If the kid has a decent arm, a lefty can be the size of Spud Webb and still be a prospect.

As I stated, seven of the ten positions on a modern baseball field are the bailiwick of the big guys.

So what chance does a little guy have? Other than being a left-handed pitcher or the son of a front office executive, to get drafted, a smaller player must possess speed, fielding skill, a bat, and an arm which belie his size. Undersized prospects have a built-in disadvantage. They are limited to one of three spots (center field, shortstop, second base) and must outperform their bigger competitors by an eye-catching margin.

Still, several organizations will ignore a smaller player. When I worked for the New York Mets, I was given the assignment of scouting one of the assembled Area Code teams in Long Beach, California, in August of 2005. On the second day, I was impressed by an undersized righty who showed a decent fastball, excellent secondary pitches, and advanced command. The prospect was 5'10" and 175 pounds. After his outing, I ran up the stairs of the stands on the first base side to report to my scouting director.

"Let me tell you about this guy!" I said excitedly. Our director, a man whom I've always had immense respect for, cut me off before I could utter another word.

"Forget about him," he said, shrugging his shoulders. "Little guy."

Tools
Runs
Of the five tools, speed is the only tool which improves other tools.

If combined with first step quickness and a proper "route" to the ball, a fast player will exhibit substantially better range than an average or slow player, thus improving his fielding grade.

A plus runner automatically has an advantage as a hitter, for he will beat out more infield hits than his slower counterparts, thereby upping his batting average and on-base percentage.

As odd as it may sound, speed also gives a hitter more power at bat, particularly from a statistical standpoint. The speedy hitter can stretch a single into a double or a double into a triple, thereby increasing his number of total bases and, by extension, his slugging percentage.

Despite its unique influence on other tools, speed—and a scout's emphasis on speed—has significantly diminished in recent years. One team in particular, for instance, places no importance on speed whatsoever.

A few years ago, a scout for that team told me, hypothetically, that if one of his supervisors learned he had gone onto the field to time 60-yard dashes at a showcase, he would be verbally berated and possibly fired.

Many other organizations have lessened their grading standards for running times, reflecting the current nature of baseball. Today's game emphasizes physical size and power at the expense of speed. Run times are the only area which, in general, many ball clubs of the relatively recent past were clearly superior to modern teams.

Individual and team speed was prevalent in the '70s and '80s in baseball. That style of play has almost completely vanished in today's game. For instance, it is exceptionally rare to see a modern American League team attempt a squeeze play or double steal.

On the 20–80 scout grading scale, here are the modern standards for running speeds. Keep in mind that this chart is not universal, as some organizations have slight variations.

60 Yard Dash	
Time	Grade
6.4	80
6.5	75
6.6	70
6.7	65
6.8	60
6.9	55
7.0	50
7.1	45

7.2	40
7.3	35
7.4	30
7.5	25
7.6+	20

Sports fans are familiar with the 40-yard dash standard used in pro and college football. Baseball uses the 60-yard dash standard as a speed gauge because of its commonality in the game: 60 yards (180 feet) is the distance from home to second, first to third, and second to home.

Home to First Right-Handed Hitter		
Full Swing	Bunt	Grade
4.0	3.8	80
4.05	3.85	75
4.1	3.9	70
4.15	3.95	65
4.2	4.0	60
4.25	4.05	55
4.3	4.1	50
4.35	4.15	45
4.4	4.2	40
4.45	4.25	35
4.5	4.3	30
4.55	4.35	25
4.6	4.4	20

The fastest prospect I have ever timed was DeSean Jackson, now a superstar wide receiver with the Washington Redskins of the NFL. As a right-handed hitting outfielder for Long Beach Poly High School in 2005, Jackson rapped a ground ball to shortstop in his first at bat in game versus El Segundo High, getting down the line in 3.79 seconds. In his second at-bat that night, Jackson tried to bunt his way on base. I timed him in 3.58 seconds.

I was lucky that evening. Many scouts can spend thirty, forty, possibly fifty years in the business and never time a player who was as fast as DeSean Jackson.

Home to First Left-Handed Hitter		
Full Swing	Bunt	Grade
3.9	3.7	80
3.95	3.75	75
4.0	3.8	70
4.05	3.85	65
4.1	3.9	60
4.15	3.95	55
4.2	4.0	50
4.25	4.05	45
4.3	4.1	40
4.35	4.15	35
4.4	4.2	30
4.45	4.25	25
4.5	4.3	20

Knowledgeable baseball fans are acutely aware that running speed is useless if a player does not know how to utilize his speed.

A veteran scout once informed me that Rickey Henderson's best 60-yard dash time was around 6.6. That is outstanding speed, but dozens, perhaps hundreds, of players in big league history have had superior times.

The key is that Henderson knew how to use his speed. Rickey's first step quickness was extraordinary, plus his ability to read a pitcher's pickoff move and time his jump perfectly was remarkable.

By contrast, Herb Washington may have been the fastest player in baseball history. A world class sprinter from Michigan State University, Washington was employed as a designated pinch runner by the A's in the mid-'70s.

In the second game of the 1974 World Series, Washington came in to pinch run in the top of the ninth, representing the tying run. Dodger reliever Mike Marshall picked Washington off by two feet, effectively ending the game and the designated pinch runner experiment.

Unfortunately for Herb Washington, bases are not stolen by using sprinter's blocks or a starter's pistol.

For the majority of position players, speed is the one tool that dissipates most rapidly. As ballplayers progress into their thirties, most retain their bat and arm strength but their legs deteriorate. Vladimir Guerrero is a prime example. A 30–40 per year base stealer as a youngster, Vlad could barely get down the line in his mid-thirties.

On occasion, a scout will give a player a reverse run grade. Let's postulate that a D-1 college catcher is a top draft prospect. He has a strong, mature build; a classic backstop's frame. Most scouts, taking note of the catcher's body and the rigors of his position, will assume that his running speed will lessen as he nears age thirty. Therefore, this type of player may receive a current speed grade of 45 but a future speed grade of 35.

Unlike the NFL and NBA, advanced speed training is rarely part of a ballclub's strength and conditioning regimen. Combined with modern offensive philosophies, this depressing reality has reduced modern stolen base totals, even among players with outstanding speed. Jeff Francoeur and Justin Upton received 80 speed grades as amateur prospects. Last year, Francoeur had two steals, while Upton had eight.

I maintain that running speed is the rarest and most exciting of the five tools. It is the only tool that profoundly affects the other tools. MLB scouts should be embracing speed, not downplaying or rejecting it.

Hit/Power
Hitting is by far the most difficult tool to judge.

"No one really knows if a guy is going to hit," a cross checker once told me. That opinion is a common one in the scouting industry for one simple reason: it's true.

A scout attempts to determine if an eighteen-year-old high school kid can, seven years from now, hit major league pitching well enough to maintain a starting job. Hitting is perhaps the most difficult skill in all of sports, and "projecting" hitters is just as problematic.

Judging hitting is tough for a variety of reasons. An amateur player faces pitching which is vastly inferior to professional pitching. College and high school infielders and outfielders are not as adept defensively as professionals; so many batted balls that would normally be routinely fielded will drop in for hits in amateur ball.

Most high school ballparks are also significantly smaller in outfield dimensions and in foul territory than are big league fields. Many fouls that are out of play in a high school park would be caught in a pro park; the same with home runs.

The composition of the baseballs is another factor. Amateur baseballs have raised seams and less lively inner cores. (The NCAA will use flatter seamed baseballs soon, but they will not have lively pro style cores, as of yet.)

College and high school baseballs have a COR (Coefficient of Restitution) of .555. Flat, or rolled, seamed pro balls have a COR rating of .578. If struck with the same amount of force, a pro ball will travel approximately 20 feet farther than an amateur baseball.

Of all the factors, the bat is the main differential between amateur and pro baseball. All bats in pro ball, major or minor leagues, must be made of wood. The two most popular types of wood for use in pro bats are maple and northern white ash.

Gone with the wind are supercharged metal bats that produce 21–14 NCAA D-1 title games. Colleges and high schools now use BBCOR bats (Ball-Bat Coefficient of Restitution). These bats are also made of metal but are manufactured to more closely approximate the qualities and impact response of a wood bat but without the cost or danger of breaking.

All of these variables make hitting more difficult to judge than speed, for instance. Sixty yards in the majors is the same distance as 60 yards in high school: the distance between home and first in high school is 90 feet, same as the big leagues.

Despite the advent of advanced sabermetrics, grading, fielding, and hitting remain a subjective exercise for scouts. Radar guns can measure the velocity of a thrown baseball, stopwatches can measure running speed, but even in the modern world grading fielding and hitting is done almost solely by "gut" reaction. Lots and lots of observation, but still, a gut instinct.

Naturally, a scout hopes to observe a top hitting prospect in an environment which resembles pro baseball, however faintly.

Ideally, scouts want to see a hitter square off in his spring season against a pitcher who also has top-notch ability.

Summer showcases serve a useful purpose for scouts. We can see the best hitting prospects face the top pitching prospects. Scouts get the critically important opportunity to observe a hitter using a wood bat in both batting practice and game situations.

A quick bit of inside info: When scouting high school hitters, scouts hope to watch the youngster in a road game, not a home game. With high school games lasting only seven innings, watching a road game gives the scout a much better opportunity of seeing an extra at bat in the seventh inning.

What does a scout look for in a hitter? Of the four basics (frame, tools, mechanics, production), frame is the least important. In baseball history, truly great hitters have ranged from the tall and lanky (a young Ted Williams) to short and pudgy (Kirby Puckett). Perhaps no one skill in any sport has seen such a diverse range of body types succeed than in the art of hitting a baseball.

Need some proof? In NBA history, have any great scorers been tall and rangy? Yes, of course. Have any been built like Kirby Puckett, Yogi Berra, Hack Wilson, or Thurman Munson? No. In NFL history, have any great quarterbacks been built like the latter baseball players? No.

In my view, success in hitting is based on three factors:

1. Talent
2. Knowledge
3. Work

Raw talent in hitting encompasses two items: Vision and bat speed.

Vision—extraordinary eyesight—is the one common gift amongst almost every outstanding hitter. In perhaps no other athletic endeavor is visual acuity as crucial as in hitting a baseball.

Dating back to Rogers Hornsby, Babe Ruth, and Ted Williams and continuing to the modern day, nearly every legendary hitter has been blessed with phenomenal natural vision. Exceptional eyesight is the single most important physical trait a hitter can possess.

We're all familiar with the Snellen eye test, in which lines of black letters of gradually diminishing sizes are set against a white background. Measured in feet, preferred vision is 20/20 (or 6/6 by European metric standards).

Additional vision exams are far more detailed and complicated than reading letters on a chart. Hitting entails the ability not only to identify a baseball hurtling toward the plate and to separate it from background objects, but to "read" its speed, spin, and location.

Other types of eye exams can test peripheral vision, object identification, etc. Therefore, ball clubs are interested not only in Snellen results but in the results of more complicated, in-depth eye exams.

Many ball clubs do not conduct these tests themselves. Instead, they rely on vision test results performed on each prospect which are provided by the Major League Scouting Bureau. Selected ball clubs perform their own vision exams, independent of the Bureau. The Kansas City Royals have long administered their own eye exams.

In an article published by *Sports Illustrated* on August 8, 2011, entitled "Major League Vision," writer David Epstein pointed out that the *average* visual acuity for pro baseball players is 20/13. 20/13! A tiny percentage of players scored 20/9 or better. Interestingly, Epstein states that big leaguers on average recorded better vision scores than minor leaguers.

What is so important about vision in hitting? Let's compare a person with normal 20/20 sight and a big leaguer with 20/10 sight. The big leaguer can see an object with clarity and specificity at 20 feet; the average Joe must be 10 feet away to see the object with the same precision.

A major league fastball traveling between 90 and 100 miles an hour requires only between .36 and .45 of a second to reach home plate. A hitter with 20/10 vision can identify that pitch 10 feet sooner than a person with 20/20 vision. That extra fraction of time permits the 20/10 hitter to make a better, more informed decision as to whether that pitch is one he wants to swing at or one he prefers to take.

When evaluating amateur hitting prospects in preparation for the draft, scouts compile reams of information. From my perspective, the most important measurement an organization compiles—far more important than saber stats—are the results of a youngster's in-depth vision exam. No single bit of information is as accurate a harbinger of a batter's potential for future success.

The second component of raw talent is bat speed, but don't confuse exit speed with bat speed. Exit speed is the velocity at which a batted ball leaves the bat after contact with an incoming pitch. Exit speeds for big league hitters are often at or well in excess of 100 miles per hour.

Bat speed is the speed at which the bat itself is traveling as it is propelled by the hitter. Major league bat speed ranges, generally, from 70 to 85 mph. A small coterie of hitters can exceed 85 mph.

Bat speed has several ingredients. The three main ingredients are hand-eye coordination, quick reflexes, and physical strength. Along with proper hitting mechanics, bat speed can be improved as a player develops. However, the majority of bat speed is a "either you got it or you don't" proposition. That is, natural, God given, raw talent.

Scouts commonly judge bat speed by simple observation, noting how the ball reacts off a hitter's bat or the velocity with which a batter swings his bat. Being able to "turn on" an inside fastball is another way scouts gauge bat speed.

Measuring bat speed is actually fairly simple. Give a prospect a wood bat and then place a baseball on a tee. To prevent decapitation, hide behind some sort of screen. With a radar gun, measure the speed of the ball as it launches off the tee. Because the ball in this drill begins in a stationary position, there is no impetus from an incoming pitch to add to the ball's exit speed; the bat alone imparts velocity to the ball. Voila! Bat speed.

Among modern hitters, my educated guess is that Giancarlo Stanton and Yoenis Cespedes possess the fastest bats in big league baseball. Mike Trout, Yasiel Puig, Bryce Harper, Mark Trumbo, Prince Fielder, Robinson Cano, and Miguel Cabrera are probably in the plus 85 mph range.

Historically, Willie Mays, Mickey Mantle, and Hank Aaron probably had the best bat speed of the '50s and '60s; Reggie Jackson and Richie Allen in the '70s; Andre Dawson and Bo Jackson in the '80s; Ken Griffey, Jr. and Barry Bonds in the '90s; and Gary Sheffield in the 2000s. While there was no measuring device in existence in the '30s and '40s, my assumption is that the all-time king of bat speed was Josh Gibson, the Hall of Fame Negro League catcher.

It is vital to note that bat speed alone does not make a great hitter, as many other factors are involved. The fastest bat speed I have ever witnessed belonged to Ruben Rivera, who in 2001 played with the Cincinnati Reds. In batting practice, Rivera would take a ridiculously easy swing and loft the ball halfway up the outfield pavilion at Dodger Stadium. Rivera hit .216 in nine big league seasons with a grand total of 64 home runs.

Conversely, lack of superlative bat speed is not a death sentence. In 1994, the Toronto Blue Jays conducted bat speed tests on their hitters. Turns out the slowest bat belonged to John Olerud, the Jays first baseman and best hitter, who had just led the AL with a .363 batting average. Olerud's relatively slow bat had a reverse advantage, for his bat remained in the hitting zone longer than other players'.

Science, medicine, and high-tech training can improve vision and bat speed, but only slightly. The basic, raw talent required for hitting a baseball can be suitably summed up in this line from the Oscar winning film *Chariots of Fire*: "You can't put in what God left out."

Baseball experts and fans have long engaged in this debate: Is a hitter born or made? My answer is both. A hitter is first born and then made. It's important to understand that this equation is unbalanced. In my opinion, a great hitter is approximately 75 percent born and 25 percent made.

It is a common sight today for parents to shuttle their child from one private hitting coach to another, hoping one particular coach has that magic piece of advice or rare bit of insight that can transform his kid from a .150 Little League hitter into Ted Williams. Coaching quality varies wildly from teacher to teacher, but parents must understand this one fact: 80 percent of a hitter's success is determined at conception; it is genetic. Even the smartest coach can't overcome that truth.

Next is knowledge. A hitter has to thoroughly understand the proper fundamentals and mechanics of his craft. He then has to implement those correct mechanics into his swing on a consistent and not an occasional basis.

As a scout, these are the main technical points I look for in a hitting prospect:

Each swing a hitter takes has four sections: Stance, Load (backwards weight shift), Stride, and Swing. The first critical component dictates that a hitter maintains his balance through-out all four sections of his swing.

When a hitter completes his stride, he is in the "launch" posi-tion. Swings taught by amateur coaches often differ from swings taught by pros, but these are the classic characteristics of a pro launch position:

- The back foot should be pointed straight, not angled in or out.
- The front foot should be angled open to 45 degrees.
- The knees should be in a slight "knocked" position, with the weight centered on the inside, not the outside, of the thighs.
- Both feet must be positioned inside of the knees.
- The front hip and shoulder must be closed, not open.
- The front shoulder should be tucked underneath the chin.
- The head's position should be square, so that both eyes look directly at the pitcher, no angling or tilting of head.
- The back elbow must be pointed with wrists cocked so that the bat is held at a 45 degree angle above the helmet (not behind the head).
- A "bridge," meaning the front elbow is bent and not stiff or straight.

Separation is also critical at this stage. This term means that a hitter's hands should be spaced away from his body properly, so that his hands and arms can work freely and independently as he swings. This can be a bit tricky; not enough space and the arms get pinned to the body, too much and the swing becomes far too long. A consensus among pro hitting coaches I have spoken with indicates that proper separation is achieved when the hands are positioned even or slightly beyond the back shoulder and almost directly over the back foot at the launch position.

From the launch position, a hitter makes a critical decision: To swing or not to swing? When a batter begins his swing, the first component I look for is a compact backswing. The backswing must be free of unnecessary length or movement, and a batter's path to the ball must be direct. I have never seen a successful hitter with a long, hitched, or otherwise poor backswing.

Dropping the back elbow initiates a hitter's swing, beginning a chain reaction of activity. For me, the three crucial factors are front shoulder, head position, and swing path.

First is a hitter's front shoulder. The lead shoulder must begin in a closed posture; a hitter then drives it down slightly and at the target, which, of course, is the ball. Far too often scouts observe what I call the "High School Drift," in which an amateur hitter pulls his lead shoulder up, out, and open.

Second, a hitter must track the ball with his eyes before it leaves the pitcher's hand, all the way to contact (he hopes) with his bat. Imagine a sniper or an Olympic sharpshooter staring down the length of his rifle. He's not looking up, down, left, or right; he is staring directly down the barrel of the weapon. That is what a big league hitter does—he looks right down the bat barrel at contact and often keeps his head down in that position until his hands have cleared his front knee.

Third is swing path. The single most important fundamental of hitting dictates that a hitter, as he starts his swing, keeps *his hands inside the ball.* Swinging outside or around the ball is death to a hitter at any level. Keeping the hands inside increases bat control, power, and allows the hitter to drive the ball to all fields with authority. Next, the batter pulls his hands across his chest, dropping them into the proper slot to start the bat to the ball.

Keep in mind that the exhortation of your Little League coach to "Hit down on the ball" is useless. A correct swing path is on a slight upward angle of about 10 degrees. This upward path permits the bat to remain generally on the same plane as the incoming pitch (which usually is descending) and allows the hitter a much larger "zone" to make contact in.

Ideally, a hitter will make contact with the ball when his hands are in the classic "palm up, palm down" position. The palm of the bottom hand should face down and the palm of the top hand should face up. At this stage, it is critical that the batter avoid the "tennis forehand." In order to keep the ball in the court, a tennis player rolls his/her wrists immediately when hitting a forehand shot. If a batter makes this mistake, he will put topspin on the ball; almost all pro hitters aim to put backspin on the ball.

After contact, a hitter avoids rolling his wrists and then fully extends his arms into a "power V." At this stage, the hitter's bat should be pointing directly toward the middle of the diamond, his extended arms forming a "V." He then rolls or snaps his wrists and completes the swing by finishing or clearing his hands high, typically above his head.

One aspect of hitting frequently ignored by amateur coaches and players is the concept of "letting the hands go." Study videos of Willie Mays, Hank Aaron, Ernie Banks, and Frank Robinson. Notice how each of these hitters uses his hands to violently whip the bat head at the ball, generating bat and exit speed. Too many hitters in modern amateur baseball push or shove the bat through the strike zone, drastically robbing themselves of power.

Proper hitting fundamentals are critical, but a scout should not obsess on mechanics when evaluating an amateur hitter, particularly one in high school. Scouts are primarily searching for raw talent, bat speed, and aggressiveness in attacking a pitch. If a talented youngster has a few flaws in his swing, a scout can accept that on the assumption that the organization's player development personnel can perform corrections.

Assume you are watching a "nature" program on cable TV. A feline predator is crouched in the brush, waiting to pounce on his prey which will provide that day's meal. The lion, tiger, panther, etc., is not worrying about his mechanics. He doesn't say to himself, "You know, my fundamentals on that last kill were poor. I need to position my left paw in a 12 degree inverse axis ratio in relation to the posture of my inverted . . ." A predator cares only about picking the right moment to strike and attack, using his innate natural ability—speed, quickness, and strength. These talents are often breathtaking, despite their viciousness.

Primarily, that is what scouts want to see in a hitting prospect—natural ability. Attack the pitch like a panther, using your bat speed and quickness. Don't sweat the details too much at this early stage. Mechanics are important, of course, but if a hitting prospect's fundamentals aren't perfect, it's not a disqualifier. We'll work on that part.

The final component for every successful hitter is work. Years of practice and game experience are required for any athlete to have the slightest chance to be a productive professional hitter.

Remember that *no* hitter can be successful with one or two of the three factors; every successful hitter requires all three factors: talent, knowledge, work.

Let's postulate that a scout has zeroed in on a hot hitting prospect in his area. Off and on for two years, the scout has followed this player. He's seen the youngster perform in wood bat showcases and metal bat spring high school games. The scout has evaluated the hitter's talent, knowledge, and work ethic; he's examined—by video and observation—every detail of the hitter's mechanics and fundamentals.

Now the scout is prepared to grade the prospect.

All organizations grade a prospect in hitting, power, and power frequency. Two separate grades—present and future—are given in each of the three areas. The future grade is the most important score because what an amateur player will be is far more critical than what he is now.

Future "OFP" grading scales for hitting and power generally break down along these parameters:

Batting Average	Grade
.310+	80
.290–.309	70
.275–.289	60
.260–.274	50
.240–.259	40
.230–.239	30
.229 -	20

Home Run Frequency	Grade
40+	80
30–39	70
25–29	60
16–24	50
10–15	40
5–9	30
0–4	20

Remember that this scale is not universal in pro ball; it may vary somewhat from club to club. Grade scales are often adjusted in accordance to the type of "era" baseball is experiencing. During the steroid era, 45 + was 80 power frequency; but in our more tame current offensive era, the standard has been altered downward by some clubs.

After meticulous consideration, the scout will then assign a number grade to the youngster's hitting and power tools. Next the scout will hope to avoid an irate, screaming phone call from his cross checker or director.

How difficult is it to forecast hitting and power? Let's examine one of many, many examples. In 2007, the third overall pick in the draft was Josh Vitters, a third baseman from Cypress High School in Southern California. Vitters, selected by the Cubs, has had a "cup of coffee" in the majors, but is currently mired in the minors. (As of the beginning of the 2014 season, Vitters was playing for the Cubs AAA affiliate in Iowa.)

Both Giancarlo Stanton and Freddie Freeman were buried deep in the second round of the 2007 draft. Obviously, if the Cubs (or any organization) knew in 2007 what they know now, Stanton would have been the third overall pick, followed closely by Freeman. Vitters would have been the guy selected deep in the second round.

One firm conclusion can be reached: Hitting and power are by far the most difficult tools for scouts to judge; they are also the most important tools for scouts to judge.

Throw
One of the endearing oddities of baseball is that each position on the field has its own separate throwing arm requirements.

A right fielder, shortstop, or third baseman must have a cannon; a first baseman's arm is nearly irrelevant. It's a pleasant convenience for a center fielder, left fielder, or second baseman to have a strong arm, but other attributes are far more prized at those positions.

Few fans contemplate that a catcher, when he attempts to throw a runner out at second base, is delivering the ball over 42 yards. That's nearly long bomb or "9" route distance in football. The catcher has to deliver the ball in less than two seconds and typically releases the ball next to his right ear.

A strong throwing arm is classically the first tool to develop and is noticeably evident as early as little league. Scouts zero in on two basic elements in evaluating arms.

First is ease of the throwing motion. Any arm action that is awkward, stiff, or truncated is a warning flag for talent evaluators. Almost every top-notch baseball player has a throwing motion which is full, easy, and fluid.

Second is velocity and trajectory. Scouts look for raw speed on throws and a flight path which follows a straight line instead of arching trajectory. One telltale sign of a powerful throw, particularly from the outfield, is how the ball reacts if it is intentionally bounced into the target. Weak throws lose steam and roll; strong throws skip quickly and pick up momentum.

On rare occasions, scouts will aim a radar gun at a position player during a game. I'll never forget the sight of scouts clustered behind first base when Troy Tulowitzki was a draft eligible shortstop at Long Beach State. His best throw across the diamond was clocked at 94 mph.

Pre-game infield/outfield drills at ball games or showcases openly reveal who can throw and who can't. Velocity and trajectory are closely watched by scouts as outfielders and then infielders make their tosses. At showcases all outfielders throw from right field. It makes no difference if an infielder is a second baseman, third baseman, or shortstop during games, for in a showcase all infielders throw from deep in the shortstop hole . . . and for good reason. During a pre-draft workout in 2006, one of my colleagues with the New York Mets told a player during infield drills, "You need to show 'em arm strength. That's what they're lookin' for!"

Catcher's arms are the only ones evaluated by a stopwatch. At showcases, a coach stands about halfway between the mound and the plate and slightly off to the right side of the diamond to avoid getting beaned. He flips a series of throws to all catchers, who are in full equipment. Each backstop fires between three and five balls to second. The elapsed time from the instant the catcher receives the ball to the instant it touches a middle infielder's glove is called a "pop" time.

Here are the general grading standards for catcher's pop times:

Time	Grade
1.70	80
1.75	75
1.80	70
1.85	65
1.90	60
1.95	55
2.00	50
2.05	45
2.10	40
2.15	35
2.20	30
2.25	25
2.30	20

The quickest pop times I have ever recorded were posted by two high school catchers. The second fastest was Austin Hedges, currently a rising star in the Padres organization. I timed Hedges in 1.78.

The fastest was Chris Rivera, currently an infielder in the Cardinals organization. Rivera almost never caught during a game, so I was shocked when he took a turn behind the dish at a showcase and fired off a 1.77 throw to second.

Throwing arm strength is an easy tool to judge. With the possible exception of catchers, the throw tool is not the most important position player tool, but it is still vital.

A strong outfield arm nails runners on the bases and prevents many from attempting to advance. Infielders with strong arms can play deeper than normal and improve their range. Most critically, a powerful arm is often the deciding factor in a close play.

A powerful arm ensures a player at least some playing time. An old-time scout once told me, "If a guy can't run, hit, or field, but has a big arm—Christ, we'll find somethin' for him to do!"

Field

In baseball, the most spectacular, visually stunning portion of the game is fielding. On a daily basis, big leaguers make plays that defy both gravity and belief.

Yet fielding gets the least attention from scouts among the five tools . . . as well as the least respect. The Hit-Power-Throw-Run tools are all more highly prized at almost every position than is the Field tool.

Imagine that a scout has within his territory a prominent D-1 college program. The school's first baseman is 6'4" 230 pounds, and receives a 70 OFP hit and 75 OFP power grade from the scout. Next, the scout drops a 35 OFP score on his run, throw, and field tools. This places the player's total OFP at 50 (250 divided by 5).

This school's shortstop is 5'10" 170 pounds. Our scout places a 40 grade on his hitting and 30 on his power, yet he awards a 60 OFP on his glove, arm, and speed. When totaled, this player's OFP is also 250/50.

Both players received the exact same OFP scores, but who is the first round candidate? The answer is the first baseman, since hitting and power are much more prized in the draft than are arm, glove, and speed. The shortstop will probably get drafted in a later round. He will be offered hundreds of thousands or millions of dollars less in bonus money than the first baseman.

While not as lucrative as hitting, fielding is a critical part of baseball. In judging defense, scouts focus on three areas: Actions-Jump-Range.

An "easy actions guy" is a defensive player—usually an infielder—whose fielding actions are smooth, fluid, and devoid of any stiffness or awkwardness. Omar Vizquel would be the poster boy for an easy actions fielder.

Judging actions is a purely subjective exercise, since no stat, radar gun, or stopwatch can measure it. Still, it is a skill that is exceptionally easy to notice. When watching pre-game infield/outfield warm-ups, everyone from novice to expert scouts can identify the rare player who can "pick it."

Jumps are trickier to assess. "Getting a Jump" is an ancient baseball term which refers not only to how quickly the fielder reacts to a batted ball, but if his initial steps are taken in the correct direction. (How many times have you seen an outfielder react instantly, start in for a ball, but then have to backpedal furiously? Or start back and then rush in?)

In evaluating jumps, scouts look for two red flags. First is "freezing." In some instances, a fielder must pause immediately after the ball is hit to gauge it, but in most cases freezing indicates a fielder's inability to read the ball as it comes off the bat.

Second is "standing up." All fielders begin in a slight crouch. On a fly ball or ground ball, if a fielder stands up *before* taking his crossover step toward the ball, he robs himself of range.

I can't find a reference to this anecdote on the Internet, but I recall about thirty years ago reading that Bill Mazeroski, the Hall of Fame defensive second baseman wizard for the Pirates and World Series hero, worked with Tim Wallach, then a young Expo third baseman. Maz noticed that Wallach, when a ball was hit in his vicinity, was standing up out of his fielding crouch before making his move to the ball. Maz helped Wallach make the correction and Wallach, despite the fact he was not particularly fast, improved his jumps and range immensely to become one his era's best defensive third basemen.

Range (a fielder's knack for consistently "getting to" the ball) is a combination of several factors: speed, jump, and route. Speed is an obvious aid to a defensive player's range, but not every fast player has great range. Rare players without superlative speed often have terrific range, due to their quick jumps and ideal routes. Think Jim Edmonds.

Strong arms, especially on the infield, can increase range. Cal Ripken Jr., whose speed was below average, handled a remarkable number of chances as a shortstop. His arm permitted him to play deeper and get to balls others could not and his magically quick release was extraordinary.

A quick and proper jump greatly increases a fielder's range, since success on the majority of defensive plays is determined in the first few milliseconds after a ball is hit.

Be careful in judging defensive stats from the past and comparing them to modern players. Let's next cover center fielders. In the 1950s, many ballparks had deep center-field fences: Yankee Stadium, Polo Grounds, Tiger Stadium, Forbes Field, etc. With the exception of Minute Maid Park in Houston, modern center field dimensions rarely exceed 400–410 feet.

Ballpark factors, combined with the fact that modern hitters strike out much more frequently, serve to depress putout totals of modern outfielders. We may never see another center fielder record 500 plus putouts in a season, as Richie Ashburn did several times in his career. That does not mean, however, that today's outfielders are inferior to those of the past; they simply have fewer opportunities to make plays.

Route refers to a fielder's path to a batted ball. A direct path is usually preferable; however, there are selected plays in which a fielder will need to circle the ball.

In amateur games it is not uncommon for scouts to see outfielders take routes which resemble an escaped prisoner being chased by bloodhounds. Let's say a scout is watching a center field prospect. A drive is hit to the player's right, into the left field gap. The scout wants to see actions, speed, and a jump, but in this case he is focusing on the route.

Many amateur outfielders will move laterally in a straight line to their right and then directly back in a sort of 90 degree angle or "L" route. The correct route is a diagonal route, approximating a back slash on a keyboard.

Scouts fully understand that the majority of top prospects have spent far more time working on their hitting and throwing than they have on fielding. Scouts are not expecting to see refined defensive skills even on elite draft prospects. As with other tools, scouts are searching for the basics: instincts and raw ability, which, they hope (and often pray) the coaches in their organization can fully develop.

For me, improving fielding is also a revealer of character. Everyone loves to hit. Outstanding hitters love to show off, plus they enjoy the glamour that comes with being an elite hitter. Working to improve as a hitter is fun. Enjoyable.

Improving from a below average or average fielder to an above average defender is difficult, often dreary work, containing little glamour and receiving scant notoriety. When a fielder has improved drastically, the change is obvious and dramatic. The prospect who dedicates himself to that effort has shown me outstanding makeup and character.

· · ·

Having covered the five position player tools, let's now concentrate on pitching.

Due to the paucity of quality left-handed pitching available in baseball, scouts basically ignore the build and frame of a lefty pitching prospect. This is not the same with right-handers. Few short and/or stout righties receive much early round draft attention.

When observing a right-handed pitching prospect, scouts prefer a tall (at or above 6'2") youngster with a lanky "projectable" build. Additional preferred physical traits include big hands, long fingers, long arms, long legs, and broad shoulders.

This type of body contains several built-in advantages. Projection is the first advantage, for this body type indicates the pitcher can add positive weight (muscle) as he matures, increasing the likelihood he will throw much harder at the age of twenty-five than he does at eighteen.

The second advantage is the tall pitcher's increased ability to deliver the pitch on a consistent downward plane. A 6'4" righty standing on a 10" mound delivering the ball on a downward plane creates a severe tilted angle, permitting his pitch to catch a very small sliver of the strike zone. Michael Wacha, the brilliant young pitching star of the St. Louis Cardinals, is particularly adept at this tactic.

Creating angles is exceptionally important to a pitcher's success. No pitcher aims to have his delivery catch a large portion of the strike zone, since that makes a pitch substantially easier to hit. Every hurler aims to throw strikes which nick a tiny portion of the zone. One longtime pitching coach, a former big leaguer, was recently quoted thusly: "It's all about creating angles!"

Height and long arms create a final advantage by "shortening the distance." On average, a pitcher releases the ball 4 feet in front of the rubber. Therefore a fastball typically travels 56.5 feet from the pitcher's hand to the front of home plate.

Tall pitchers with octopus arms can reduce that distance, enabling, say, a 92 mph fastball released 5 feet in front of the slab to arrive at the plate as quickly as a 94 mph fastball released from 4 feet in front of the slab.[1] Shortening the distance gives a pitcher with average velocity (50 on the grading scale) a fastball that arrives in the same amount of time as a fastball graded at 55 or 60.

Whilst observing pitchers, scouts pay rapt attention to the ease of delivery. We prefer to see an arm action which is smooth, fluid, and free of stiffness, awkwardness, and restriction. Looseness in the hips is also a valuable asset for any pitcher. During the delivery of a pitch, a hurler's hips will turn and torque quite severely. Therefore, it is essential that a pitching prospect show a strong core and an easy rotation through the midsection.

Understand that the terms "control" and "command" in baseball circles does not mean simply getting the ball over the plate. Any dope can do that. Pitchers need to pinpoint the ball into specific, restricted areas of the strike zone—not the heart of the plate.

Scouts hope to see command and control in pitchers that is consistent and not occasional. Pitching prospects must also display the ability to command *all* of their pitches—from the beginning of an outing to the end of an outing.

In scouting, the words "secondary pitches" or "secondaries" refer to any offering that is not a fastball. This includes the obvious curve, slider, and changeup, but can also refer to more exotic offerings such as a splitter, screwball, palmball, or knuckler (if that is not the pitcher's primary weapon).

---

1 My calculations show that a 92 mph fastball takes .411 of a second to travel 55.5 feet. A 94 mph fastball travels 56½ feet in .410 of a second.

Scouts note the consistency of the secondary pitches and their shape, command, and spin tightness. One scouting director once told me that if you pay close attention, you'll find there are almost as many curve types as there are pitchers.

Scouts are always asked in their reports to compare an amateur pitcher to an established big leaguer in order to give the front office types a mental picture of what the kid looks like.

A scout friend of mine once told me that the great scout Jesse Flores once said to him, "Don't worry about who the guy reminds you of. Ask yourself: Whose *stuff* does he remind you of? That's a better comparison."

Now for a quick diversion regarding the changeup. Baseball, like any other profession, goes through eras and fads. The "it" pitch of the 1980s, for instance, was the split fingered fastball.

Today's "it" pitch is the changeup. In big league baseball, we see changeups thrown in situations that we never would have twenty plus years ago: on a first pitch, back to back, behind in the count, etc. This trend shows no sign of abating, so pitching prospects take notice: your change should not be an afterthought. In modern baseball, the change is as important to develop and use as is the fastball and breaking ball.

In observing pitching prospects, scouts always evaluate mechanics. Scouts concede that the quality of pitching mechanics in amateur hurlers varies wildly and is often horrendous. Yet scouts understand that poor command is often the result of poor mechanics; that is, command and mechanics are flip sides of the same coin.

A scout notes what a pitcher is doing right and wrong mechanically, keeping in mind that correct mechanics not only improve a pitcher's performance, velocity, and stamina, but serve as a buffer against injury.

The first key mechanical point a scout looks for in a pitching prospect is a full, easy, unrestricted arm stroke on both the backswing and follow through. We take note of his release point, how consistent that release is, and if the pitcher is "tipping" his pitches by altering the release point.

Using the legs properly and driving toward the plate with a closed front shoulder is also crucial, for every fan has heard a TV commentator mention if a pitcher is "flying open." Finally, we look for a finish that is full and balanced. A pitcher should drive toward the plate and not away from it, all the while finishing out over his front foot.

By far the most critical tool a scout looks for in a pitcher is the fastball. The heater is baseball's foundational pitch. It is the one pitch scouts focus the majority of their attention on when scouting amateur prospects.

There are three main varieties of the fastball: A four seam fastball, as the name portends, is released so that all four seams of the baseball spin in unison. The four-seamer flashes the highest velocity of all fastball types and, if thrown properly, will rise slightly as it reaches the strike zone.

A two-seamer—or sinker—is thrown so that top spin is imparted to the ball, forcing it to drop suddenly or gradually as it approaches home plate. All fastballs are delivered by gripping the baseball with only the index and middle finger of the pitching hand. Imagine a "V" for victory sign as the ball is gripped.

By varying finger pressure (heavier on the middle finger, lighter on the index finger, or vice versa), a pitcher can get the ball to move to one side of the dish or the other. Scouts refer to this phenomenon as "arm side" or "glove side" movement.

Rising or dropping movement on a fastball is governed by the Bernoulli Effect. This effect is a scientific principle, which, put simply, means that when topspin is imparted to a ball, the air above the ball becomes heavier and the air beneath the ball becomes lighter. The heavy air at the top forces the ball on a downward path.

Backspin, as in a four-seam fastball, causes air beneath the ball to be heavy and air on top to be light. The heavier air underneath the ball in this instance causes the ball to rise. For both topspin and backspin, the velocity and intensity of the spin (tightness) increases the severity of the downward or upward movement.

A cut fastball is a relatively modern creation. Known in the industry as a "cutter," it begins life looking like an ordinary garden variety fastball. But at the last possible instant, the ball bores in on a hitter's hands or darts away from him. A cutter normally stays on a flat plane, that is, it doesn't show drastic up or down motion as does a four-seamer, sinker, change, or curve. Mariano Rivera possessed the greatest cutter in baseball history.

Fans and scouts are rendered giddily excited if they spot a pitcher with exceptional fastball velocity. Remember, however, that in advanced levels of baseball, velocity is irrelevant without command. Proof? Compare the first six years of Sandy Koufax's career with the final six years of his career.

Fastball movement—especially late movement—is also crucial. Neither Roy Halladay nor Greg Maddux possessed blazing heat, but the sudden, drastic, darting late movement of their fastballs made them almost impossible to hit.

An ancient scout once told me, in a discussion regarding amateur pitching prospects: "Velocity will get you drafted; command and movement will get you to the big leagues." And keep you there.

In attempting to understand fastballs and fastball grading, keep in mind one of my main points in this chapter and in the preface: Baseball is now the nearly exclusive property of big, strong, physical guys. Scouts are looking for big dudes with huge bodies and power arms.

Fastball velocity standards have changed. Thirty years ago, a kid throwing 92–93 would cause a panic among scouts. Today, blasé scouts will banish a 92–93 guy to the back of a rotation as a fourth or fifth starter. Short inning relievers in the modern game almost always bring heat at or above 95 mph.

Before I detail grading scales for fastballs, take note that within the baseball industry, there is a debate about radar guns. That debate questions if today's pitchers really do throw significantly harder than their predecessors, or if radar gun equipment is now so advanced and sensitive it only *seems* as if kids throw harder today. Skeptics contend gaudy modern velocity readings are an illusion of modern technology.

I won't try to settle that debate here. Neither side in the discussion has provided verifiable proof, just speculation. My hypothesis is that baseball has always had guys who throw exceptionally hard. Today there are just more of those pitchers; they are a rule instead of an exception.

With the plethora of hard throwers present in the big leagues today, organizational grading scales for fastball velocity have tilted upward in the past five years. In discussions with scouts, this is a fastball grading scale which generally reflects current industry standards. In parentheses, I've placed the standards used by the New York Mets in 2006 as a contrast.

Velocity	
98 (96) mph	80
97 (95)	75
96 (94)	70
95 (93)	65
94 (92)	60
93 (91)	55
92 (90)	50
91 (89)	45

90 (88)	40
89 (87)	35
88 (86)	30
87 (85)	25
86 (84)	20

Fastball velocity grades—both current and OFP—are always based on the pitcher's average velocity, not his peak velocity. In scouting vernacular, the average speed of a pitcher's heater is where his fastball "sits." However, peaks are always noted in the body of the report.

In 2013, the average speed of a major league fastball was 91.9 mph.

In a final comment on pitching, note that the primary difference between a minor league pitcher and a major league pitcher is consistent command and the quality of curves and off-speed pitches. Minor league pitchers—particularly at AA and AAA—throw just as hard as the big leaguers, but their ability to command and obtain consistent late movement on their secondary pitches is not as good as the major leaguers.

Keep this factoid in mind: When big league hitters swing at a curve and either miss it on a two strike count or put it in play (a hit or an out), their batting average is around 50 to 60 points *lower* than when swinging at a fastball. For all the hype attached to fastball velocity, curves and off-speed stuff are baseball's true "out" pitches.

· · ·

Now, let us postulate that a scout has thoroughly observed a prospect and is now prepared to file a report on that player.

Prior to filing a report, scouts may also conduct a home visit with the player. Visits are intended to introduce the scout and his organization to the prospect and his family. During these home visits, scouts hope to get a "read" on the kid and his family, while achieving a measure of comfort, trust, and interaction. That goal is frequently, but not always, achieved. Success depends on a scout's people skills. Some scouts excel in this, while others do not.

In modern amateur scouting, the majority of ballclubs also insist that their area scouts record video of each prospect.

That video, in raw form, is sent to an editing specialist in the front office who condenses and splices the footage, making it viewable and palatable for the general manager, scouting director, and cross checkers. Some scouts use independent or freelance video editors for this type of footage.

Scouting video is almost always recorded from a player's "open side." For a left-handed pitcher or right-handed hitter, the scout will station himself down the first base or right field line. For a right-handed pitcher or a left-handed hitter, scouts station themselves down the third base or left field line.

All organizations utilize a computerized report form. This is true for all types of reports that an organization's scouting department generates: amateur reports, pro reports (minor or major leaguers), and advance scouting reports.

We'll focus on amateur reports. Typically, the computer program gives the scout the option of filing a report on a pitcher or a position player. Once the intended option is selected, the blank report form then appears on the screen.

The upper half of the form provides a player's basic information: Name, school, height, weight, date of birth, etc. The central part of the report contains the grade breakdown.

Each tool is assigned a number grade on the 20–80 scouting scale. Those figures are added together and divided to reach a total score. Two separate grades are provided. The first grades evaluate a prospect's current ability and compares it to accepted big league norms.

This grade is inherently unfair to draft prospects, especially high school athletes, since at seventeen to eighteen years of age, they are being compared to grown men playing in the majors who are between twenty-five and forty.

In any report on an amateur prospect, the second grade, or OFP grade, is the most important portion. A scout attempts to peer into his crystal (base) ball and predict a player's future performance.

For each individual tool, the scout predicts how a prospect will grade out several years in the future when he is between twenty-four and thirty-two years of age. Again, the numbers are added up and divided to provide an OFP score on the prospect.

The OFP is, by miles, the most important portion of the report. It is the scout's bold statement of what type of big league player this prospect may become. It is what a scout gets paid for; the primary function of his job.

I've had scouts tell me that their own general managers rarely read reports and simply just scan the OFP scores, which are usually placed in the upper right corner of the report. If they see a high score, they read on.

Let's examine grades a longtime scout awarded to Daryl Strawberry. Strawberry was the first pick in the MLB draft out of Crenshaw High in Los Angeles in 1980. Ninety-nine percent of grades given amateur prospects are more conservative than the ones my friend gave Strawberry, but this serves as a fine example of how a scout approaches grading.

	Current	Future
Hit	20	70
Power (raw)	55	80
Power (frequency)	20	70
Throw	70	75
Field	40	65
Run	65	70

This scout explained to me he was convinced that if Strawberry went to the majors out of high school, he would be overwhelmed by big league pitching, hence the low current hit and power frequency scores. Said this scout, "I'm always cautious with the current scores. I try to be realistic. With future scores, I try to be optimistic."

His scores on Strawberry reflect both caution and optimism. The scout gave Strawberry a 45 current score but a 72 OFP score. This scout confided that Strawberry's immense raw talent gave him the courage to file a report with such a large numeric discrepancy. "I was projecting!" he said.

Projection is the heart of amateur scouting.

The lower half of the form contains four separate paragraph-sized empty boxes. Inside each box, the scout writes a mini essay on the prospect. The first box contains a physical description of the player; the second box outlines his strengths; the third box details his weaknesses and the fourth box is a conclusion and/or summary.

Physical description paragraphs are straightforward. The scout describes the prospect's height, weight, "projectability," and body type—tall and lanky, mature and muscular, etc. Next, the scout compares the player's look and build to a well-known current big leaguer. This gives the front office a general mental image of the player's frame.

Let's say a scout is filing a report on a tall, skinny high school right-handed pitcher. Perhaps a Chris Tillman comp would be in order. Maybe the scout is writing up a college first baseman who is a behemoth. Adam Dunn could be a fair comparison. Or perhaps the scout has his eyeballs set on a shorter outfielder with a strong, athletic body—an Andrew McCutchen might work.

In writing and submitting player physical comparisons, it is important to note that the scout is *not* stating that a prospect will become Andrew McCutchen; he is simply stating that the prospect *resembles* the great Pirate center fielder physically.

The "strengths" paragraph provides a brief, concise description of all the prospect's perceived strengths. This paragraph provides written details of the number grade the scout has previously assigned to the player in the grading portion of the report.

Scouts almost always describe a player's most noteworthy tool at the outset of the strengths paragraph. Lesser strengths or more subtle talents are mentioned typically toward the end.

"I've never left the weaknesses box blank" a veteran scout, who has signed dozens of major leaguers, once told me.

Scouts try to be delicate while writing up weaknesses. They try to alert the front office to a player's drawbacks and to areas development personnel may need to improve upon. At the same time, scouts want to strike a positive, not negative, tone and they seek to avoid poisoning the supervisor's opinion of the player. After all, the mere fact that a scout is taking the time and effort to write and file a report on a prospect means there is *something* he likes about the player.

The summation/conclusion paragraph usually begins with the scout's opinion as to how the player "profiles." Is he an everyday player? A backup? A starting pitcher, middle relief specialist or a closer? An All-Star, Hall of Famer, or a reliable if unspectacular everyday guy? What position will he play, where does he fit in the batting order? How well will he do in his first year of pro ball in the minors? How quickly will he ascend to the big leagues?

If the report focuses on a high school player, his college choice is mentioned. For college players, the remaining amount of a player's eligibility is noted.

Finally, the concluding paragraph discusses the player's "signability." For most prospects, signability is not revealed until a month prior to the draft, if at all. Therefore, signability descriptions are usually vague if not non-existent in early reports; details are included when they are available.

The scout proofreads his report and if he is satisfied with the product, he clicks the "send" button. This action submits the report to the organization's front office, where all approved parties can view it. Report programs retain a feature which permits the scout to view his past reports on all players he has written up, or, in scout slang, "guys I have in."

Prior to the June draft, most organizations impose a report deadline. This mandates that all reports be sent by a predetermined date and that no reports can be sent after that date.

As draft day nears, all organizations intensify their preparations. Meetings are held involving the scouting director, cross checkers, area scouts, analytics experts, and additional critical personnel.

Each prospect the organization's scouts have filed a report on are discussed in the various meetings. Subsequently, all potential draftees are ranked in order of the ballclub's preference. Each year approximately 1,200 players are chosen (40 rounds and 30 picks per round) in the MLB draft. For every scouting department, sifting through 1,000 plus reports is a tedious—but necessary—process.

Only eligible players from the United States, Canada, and Puerto Rico are considered for the draft; prospects from baseball rich hotbeds such as the Dominican Republic, Venezuela, and the Far East are not. Players from those parts of the globe are subject to a different acquisition system.

In the days leading up to the draft in early June, each club forms a draft board and a draft war room. On the draft board, small, moveable magnetic tiles contain the name of each player the ballclub has its eye on. If a player is selected, his name moves from the available side of the board to the selected side of the board.

Inside the draft room on draft day sits the organization's top baseball brass. General managers are heavily involved in a ballclub's early picks but are rarely involved in later round choices. On day one of the draft, the first and second round is conducted. Clubs have five minutes to make their selections.

On days two and three (rounds 3 through 40), pick "windows" narrow down to thirty seconds. This condensed time frame can make a draft room a place of frantic activity. Phone calls fly from the scouts in the draft room (or those who remain at home on draft day) to advisors and prospects not yet drafted. Organizations try to determine if a player will agree to sign if he is drafted in later, double digit rounds and what his bonus demands might be.

Once the draft has concluded, an organization attempts to sign their draftees by negotiating with players and their advisors. The signing deadline nowadays is on or around July 15.

Once bonus amounts and contract terms have been finalized, each player signs the Standard Minor League Contract. Physical exams are given each new player. Now an employee of the ballclub that drafted him, the player is assigned by the organization to one of its Minor League affiliates.

This begins the long and arduous road to the big leagues. Most draftees (around 92 percent) don't make it. For the few who do, the journey is well worth it. Not only is Major League Baseball a great and popular game, it is now an extremely lucrative profession for the player.

Scouting and the draft has changed drastically over the years. Scouts no longer prepare handwritten reports on triplicate forms. Radar guns and sabermetric stats have arrived to assist, if not replace, gut feelings.

As recently as 2001, the Los Angeles Dodgers draft was conducted inside the nursery used by the player's children on the eighth floor of Dodger Stadium. To set up the necessary equipment, scouts had to move toys, stuffed animals, and tiny tables and chairs aside.

In 2004, the Angels conducted their draft from a conference room in a tourist hotel across the street from Disneyland. Those days of simplicity and innocence are long gone.

Baseball today is a corporate entity, obsessed with the two pillars of modern mega business: One, using public relations to maintain a positive public image; and two, the hallowed bottom line.

Today's Major League Baseball Draft and the scouting that leads up to it is now computerized and driven by technology and statistics. Cold, hard, efficient big business. (Like so much of current society, the first round of MLB's draft is a television show. Unlike embarrassing TV trash, televising the draft is a positive step for MLB since it makes the process so much more accessible to the public.)

Despite the application of business philosophies and the advent of modern technology, the importance of the amateur scout can never be obscured.

It is the scout's encounters with a prospect—watching him play, getting to know him and his family, filing reports—that initiates a player's career. It may be a career that benefits the player, his ballclub, a city and the sport itself.

Common popular clichés insist that "Scouts are the foundation of baseball," or "Scouts are the lifeblood of baseball." I don't mean to denigrate the importance of scouts, but I am not sure I agree with those clichés. Players are the lifeblood and foundation of baseball, from tee-ball to the majors.

I see amateur scouts as a type of doorman one might see guarding the entrance to a swanky, hip dance club where eager twenty-somethings yearn for admittance on a Saturday night. (Scouts are never as well dressed as the doormen.)

The doorman surveys the crowd behind the velvet rope line, using his own personal judgment to determine who deserves entrance and who doesn't. He evaluates each candidate by a well-established set of internal criteria and decides if a hopeful should be let inside.

As I see it, that is what amateur scouting in baseball comprises. The doorman asks himself, *Do I drop the velvet rope for this person and let him in?*

In a similar vein, the scout asks himself, *Is this player good enough to file a report on? Does he have a chance to play in the big leagues?*

That, I contend, is the essence of amateur scouting in baseball.

. . .

As an addendum, as well as an indulgence, I've added two lists to this chapter: The first list is of the best tools and best players among those I have scouted from 2000 to 2013. My second list comprises the best tools and best players I have seen among Major Leaguers from 1964 to 2013.

Amateur Prospects, 2000-2013:
Best all around, College: Troy Tulowitzki, Long Beach State, 2005
Best all around, High School: Adam Jones, 2003
Best Pitcher, College: Tim Lincecum, Washington, 2006
Best Pitcher, High School: Lucas Giolito, 2012 (Injured early in senior season.)
Best Defensive player, College: Troy Tulowitzki
Best Defensive player, High School: Matt Dominguez, 2007, and Francisco Lindor, 2011
Best Hitter, College: Bryce Harper, College of Southern Nevada, 2010
Best Hitter, High School: Mike Moustakas, 2007
Best raw power, College: Nick Akins, Vanguard University of Southern California, 2009
Best raw power, High School: Giancarlo Stanton, 2007
Best arm, position player, High School or College: Anthony Gose, High School, 2008
Fastest, High School or College: DeSean Jackson, High School, 2005

Major League Rankings: This list reflects my rankings of Major Leaguers from 1964 to 2013. I have included only players I have seen personally, therefore, deserving all-time greats active before 1964 are not included.

Field: Ozzie Smith
Run: Bo Jackson
Throw: Roberto Clemente
Hit: Tony Gwynn
Power: Mickey Mantle
Best All-Around hitter (power and average): Miguel Cabrera and Albert Pujols
Fastball velocity: Aroldis Chapman, lefty, and Nolan Ryan, righty.
Best All-Around player: Willie Mays

Position by Position:
1B: Albert Pujols
2B: Joe Morgan
SS: Ozzie Smith
3B: Mike Schmidt
OF: Willie Mays, Hank Aaron, Ken Griffey, Jr.
C: Johnny Bench
RHP: Bob Gibson
LHP: Sandy Koufax

Best single season by a position player: Carl Yastrzemski, 1967 **(189 H, 112 R, *44 HR, 121 RBI, 326 BA, .418 OBP, .622 SLG)*[2]**
Best single season by a pitcher: Sandy Koufax, 1965 (***26–8, 2.04 ERA, 27 CG, 382 K, 335.2 IP***)

---

2 Bold: Led League
   Bold and Italics: Led MLB

3

Make Sure You Relax and Have a Great Experience

P APERWORK, IN THE majority of American businesses, is seen as a mundane nuisance. Cubicle dwellers nationwide, burdened by Himalayan stacks, curse it every day. Administrators and office managers grudgingly tolerate it, toiling with one eye on the pile, one on the clock.

In amateur scouting, paperwork is a ritual game of "chicken," a stare down contest involving will and nerves played out over computer generated forms. Baseball scouts distribute two types of paperwork: a postcard-sized "Information Card" and a multi-page, wide-ranging questionnaire. Both are always accompanied by a self-addressed stamped, or metered, envelope.

In the paperwork ritual, the Information Card is first up to the plate.

I am not certain, but I may have been the first scout to hand an information card to Giancarlo Stanton, now a superstar outfielder with the Miami Marlins and the possessor of home run power worthy of Greek mythology.

In the spring of 2006, I traveled to Loyola High School in Los Angeles to scout a Sherman Oaks Notre Dame High School teammate of Stanton's. Stanton was then a junior, his teammate a senior. I had never seen or heard of Stanton previously.

Fooled by a pitch in his first trip to the plate, Stanton waved his bat at the ball but managed to drive it off the fence in left-center field. The next time up, he launched a ball over the same fence, clearing the school's classroom buildings . . . that ball may still be traveling.

During the game, I introduced myself to Stanton's father, meeting the young man briefly afterwards. At that time, Stanton was mainly a football and basketball star and had not received much attention for his baseball exploits. Obviously, that situation has since changed.

Mr. Stanton was friendly and cooperative. I nonetheless interpreted his puzzled facial reaction to my "please have your son fill out this card" request to be one of quizzical surprise. As I drove home, I recall thinking to myself, *I'll never see that card again!*

Three days later the envelope appeared in my mailbox.

Stanton's information card, shown below, is fairly standard in the industry. Basic information, simple, straightforward. The goal is to identify the player, get him in your files, and follow up later.

Player Information Card for Giancarlo Stanton.

Next on the list comes the multipage, long form paperwork. To a prospect, long form paperwork is the equivalent of a prostate exam performed by a doctor wearing sandpaper gloves; baseball's version of a "Marathon Man" root canal. It is safe, but burdensome and colossally annoying.

Almost all organizations "time" paperwork.

Scouts will take note of the date they hand paperwork to a prospect. Most scouts hope to receive the completed paperwork within a week, preferably sooner. Any time frame beyond one week causes concern, if not outright anger, among scouts.

Phone calls placed by scouts seeking tardy paperwork run the gamut from chiding, pestering, pleading, yelling, and even screaming. A scout, you see, needs the paperwork not just for his own files, but to satisfy his stubborn superiors as well as administrators in far away front offices.

Timing paperwork serves another purpose.

Many scouts cling to the old-fashioned notion that prompt return of paperwork indicates that a player has a burning desire to play pro ball, a fire in the belly to succeed. Failure to quickly return paperwork is often seen as a quality of a slacker, a slough off, a ne'er do well.

Contrarians to this viewpoint claim that desire is shown on the field, not at the post office. In 2005, a Southern California scout handed paperwork to Troy Tulowitzki, then a draft eligible prospect at Long Beach State and now a superstar shortstop with the Colorado Rockies.

The scout is still awaiting Tulowitzki's return envelope.

Failure to return often has other root causes. A high school pitching prospect was once handed an information card by a scout with a reputation for being annoying and persistent, if not obsessive. The pitcher never returned the card and the scout angrily crossed the youngster off his "follow" list.

Later, the pitcher matriculated to a D-1 baseball program. During his draft eligible college season, I asked him why he hadn't returned the info card he was given as a high schooler.

"I returned everyone else's paperwork, but not his," he informed me. "I can't stand that guy."

Naturally, scouts prefer paperwork to be completed by the player. Often, that is not the case. Parents, agents, and others frequently fill out paperwork for prospects, who can feel overwhelmed and beleaguered by the insistent attentions of thirty major league organizations.

A prospect filling out paperwork solo and in an efficient fashion, the theory goes, is displaying initiative, responsibility and self-reliance, among other attributes. Sort of a self-filling prophecy.

Scouts are paid observers, of course. Their internal radar alarm starts to beep when they sense someone other than the player has completed paperwork. Tipoffs are numerous. Male teenage athletes have notoriously bad handwriting. Neat, meticulous printing screams a "J'accuse" at dear old Mom.

Typewritten paperwork is a blatant red flag. Anyone brave enough to venture into a teenage boy's room knows instinctively they have neither the instinct nor desire to patiently type sentences or even poke an "x" into a box via typewriter or computer word processor. Perfectly printed responses, in a scout's mind, spin the turret guns of blame toward agents or advisors.

Prospect paperwork universally contains four sections: Basic personal information, medical history, education, and signability. The forms typically run around ten pages and many begin with a preamble.

Here is a sample:

You are receiving this questionnaire to be considered for the upcoming MLB draft. Becoming a professional baseball player

begins here. The questionnaire should be viewed as an employ-
ment application and should be taken serious (sic) if you have
interest in signing a professional contract. Your application
will be viewed in many ways. . . . Make sure you relax and
have a great experience.

The first portion of the relaxation process, after the basic personal
information section is dispensed with, is a thorough medical history.
This portion is darn near invasive. That's understandable, since ball
clubs naturally want to learn about any physical injuries, surgeries,
chronic conditions, family histories, drugs, alcohol, or medications.

The numerous med questions come pressed together in single
space type, with rat-a-tat-tat machine gun rapidity:

- Do you wear glasses?
- Do you wear contacts?
- Are you a diabetic?
- Have you ever required special adhesive taping, wrapping
  or braces for competing in athletic competition?
- Have you ever used tobacco products?
- Have you ever used any drugs or medications?
- Have you ever used any illegal/controlled substances?
- The majority of emphasis in the med section is on inju-
  ries, past and present. Name any part of the body, from
  the cowlick to the arches, it's covered.

Ominous questions—ones that usually receive a "no" even when
a "yes" is warranted—are usually tucked in at the end, near the
date and signature line:

- Have you ever been convicted of a DUI?
- Have you ever been convicted of any other criminal
  offense?

"If you answer yes to one of those questions," a scout once kid-
dingly observed, "then you're qualified to be a scouting director."

Alcohol and drug usage questions, be they subtle or direct, are always asked. Given baseball's extensive history of drug and alcohol abuse, this question may, to some, smack of hypocrisy. Organizations fully understand that ballplayers are rarely ideal or model citizens, but drafting decisions are made easier by early identification of potential land mines.

Full revelation of medical facts can be sensitive. Each team's medical section contains a lead paragraph with the disclaimer, "This information will be kept confidential." That is true if you don't count the general manager, assistant general managers, scouting director, team medical personnel, cross checkers, and office administrators, all of whom have access to the information.

Complete health disclosure from prospects is a rare but welcomed surprise. One dad several years ago attended each of his son's games armed with a tall stack of stapled medical reports. He handed them out to each scout in attendance like a Hare Krishna distributing pamphlets at the airport.

One wonderfully nice dad, without my asking, voluntarily handed me a complete, thick medical file on his son. The father dutifully informed me that his right-handed son's arm injury the previous year was so serious that the kid had resorted to throwing left-handed during his games. I was grateful for the information; my guess was the player's agent was not particularly enthralled with the dad's candor.

Restricting medical information is often used by agents as a chess move in negotiating strategies. Some hold back information, some wait until the last moment to provide facts, etc. Agents fear that revelation of past or current injuries may cause ball clubs to "red flag" a prospect, a process which either drops a player far down a team's draft board or eliminates him altogether.

All the tactics and maneuvering constitute a moot point. Contracts can be voided and bonus payments reduced or eliminated by a post draft or post signing discovery of a previously unknown or undisclosed injury. This unfortunate scenario has occurred on several occasions. It befell 2012 NL Cy Young Award winner R. A. Dickey when he was drafted by the Texas Rangers in 1996.

The Rangers discovered that Dickey was born without an ulnar collateral ligament in his pitching (right) elbow. Subsequently, his bonus was reduced from $810,000 to $75,000. Texas claimed that Dickey's elbow was "an injury waiting to happen." To his credit, Dickey persevered, winning the National League Cy Young Award in 2012, as a member of the New York Mets.

Agent Scott Boras, on the other extreme, does not provide any medical information on his clients to organizations. This infuriates many baseball people who unanimously insist on full pre-draft health disclosure.

A quick digression on Boras. I have met Boras and have chatted with him. He is a pleasant, low key gentleman who does not exhibit phoniness or Hollywood-type slickness, as do several other major agents. Still, behind his public face, I always get the impression of a kind of puckish self-confidence with Boras.

Poker losers understand this look. Boras knows he has the cards to beat you; if he doesn't have them yet, he knows he will soon get them. It's the slightly amused, quietly assured face of a guy who always wins.

Contrary to popular belief, Boras does not have devilish red skin, smoke coming out of his ears, nor does he carry a pitchfork. He does not, as far as I know, travel to games on a broomstick. Boras's job is to get as much money for his clients as he possibly can, and, last time I checked, he is damn successful.

Scott Boras's combination of success and high profile visibility naturally leads to "taking sides" in the baseball industry, the public, and the media. Many insiders and journalists pinch their noses at the mention of his name; others side enthusiastically with Boras, such as Jon Heyman of CBS Sports.

No one, myself included, would ever accuse Boras of doing anything illegal or engaging in activity that is contrary to baseball's internal rules. However, there is no doubt that many people in the industry are opposed to some of the tactics he employs.

Personally, I somewhat disagree with some of the methods Boras utilizes, but I will concede that he is a heck of a nice guy. More importantly, Boras is able to procure fantastic amounts of money for his clients. No doubt hand wringers may raise "Does the end justify the means?" questions regarding Boras. Like him or not (many of his clients adore him and are fiercely loyal), Boras is a staggeringly successful agent.

By the way, if you have a sudden notion that you would like to casually drop in on Boras's office in Newport Beach, California, one of these days, forget about it. The premises are protected by an expensive, ultra high-tech security system designed by NASA engineers.

By far, the majority of space in prospect questionnaires is occupied by the medical history section. An education section is almost always included. Organizations respect a prospect's desire to get an advanced education (if the kid has such a desire) but a scout is far more interested in how a player's college plans affect his potential signability.

College players are asked how many credits they have completed, how many credits they need to graduate, and if they intend on returning to school. Bully for higher education, but still . . . scouts just want to know if the player will sign if drafted.

Junior college players are asked similar questions, plus a few add ons: "Will you return to the same school? Will you attend a four-year school? Have you signed a National Letter of Intent?" Again, scouts just want to know if the kid will sign a contract if drafted.

High school prospects are bombarded with a phalanx of education questions, beginning with their college choice then graduating to their GPA, SAT (math-verbal-essay), or ACT scores. Once more, scouts are mostly interested in how a kid's educational plans may influence his signability. A kid could range anywhere from a future Rhodes Scholar to a functional illiterate. Scouts care only if he will sign a pro contract if drafted . . . which is not to say that certain questions don't have an inherent entertainment value.

A salacious oversight cropped up in one team's education section several years ago. In a box directed at college prospects, the team inquired about each player's cumulative GPA. However, to save space on the form, the line read: "Cum GPA_____."

Having generated much finger pointing, giggling, and snickering, the line was altered the following year.

Many years ago, a scout received an urgent phone call from a high school prospect smack in the middle of filling out his paperwork. "What does 'compensation' mean?" the prospect asked the scout.

After gently relaying a definition, the scout suddenly realized: This kid is signable. No way on earth he's going to college.

The education section of prospect paperwork provides a wealth of information: Units earned, units needed, test scores, GPAs, a player's attitude toward higher education. In those factoids, which, to be honest, scouts find superfluous teams are looking for tip-offs beyond the basic tidbits provided. As I've stated, organizations are primarily searching for indicators that a prospect will sign if drafted.

Let's focus on high school prospects. Their education section typically includes a series of key questions. The first is along the lines of "Do you plan to attend college next year?" That is accompanied by the standard queries, "What school will you attend?" and "What is your scholarship percentage?" A few clubs love to toss in a "How important is education to you and your family?" question, usually followed by a request to list all family members who have attended college and the degrees, if any, they have earned.

Keep in mind that scouts are looking for hints, subtle or blatant, that a player is signable. An emphatic yes to the first question indicates an unwillingness to sign; any wavering signals wiggle room.

Scholarship percentages are massively important. Understand that under current NCAA rules, Division-1 baseball programs are permitted only 11.7 scholarships for baseball. Those scholarships must be sliced and diced to cover an entire thirty-five-man roster, twenty-seven of whom must have at least a 25 percent scholarship. D-1 football and basketball programs have no such restrictions, for all of the scholarships they award must be, under NCAA rules, 100 percent grants.

A high percentage scholarship to a top school (85 percent to Stanford, let's say) signals that a player will be nearly impossible to sign or will ask for a sizeable bonus amount in order to be "bought out" of his commitment. Scouts know that smaller percentages or commitments to less prestigious or expensive college programs make the lure of a tidy signing bonus difficult for the player to reject.

Perhaps the most significant education indicator for a prospect is family history. If parents, grandparents, and siblings all boast advanced educations, the odds of a player foregoing college to sign for anything other than a hefty dollar figure are practically nil.

You may ask: "If the true purpose of the Medical Questionnaire and the Education Survey are to determine signability, then . . . why don't the forms just ask the prospect about signability directly?" That's a hell of a good question.

Uh, well, prospect paperwork forms *do* inquire regarding signability. Boy, do they ever.

Nuance and subtlety are never hallmarks of the signability section. These questions are taken directly from one team's prospect paperwork form:

- "Is signing now and attending college in the offseason an option?"

- "Have you and your family decided what round(s) you would need to be drafted in for you to sign?"
- "Is there a round which you believe the chance of signing would be slim?"
- "Ultimately I see myself: Attending/Finishing College"

Give this ball club kudos for inventing multiple ways to ask the same freaking question.

Wait, there's more! From the same team's form:

- "How important is the college experience to you?"
- "How important is playing professional baseball to you?"
- "How important is starting your professional career now?"
- "Do you expect to be drafted?"
- "Explain the percentage of attending/finishing college versus signing professionally (College %/Professional %)
  - My Personal Preference:
    95/5—75/25—50/50—25/75—5/95
  - My Family's Preference:
    95/5—75/25—50/50—25/75—5/95"

Assuming the prospect at this stage has not gone berserk and shot up a Post Office, he still must answer these delightful questions:

- "Do you feel your chances of playing in the big leagues would be helped or hindered by attending/finishing college?"
- "Do you see the advantages to beginning a pro career immediately?"
- "Are you prepared to handle the rigors of professional baseball?"

Notice a thread here, a theme perhaps?

Another organization's paperwork form extends this line of inquiry further:

- "Do you have an advisor?"

A quick note: Advisor is a code name for an agent. It is exceptionally important for a scout to know who is representing a player. This signals if a signing negotiation will be simple, easy and quick or as contentious as the Battle of the Marne.

- "Who will be the ultimate decision maker when deciding to sign a contract: you, your family, or your advisor?"
- "What are your expectations for the upcoming draft?"
- "Are you more concerned with the round in which you are selected, or the amount of the signing bonus?"
- "Do you have a set dollar amount that you will require in order to sign?"
- "Will you sign for slot money?"
- "Realistically, in what area of the draft do you expect to be drafted (please check no more than two areas):

1st round
2nd-3rd rounds
4th-7th rounds
8th-12th rounds
13th round on"

These examples are culled from only two organizations' paperwork forms. All other ball clubs are equally as relentless and obsessive regarding signability.

Instead of asking the same question in differing formats time and time again, why not ask just two questions and be done with it?

Those questions would be: Will you sign? If you sign, how much bonus money do you want? This solution would save time, space and half a rainforest.

This does not happen for two reasons. Number one, almost nothing in baseball makes any sense. Proof? Bud Selig has been commissioner for almost twenty years.

Number two, determining signability is absolutely paramount for all scouts. The quickest way for a scout to get fired is to guarantee his superiors that a player will sign in a designated round and/or for a designated amount and then have the player refuse after being drafted.

If the prospect reneges on a pre-draft agreement, the scout and the ballclub have not only wasted a valuable draft pick, but are embarrassed and made to look foolish. That is positively unacceptable, especially with an early (single digit round) selection. Ceaselessly repetitive signability questions are both a sign of extreme thoroughness and a paranoid reflection of the dread of being fired.

Herein lies the structure of the aforementioned game of "chicken." Ball clubs, through scout provided paperwork, go to obsessive lengths to try to coax an implied or, preferably, a direct signability commitment from a prospect.

Agents representing players have an equally clever agenda in filling out paperwork. Advisors strive to avoid providing a "tell." They attempt to provide as much information as possible without revealing anything.

On a direct line collision course, who will flinch first?

That is the real purpose of prospect paperwork. Can the scout nail down a player's signability or, seeking added negotiating leverage after the draft, can an agent avoid caving?

This bizarre dance can cause awkward confrontations. During home visits, scouts commonly complain that a prospect has not completely filled out his paperwork, leaving the signability section blank. (A common tactic often encouraged, if not ordered, by advisors.)

If thwarted, a popular ruse used by scouts is to verbally toss out a round or, more likely, a figure. A common range is $500,000 to $700,000.

"What if I tell my bosses your figure is $500,000?" a scout will ask. Designed to elicit a visceral response, the scout will read the facial reactions and body language of the player and his parents to determine if his dart has hit the bull's-eye.

Naïve prospects and parents fold; those well-schooled and coached by advisors hold firm, avoiding getting locked in or nailed down to a figure. Savvy agents insist their clients not engage a scout when this tactic is used so as not to lend it credibility.

All of this maneuvering and gamesmanship veers a prospect away from the stated purpose of organizational paperwork, which is to ostensibly act as a job application. That idea is nonsense.

As a game, baseball (when played well) is beautiful, elegant, and timeless. As a business, it's cold, harsh, and ruthless.

Instructions which appear in one ballclub's paperwork states a perfect warning:

". . . For players and parents alike, this is an important decision and should not be taken lightly."

4

Most People Enjoy Seeing Someone Else Make a Mistake

ALL MAJOR LEAGUE organizations, as well as the Major League Scouting Bureau, administer to each prospect some form of psychological examination, known in the trade as a "psych test."

Depending on one's point of view, these exams are either a ludicrous, hilarious, needless waste of time, or a critical and indispensable evaluation tool which, if eliminated, would undermine not only the very foundation of baseball but of human civilization as well.

The majority of teams utilize a tidy two- to four-page psych test. When I worked for the Mets, we tortured players with a two-and-a-half-hour antediluvian monstrosity, the mental equivalent of being placed on the "Rack."

Many of the questions are of the Barbara Walters-Katherine Hepburn variety. In a widely satirized and ridiculed 1981 TV interview, Baba asked Kaf-win, "What kind of tree are you?"

Here is a sample of actual True/False questions from a psych test administered by a major league ballclub:

"I am not very smart."

"Most people enjoy seeing someone else make a mistake."

"I have never had bad habits."

"When I give a gift, even the paper it is wrapped in is important."

"I do not think dirty jokes are funny."

Test proponents feel these queries reveal deep and important inner truths. Critics maintain the questions are silly nonsense and that the exact same results could be garnered by flipping a coin.

Naturally, the test also veers into the Baba Wawa tree (twee) realm by asking: "If an animal, I see myself more like a: A. Dog B. Cat."

Undoubtedly, several questions evoke a *Princess Bride* reaction. In that classic film, Westley (Cary Elwes) challenges Vizzini (Wallace Shawn) to drink from one of two cups. One cup is poisoned, supposedly, and the other is not.

Loudly, Vizzini vocalizes his theories as to which cup contains poison, rationalizing, "If you think that I think that you thought that I thought . . ." etc. Vizzini ties himself up into paralysis by over analysis, a kind of logical Gordian knot. He drinks from one cup and falls dead. Both cups were poisoned.

Such a question is this one: People who work hard, even when paid little:

A. Will be rewarded in other ways,

B. Are fools.

The correct real-world answer is, of course, B. The correct "test" answer is A.

I am certain many prospects are conflicted with a *Princess Bride* internal debate when confronted with these types of psych test questions.

Why then, you ask, are these tests *actually* given? Ball clubs genuinely hope to gain insight into a players personality; specifically

his level of confidence and aggressiveness. Identifying and eliminating dangerous sociopaths, drug users, drunks, and miscreants
is an added benefit. However, if a certifiable nutcase can throw
or hit a 95 mph fastball, a negative psych test result has a higher
probability of receiving a downgraded emphasis.

The main goal, however, is a tad more succinct. Organizations
mainly want to know if a youngster is going to quit on them. To
best explain this, let me set up a scenario.

Let's say that a draftee signs for $500,000. Nowadays, that
is low second, early third round money. After his agent gets his
cut and the IRS takes theirs, the ballplayer has a retention rate
of around 56 to 60 percent—$300,000, let's say. Take note that
apart from the signing bonus, a player's agent can negotiate to
have the organization pay for the player's college education.

Kids being kids, let's further postulate that our hypothetical
player spends around $75,000 combined on a fancy car, new
clothes, vacation, and other goodies. He then places $225,000 in
the bank or in some type of investment.

Two years after signing, our friend is hitting .218 in the lower
echelons of the minor leagues—the Low-A Sally League, for
instance. Our player is enduring the oppressive heat and humid-
ity of the Carolinas for paltry minor league pay. During a seven-
teen-hour bus trip from Hicksville to Yahoo City, he becomes
introspective: "I have a new car, a pretty girl waiting for me back
home, $225,000 in the bank, plus these clowns have to pay for
my education. . . . What in the hell am I doing here?"

In truth, *that* is what the psych tests try to identify. Who will
quit and who will stick it out? Will a player persevere, or take the
money and pack it in? Most importantly, the organization wants
to determine if their potential investment will be a wise choice or
a regrettable waste of a substantial sum of cash.

In baseball's inner circles, most scouts and their organizations
accept psych tests as a necessary and vital aid. Numerous scouts

may snicker at psych tests and privately question their value, but like the seventh inning stretch and arguing with the umpire, psych tests are an ingrained baseball ritual and will never vanish.

Detractors can cite the following anecdote:

In 2004, Matt Bush was the first pick in the draft, selected as a shortstop by the San Diego Padres out of a high school in San Diego. Later that year, Bush was involved in a scuffle with a security guard in a nightclub near the Padres training complex in Arizona.

In 2009, Bush was allegedly involved in a drunken assault at a San Diego area high school. While driving under the influence in Florida in 2012, Bush caused a hit and run crash which seriously injured a seventy-two-year-old man. Bush pleaded no contest to the charges and was sentenced to four years and three months in prison.

Prior to being drafted in 2004, Matt Bush took the exact same test from which I have quoted selected questions in this chapter.

Bush passed.

5

SparQ at the Ball ParQ

This story originally appeared on the Baseball America *website on August 9, 2008.*

ONE OF THE premier features of the annual Area Code Games is SPARQ testing, which was first instituted at the Long Beach event in 2003.

In the chronologically distant and technologically backward 1990s, scouts timed players with stop watches as they ran 60-yard dashes across the outfield turf. These and other Neanderthal methods were used to measure a player's speed, leaping ability, and throwing arm strength.

Of course, these tactics are pathetically and hopelessly outdated in the computer dominated and scientifically advanced world of the twenty-first century. SPARQ tests are designed to measure rotational strength, fast twitch muscles, and explosive core power.

In other words, speed, leaping ability, and arm strength. (Apparently, no athletes had cores prior to 2002.)

The Nike/SPARQ website claims that such testing is "The continual, dynamic process of assessing and analyzing athletes at a granular level." Such methodology permits the athlete to incul-cate equal measures of both gobbledy and gook.

SPARQ testing was conducted at a softball field just north of Blair Field in Long Beach, host site of the Area Code Games.

Tiny, fit, perky, and immaculately groomed young SPARQ testers shuttled players from station to station. First was the ultra high-tech height and weight calculation zone. Each player stepped on a scale to determine his weight. He then had his height measured by standing next to a white paper banner marked in feet and inches. It's stunning how far exercise sci-ence has advanced!

Off next they go to the vertical jump station. The goal here, cleverly devised, is to jump as high as possible. No cores exploded, but several participants may in reality be kangaroos.

Jake Marisnick (Riverside Poly High, California) jumped a stunning 35.8 inches and scraped the underside of a jet landing at Long Beach Airport. He was followed by Kenny Diekroger, Kyrell Hudson, and the wonderfully named Slade Heathcott, all of whom pogo-sticked between 34.9 and 34.7 inches.

Prior to running the 60-yard dash, each squad is led through a series of bizarre warm-up exercises. No one on the Brewer Blue team was able to maintain a straight face during an awk-ward squatting drill which appeared to simulate the beginning of a sumo wrestling match. One player keeled over on his side, eliciting good-natured howls of laughter from his pals.

Off to the races they went. Hudson smoked the competition; clocking one of the fastest ACG SPARQ times ever—6.33. Second was Mike Trout, a heretofore unknown outfielder from Millville, New Jersey, who ripped off a 6.52 clocking.

Matt Moynihan (Cathedral Catholic High, San Diego) turned in a 6.58 effort, made all the more remarkable by his unconventional snorting, arm flailing, and leg spinning running style.

One racer veered off course at the start, circling like a slalom ski racer outside of one of the fluorescent green cones used to mark the running lanes. "We won't count that time" one of the SPARQ attendants informed him diplomatically.

The next nuisance is the 20-yard side to side shuttle test. Each contestant begins by shuttling five yards to his right, then ten to his left, and then five yards back to his right. Cruelly, this particular discipline is designed to determine how quickly one can fall flat on their face. The shuttle is the most difficult and frustrating test, since the turf is slippery and footing is difficult to maintain.

The final humiliation is the rotational power ball distance throw. Each athlete heaves a heavy black ball in the general direction of Disneyland. Imagine a kilt-wearing Scot straining to unload a towering tree stump at the Highland games and you'll get the idea.

The final SPARQ rankings indicate the presence in Long Beach of several exceptional athletes. Diekroger finished first with a phenomenal 85.96 overall score. Trout, Heathcott, Marisnick, and Moynihan all finished in the top ten.

With all kidding aside, the SPARQ tests are invaluable aids to scouts in determining the athletic ability of prospects participating in the ACG. Whatever modernistic labels one may want to attach, scouts have and always will be interested in raw skills and tools.

In scouting position players, hitting ability trumps all else. Non-hitting tools are of secondary consideration, but are important nonetheless. Philosophies change over time and fads come and go, but baseball is a sport played by athletes, John Kruk's viewpoint notwithstanding. ("I'm not an athlete, lady—I'm a baseball player.")

Everyone has their own method of evaluating players. Most welcome modern technology, while others eschew it. One of my favorite scouts is loveably cranky and outspoken, but a wise and perceptive observer.

His credo, oft repeated, is: "I don't need no one or nothing to tell me who can play! I can tell who can play and who can't!"

Mike Trout was a first round draft choice (25th overall pick) of the Los Angeles Angels in 2009. He made his major league debut in 2011.

In 2012 and 2013, Trout was selected to the American League All Star team and was named AL Rookie of the Year in 2012. He placed second in the 2012 and 2013 AL MVP voting. Trout's performance in his first two full major league seasons (2012 and 2013) compares favorably to the freshman and sophomore seasons of both Joe DiMaggio and Ted Williams.

SPARQ testing has since been discontinued at the annual Area Code Games.

6

Prospects

A MATEUR SCOUTS CONCENTRATE on two events: Games and Showcases. Naturally, the games a prospect plays for his high school or college team are the most important venues in which scouts observe players.

"Showcase" is a blanket term which refers to summer and fall off-season events in which top prospects band together to flash their skills and compete head to head. The premier college spectacles are the Cape Cod Summer League and the schedule played by Team USA.

Showcases involving high school prospects have exploded in number in the past ten years to a point beyond saturation. The four most prominent off-season prep showcases are the weeklong Area Code Games, staged in Long Beach, California; the Perfect Game/Rawlings All American Game held in San Diego (formerly known as the Aflac Game); and a separate All American Game at Wrigley Field in Chicago hosted by Under Armour. All three events annually occur in August. Finally, the World Wood Bat Association Championships are presented in late October in Jupiter, Florida.

I joined *Baseball America* as a Scout and Correspondent in the summer of 2007, and for the next three years filed a series of dispatches on top amateur prospects:

The Rorschach Test

August 2007

An old-time movie mogul like Louis B. Mayer or Samuel Goldwyn would be infuriated by the first two days of this year's Area Code Games.

Clark Gable is in a picture that is getting stolen by Walter Brennan. Marilyn Monroe's starring vehicle is getting upstaged by Hope Lange.

Many of the most prominent players in the 2008 high school draft class have assembled at Blair Field. Several of them are struggling like a one-armed man caught in a riptide.

Except for one player who distinguished himself.

In a sense, scouting is an elaborate Rorschach test. Some look at the ink blot and see a leaf; others see a butterfly; still others see a fire hydrant.

It can be stated with certainty that amateur scouting consists of three factors: observation, evaluation, and imagination. The latter is perilous. Why? Because the most difficult task in any profession by far is to predict the future.

Yet scouts are required to peer into a horsehide crystal ball and determine how a gawky seventeen-year-old will perform as a major leaguer eight years from now. This method produces the rare glittering success, such as Ken Griffey Jr. or Alex Rodriguez.

More commonly, the result is Brian Bullington or Matt Bush . . . busts.

Another dilemma scouts face is deciding which skill they prefer in a player who does multiple things well—for instance, a youngster who shows potential as both a pitcher and a position player.

One player causing double vision this week at the Area Code Games in Long Beach is Tyler Chatwood from Redlands East Valley High School in Redlands, California.

As a right-handed pitcher, Chatwood fires a fastball in the 90–93 mph range and mixes in a wicked hard, sharp curve. Yet Chatwood is a terrific all-around athlete, possessing physical tools which make him a big league prospect as a hitter and position player. His 6.77 second speed in the 60-yard dash is well above average. At bat, he displays the ability to rip the ball to all fields and his drives have a distinctive sharp, concussive crack.

Chatwood's glove, range, and arm easily fit either corner outfield spot. He concluded an impressive performance in today's game by unleashing a one hop laser from left field that cut down a runner by a cozy margin.

Add to this conundrum the fact that Chatwood is just 5'10" and weighs 180 pounds. His strong, undersized, but mature frame offers little projection.

> Scout Speak: He doesn't have much more room to grow and fill out.

His tools fit best in the outfield since his brave attempts to play 3B have been cringe-worthy. As a pitcher, Chatwood no doubt has the raw stuff to be successful but shows a limited "ceiling."

What, pray tell, is a scout to do? File a report on Chatwood as an outfielder or as a pitcher? The answer isn't easy, but if I was forced to make a decision, I'd draft him as an outfielder.

How tough is it for scouts to get it right?

Here's a good example: A pro scout in the early 1950s filed a report on a young second baseman playing in the Braves minor league organization at Jacksonville, Florida. "He plays second base now, but should shift to the outfield," the report began. It continued:

"He's a tremendous hitter but will never have any power."

The subject of the report?

Henry Aaron.

At least the scout got part of it right.

Tyler Chatwood was selected by the Angels in the 2nd round of the 2008 draft (74th overall pick) and received a $547,000 signing bonus. He made his major league debut for Los Angeles in 2011.

On November 30, 2011, Chatwood was traded to Colorado. In the 2014 season, he has split time between the Rockies and their AAA Colorado Springs affiliate.[1]

Hicks Clicks to Nix Tricks
March 6, 2008

Way back in the 1950s, flamboyant theater star Ethel Merman was asked her opinion of Mary Martin, who was then starring on Broadway in *Peter Pan*.

"She's ok," Merman deadpanned, "if you like talent."

Ethel Merman would have loved Aaron Hicks.

Hicks, a 6'3" 180 pound pitcher/outfielder from Wilson High in Long Beach, took the mound Thursday in a day game against El Dorado High of Orange County. A safe bet to be a first round selection in the June draft, Hicks tossed five innings, striking out 9 while allowing 1 run on 3 hits.

A right-hander, his four-seam fastball sat in the 93 to 95 mph range, peaking at 96. Hicks possesses a wicked 82–84 curve

---

1 Through the 2013 season, Chatwood had a career record of 19–22, with a 4.33 ERA. As a hitter, in 73 plate appearances, he has a .305 batting average with 18 hits (2 doubles), 5 runs scored, and 8 RBI.

which exhibits nasty 11 to 5 two-plane break. He compounds a hitter's misery with a hard cutter and a change which shows late arm side movement.

In the fifth inning, El Dorado third baseman Ryan Remlinger engaged Hicks in an epic at-bat. Hicks fired every pitch in his arsenal, and Remlinger kept fouling them off. Remlinger then blasted a 3–2 pitch 400 feet, foul by only a sliver. I asked Hicks what he was thinking at the time. "I just wanted to strike him out." And he did so with a 96 mph fastball.

To ensure that the twenty-five scouts in attendance got an eyeful, the switch hitting Hicks had a big day at bat as well.

In his first at-bat, Hicks singled to right, stole second, stole third, and scored on Zack Wilson's single.

Next time up, Hicks smacked a double off the base of the center field fence and advanced to third on a short fly to right, but was stranded.

Hicks doubled to left center in his third plate appearance, took third on a bunt, and scored on a ground out.

The El Dorado coaching staff decided that discretion is the better part of valor and walked Hicks intentionally in his fourth plate appearance.

"Geez," remarked one spectator, "this is Little League for him."

Tension is not an issue for Hicks. He played CF in the final two innings, swaying to music from an imaginary iPod in his head between pitches.

Today's performance reestablished what many scouts have long contended: Hicks is the finest high school pitching/outfield prospect to come out of the greater Los Angeles area since Daryl Strawberry in the early 1980s. He is that rare player with 5-Plus Tool potential and has the ability to be a Major League All-Star as an outfielder or pitcher.

Hicks still exhibits a few mechanical glitches, as do most prep players. On the mound, his far right (third base side) rubber position causes him to throw across his body on many pitches. Also, Hicks often loses his balance at his delivery finish by landing on a stiff front leg and falling off to his left, permitting several pitches to sail. He has inconsistent command and his pitch counts are too high.

At bat, Hicks has finally lowered his hands into a more workable pre-swing position, but he still shows a tendency to pull his front side and head off the ball and over stride.

None of these flaws are fatal and should be easily correctable once Hicks reaches professional baseball—probably this summer.

Opinions vary, but the consensus among scouts is that the club which drafts Hicks will start him in the low minors as an outfielder. If he doesn't hit after three or so years, then Hicks should comfortably transition to the bump—most likely as a setup man or closer. However, Hicks's great arm, 6.6 speed and vastly improved bat indicate that his days as a hurler may end when he signs his first pro contract.

Over a quarter century ago, a reporter covering the NBA asked the Milwaukee Bucks head coach what type of "role" star forward Marques Johnson played on the team.

"Marques has no role on this team," the coach replied. "He does everything."

So does Aaron Hicks.

Aaron Hicks was chosen by the Minnesota Twins in the first round (14th overall selection) of the June 2008 draft.

In 2013, he made his Major debut with the Twins as a center fielder, Hicks has struggled at the plate, but is a regular on sports highlights shows for his spectacular defensive plays.

The Cutter Edge

Lenny "Nails" Dykstra spent twelve years in the major leagues, playing with the New York Mets (1985–89) and the Philadelphia Phillies

(1989–96). A lifetime .285 hitter, Dykstra starred in the 1986 and 1993 World Series. He finished second in the 1993 National League Most Valuable Player voting.

April 7, 2008

Imitation, it has been said, is the sincerest form of flattery.

Liberated from an extended sentence as a middle infielder, Cutter Dykstra of Westlake, California High School has made the switch to center field, emulating his dad, Lenny Dykstra.

Beset by steroid allegations as well as legal and financial entanglements, the elder Dykstra does not fit anyone's conception of a wall poster type of role model. Dykstra the younger, while troubled internally by his father's woes, soldiers on with admirable focus and intent.

As I observed him during a Saturday afternoon game at home against visiting San Pedro High, Cutter Dykstra is attempting to get accustomed to center field. Between pitches he pantomimes catching and throwing the ball, as if to remind himself of the different mechanics between the infield and the outfield.

Any scout looking for a tall, long-limbed, graceful Joe DiMaggio-type center fielder best look elsewhere. Both Cutter (righty all the way) and Lenny (lefty) play baseball the way James Cagney played a hoodlum in a black and white 1930s gangster flick: Short and scrappy, hustle like rapid Thompson machine gun fire, short on social niceties but long on defiant attitude. No grapefruits squashed in the face of the missus, however.

Cutter displays none of the endearing rough edges his dad exhibited. His hair is not tousled or matted, nor does a golf ball sized chunk of chewing tobacco protrude from his lower cheek. This Dykstra is clean cut and wholesome looking, sort of a blonde version of David Wright of the New York Mets.

Any discussion of Cutter Dykstra among local Southern California scouts inevitably centers on which position he will play in pro ball. His arm is sufficiently strong on short and medium length throws, but a hint of shoulder stiffness in his delivery inhibits the carry of his longer throws. Left field, center field or second base are all defensive possibilities for Dykstra, but center field as his long-term residence would not only be a safe bet, it may be a family heirloom.

All of this discussion ignores the fact that no matter what position he plays, the primary feature of Dykstra's game will always be offense. He is a tremendous athlete, as evidenced by his first place finish in the SPARQ testing at the 2007 Area Code Games in Long Beach—which included a blazing 6.58 60-yard dash clocking.

Dykstra is an aggressive yet intelligent base runner, showing no qualms in challenging catchers and outfielders in stealing bases or taking the extra base. His leg churning, arm pumping, belly sliding running style is a throwback to the "Gashouse Gang" and Pepper Martin.

At bat, Dykstra employs a square and balanced stance with a slight knee flex and a high hand position. His short, compact backswing and sweeping follow through promise average if not slightly above average big league power.

Dykstra handles the middle and inside pitch exceptionally well. He struggles with the outside pitch, showing a tendency to stab or poke at a ball in that region. As do most young, eager hitters, Dykstra will on occasion chase a high fastball out of the strike zone.

In this game, Dykstra flashed his dad's combativeness, becoming visibly upset after fouling off or missing pitches he knew he should have hammered. After two singles, Dykstra whiffed on a high fastball in his third at bat.

Proving the old adage that you shouldn't throw a good hitter the same pitch twice, Dykstra got a high fastball in his next at bat and drove a 400-foot home run over the center field fence. The ball comfortably came to rest under a stately eucalyptus tree.

In their reports, scouts are asked to compare an amateur prospect to a modern major leaguer. With Dykstra, Dustin Pedroia and David Eckstein come to mind. In the upcoming June draft, Dykstra fits in the first supplemental to second round.

Lenny Dykstra, who prior to his current woes made a fortune in the car wash business after retiring from baseball, was drafted in the 13th round by the Mets in 1981. With the talent he possesses, it is likely his son won't be waiting by the phone quite as long on draft day.

And Cutter Dykstra doesn't figure to be working in a car wash anytime soon.

Cutter Dykstra was chosen by the Milwaukee Brewers in the 2nd round (54th overall pick) of the 2008 draft. He received a signing bonus of $737,000.

Since traded to the Washington Nationals, Cutter Dykstra began the 2014 season playing at Harrisburg of the AA Eastern League. His brother, Luke, is a top prospect for the 2014 MLB Draft.

And So It Gose

June 3, 2008

Scouts representing six major league organizations gathered Monday at the indoor facility of West Coast Sports Management in Pasadena, California, to witness a throwing session featuring Anthony Gose, the rocket-armed left-handed pitching and outfield prospect from Bellflower High School.

Sidelined for most of the season with shoulder tendonitis, Gose (pronounced *Goes*) was eager to show scouts that he is now perfectly fit, and, to paraphrase Mark Twain, reports of his demise are greatly exaggerated.

For moral support, Gose brought along his best friend, Aaron Hicks, who is rumored to possess a trace of baseball talent himself. Hicks's primary contribution to the proceedings was his keen ability to consume a large submarine sandwich.

WCSM's indoor setup is too small to contain Gose's arm, so the workout was held at an aged but spacious public park nearby. In a scene that can only be described as somewhat surrealistic, Gose, Hicks, and seven scouts traipsed two blocks north up Fair Oaks Avenue. It was a parade far less impressive than the one held in Pasadena every New Year's Day.

A well-groomed German Shepherd leashed to the leg of a chair at an outdoor eatery squinted as the group passed by, puzzled as to why seven middle-aged men were following two teenage athletes up the street on a warm weekday afternoon.

Once the mob reached the park, Gose and his receiver began to play a game of catch. A squirrel paused to observe. Unimpressed, he scurried up the trunk of a large, craggy oak tree.

Only 30 feet away, a homeless man lying on the un-mowed grass slept soundly, blissfully unaware that two soon to be baseball millionaires were nearby. The prone man was motionless for several minutes. I reached for my cell phone to call the coroner when our friend slowly rolled over on his side, eliminating any concerns over his expiration. He slept through the entire workout.

The scouts, however, paid rapt attention. Gose threw easily at short and extended distances, comfortably displaying the terrific arm strength that makes him perhaps the hardest throwing left-hander available in Thursday's draft.

Suitably convinced that Gose is healthy, scouts will now turn their attention to another portsider, John Lamb, of Laguna Hills High. The silky smooth throwing Lamb was injured in a car accident several months ago and missed his entire prep season. He is scheduled to throw a series of bullpen sessions later this week.

Anthony Gose was selected by the Philadelphia Phillies as an Outfielder in the 2nd round of the 2008 draft. He was the 51st overall pick.

On July 29, 2010, the Phillies traded Gose to Houston. Later that same day, the Astros traded Gose to the Blue Jays.

Gose made his Major League Debut with Toronto on July 17, 2012, as an outfielder. In 2014, he began the season with the Blue Jays but was later optioned to their AAA club at Buffalo.

Golden Harper

Bryce Harper was selected by the Washington Nationals as the first overall pick in the 2010 draft. A stunningly gifted hitter, Harper received more pre-draft hype, attention, and publicity than any other position player in the history of the amateur draft, which was established in 1965.

I first saw Harper play when he was a fifteen-year-old high school freshman. The following articles trace my observations of Harper over a two-year period from the summer of 2008 to the doorstep of the draft in 2010.

June 16, 2008

In the spring of 1950, New York Giants scout Eddie Montague was dispatched to Birmingham, Alabama, to observe a Negro League first baseman named Alonzo Perry.

Unimpressed with Perry, Montague wired the Giants front office. "I don't know about the first baseman," he opined, "but they've got a kid down here playing center field barefoot who's the greatest player I've ever seen."

That kid's name was Willie Mays.

The dozens of scouts who attended the Major League Scouting Bureau's summer showcase at the Urban Youth Academy in Compton, California, ostensibly came to evaluate the talent available in the 2009 Southern California High School Draft class.

Like Eddie Montague sixty years ago, attention was instead drawn to another player—Bryce Harper. Only fifteen, Harper is a 6' 2" 200 pound left-handed hitting catcher/third baseman from Las Vegas High. To the dismay of every organization in baseball, Harper just completed his freshman year and won't be draft eligible until 2011.

Harper does not play barefoot, but he is perhaps the finest prospect local scouts have ever seen. He began the evening with an incredible wood bat BP display, blasting tape measure shots all over the academy grounds. Harper's best effort was a bullet that flew over the center-field wall in a nanosecond and deflected off the hitting back drop like a golf ball bouncing off a trampoline.

Harper already possesses a throwing arm that grades out to 70 on the 20–80 scouting scale. As a catcher, his POP times ranged from 1.84 to 1.91—well above major league average.

Harper's only non-celestial tool is his 7.03 speed. When asked about Harper's speed, one scout said, "Who the heck cares?"

This showcase was populated with several players who later became high draft choices, including Tyler Matzek, Christian Yelich, Jake Marisnick, Cameron Garfield, Matt Davidson, Jiovanni Mier, and Tyler Skaggs.

Two months later I ran into Harper during a Perfect Game event held at USC.

August 12, 2008

Dedeaux Field on the campus of USC hosted the preliminary workouts for Sunday's Aflac Game. After a morning scrimmage, a Perfect Game event featuring 2010 and 2011 prospects was held.

Bryce Harper was one of three catchers in the rotation to receive throws during pre-game infield/outfield practice. Halfway through warm-ups, Harper, stray baseball in hand, stepped back from home plate and turned his body toward the first base foul line.

Suddenly and without warning or provocation, Harper fired a missile down the line and over the fence in the right field corner, a distance of 340 feet. Most scouts had departed after the Aflac scrimmage, but the few remaining were stunned. Whispered comments included:

"Did you see that?"

"Why did he do that?"

"I can't believe it!"

Perhaps due to utter shock, no one retrieved the baseball.

With media hype mechanisms in full gear, Harper participated in the 2009 Aflac All-American Game, held at Petco Park in San Diego. It was an underwhelming performance.

Bryce Harper, the sixteen-year-old catching phenom, was the marquee attraction at the Aflac Game. With apologies to Winston Churchill, it was not our hero's finest hour.

Despite his howitzer throwing arm, Harper was unable to nab theft minded base runners. This is due to his habit of wrapping the ball behind his neck prior to releasing his throw to second, adding unnecessary motion and unwanted time to his deliveries.

At bat, Harper grounded out twice and struck out three times, angrily rifling his batting helmet into the dugout after his third whiff.

Over the past several weeks, scouts have been whispering that Harper was off his game. Those suspicions were validated in San Diego. He could not catch up to a decent fastball and was badly fooled by every curve, flailing and missing. Harper's swing, previously very sound, has regressed. His cut is far too long on the back end, he is lunging and diving at pitches, and his timing is drastically inconsistent.

Harper is the subject of more publicity than any high school baseball player in history; some of the hype, admittedly, coming from *Baseball America*, myself included. *Sports Illustrated* placed Harper on a recent cover and hyperbolically proclaimed him "The Chosen One." An outlandish claim insists that Harper had once struck a 570-foot home run—which is blatant nonsense.

Currently, Harper is attempting to finish high school early in order to play junior college ball at the College of Southern Nevada, which would make him draft eligible in 2010, not 2011.

Judging from his ordeal on Sunday night, no sixteen-year-old, no matter how gifted or talented, can be expected to play at fantastic or unrealistic levels. Harper undoubtedly felt the pressure of extreme expectations in San Diego. Perhaps everyone—scouts, media, agents, fans, etc.—should back off Harper a shade, thus permitting him to be a teenager and develop at a less frenzied or accelerated rate.

In 2009, I did an online chat in which, to my utter lack of surprise, the subject of Bryce Harper was raised.

Question: 2016—best catcher in baseball, Wieters, Posey, or Harper?

Answer: 2016? I don't even know what I'm having for dinner tonight, much less look ahead to 2016! Kidding aside, that is a great question. I will answer that with a shocker—Harper is not a catcher for me. I would put him in right field for two reasons: he is such a great hitting prospect I don't want to see his bat diminished by the wear and tear of catching. Second, I don't think he is a very good defensive receiver. Great arm, but the glove isn't there and he wraps the ball behind his neck when he throws . . .

A month before the June 2010 draft, I spent a weekend in Las Vegas watching Harper play for the College of Southern Nevada. In this scouting report, I evaluated him and received the input of several other scouts.

May 5, 2010

Bryce Harper, the top prospect for Major League Baseball's upcoming amateur draft, once again put his considerable talents on display this past weekend. Only seventeen years old, the young phenom led his College of Southern Nevada squad to a pair of doubleheader sweeps at home against the College of Eastern Utah.

Southern Nevada plays in the six member Junior College level Scenic West Athletic Conference. In a welcome departure from amateur baseball norms, wood bats are used in all SWAC games.

A catcher/outfielder who bats left and throws right, Harper is the most heavily hyped position prospect in the entire forty-five-year history of the amateur draft. In an unusual step, Harper passed a GED exam last year and skipped his final two years of high school in order to play at CSN. That strategy makes him eligible for the 2010 draft instead of the 2011 draft.

Last summer, *Sports Illustrated* trumpeted Harper as baseball's answer to LeBron James—a teenage prodigy and unprecedented once in a lifetime talent.

Opinions among baseball insiders are lavish but considerably more restrained. Most scouts agree that Harper is the top player available in this year's draft, despite his three strikeout quasi meltdown in last summer's Aflac All American Game. One regional supervisor said of the game, "The greatest player ever? The only thing I've seen him do is strikeout!"

That comment was overly cynical and made in jest, but it does illuminate a point in reference to Harper. He is a wonderfully gifted player but by no means a perfect one. All of the Mickey Mantle comparisons made in reference to Harper are silly. No doubt Harper possesses some skills which are incredible, but his other skills ("tools") are downright pedestrian.

Harper is blessed with two top of the scale tools—staggering raw power and a cannon throwing arm. Scouts are divided on whether he fits best as a catcher or as a right fielder. Catchers with left-handed home run power are exceptionally rare. However, some clubs believe that Harper should be placed in right field, since his unique hitting ability would be diminished by the daily wear and tear of catching.

As a catcher, Harper has average but not extraordinary receiving skills and decent flexibility. Harper's hands are not cinder blocks, but neither are they Bench-ian. Raw as a defensive outfielder, Harper's routes to fly balls are, let's say, circuitous, and his fly catching talents are decidedly off-Broadway. Few observers doubt that with substantial practice Harper's defensive skills will reach solid major league average but, in all likelihood, will fail to earn him many Gold Gloves.

Harper's throwing arm, which has been clocked at 95 mph, is easily his top defensive tool. "He can really throw," said one scout. As a catcher, his home to second "pop" time hovers in the 1.90 to 1.99 range. In truth, Harper's pop times should be in the 1.80 to 1.85 region, but he wraps the ball behind his neck prior to releasing it, adding unnecessary time to his deliveries.

If he plays right field as a pro, Harper's arm has the potential to equal any legendary outfield thrower in baseball history: Roberto Clemente, Dwight Evans, Ellis Valentine, Raul Mondesi, Willie Mays, Rocky Colavito, etc.

At the plate, Harper's prodigious power is almost entirely the function of stunning natural bat speed. His swing can get long on the back end, plus he will occasionally shift his hands downward and into his body, eliminating leverage. Harper's swing path is inconsistent and he struggles with breaking balls and off speed stuff. Like many young hitters, he has consistent difficulty in handling pitches on the outside corner at the knees.

One former big league star chimed in with a different observation. "He takes such a big cut," said the former player, "that he leaves himself vulnerable inside. I think he can be tied up on the hands with hard stuff."

In addition to his remarkable talent, Harper is one of the quirkiest players scouts have ever seen. He smears on an elaborate amount of eye black on his face, the pattern of which resembles the helmet logo of the NFL's Atlanta Falcons. Prior to entering the batter's box, Harper rubs his palms in the dirt, spits in his hands, and then rubs his palms in the dirt once more. He enters the box and rubs more dirt on his hands, takes his stance, touches the corners of the plate with his bat, and then taps his front toe with the bat barrel.

Several scouts weighed in with their views on Harper. "I like him a lot, he's a heck of a hitter" said one. "He hits the fastball as good as anybody and can drive the ball the other way. The bat plays anywhere you put him. His release takes some time, but he has an absolute cannon. He may move from catcher only because of the wear and tear. But if he stays as a catcher, the sky is the limit."

One scout praised Harper's performance this year, stating, "He's very strong. The pressure has been on him this year and he has produced."

A veteran scout with pro and amateur scouting experience stated, "As a catcher, he has much more draft value. He's not much of an outfielder. His swing has a tendency to get long, and he fights pulling off the ball. If he comes out as a catcher, he's 1/1 (first pick, first round) for me. You've got a left-handed, power-hitting catcher and you don't get those too often."

In contrast, an American League scout said he would move Harper to the outfield immediately. "He can use his tools" the scout said, "keep his legs, and his mobility is ok. He has a plus-plus arm and he has big power. I see him as a 40 home run a year guy, but .300 is a stretch . . . because of timing issues."

The AL scout added, "The minors will be his first real competition. The whole thing about him making the majors at nineteen is nonsense. The Nationals (who own the first pick) aren't stupid. They'll let him progress properly."

Another scout expressed concern, not about Harper's talent, but on the effect money and hype may have on him: "He has a ton of talent, but it's hard for a seventeen-year-old who gets that much money to stay hungry and driven to become the best player he can be. It's very hard work to get to the major leagues and the track record for teenagers who get giant bonuses is very poor. . . . They change when they get the money. If you have $10 million in the bank and you have teenage hormones, it's hard to bust your tail and slave yourself to earning a $400,000 major league minimum salary. It takes an unusually mature and motivated kid to accomplish that."

In my opinion, and in the general consensus of scouts I spoke with, Harper projects as a perennial All-Star and MVP candidate who on a yearly basis should produce 30–40 homers, 100 RBI, and an average in the .275–.290 range. He'll have a high strike-out total each season, around 125 to 150.

It is virtually impossible for anyone—particularly a seventeen-year-old—to live up to the enormous and at times ridiculous hype that has been showered upon Bryce Harper. While he is not the "second coming" and does not profile as the greatest player of all time, Harper figures to be a Hall of Fame caliber player. For the 2010 draft, Harper is without question the top bat and premier position player available.

Bryce Harper was the first pick in the June 2010 draft, selected by the Washington Nationals as an outfielder. He received a signing bonus of $6,250,000. Harper made his major league debut on April 28, 2012—at the age of nineteen.

He was named the National League Rookie of the Year in 2012. Harper was named to the NL All Star team in 2012 and 2013.

The Strasburg Method

February 23, 2009

As the 2009 NCAA Division-I college baseball season opened this past weekend, scouts based in Southern California could exit any freeway off ramp at any time of day or night to observe a variety of potential future first round draft picks.

Stephen Strasburg began the festivities. The junior right-hander took the hill for San Diego State as the Aztecs opened their campaign against Bethune-Cookman at MLB's Urban Youth Academy complex in Compton, California. Strasburg is the consensus candidate to be the first pick in the upcoming draft, and his performance helped bolster his already lofty ranking.

Forty scouts dutifully lined up outside the chain link fence adjacent to the right field bullpen to watch Strasburg warm up. None could be blamed for wishing that pre-1965 signing rules were still in effect. In those long ago days there was no draft, and each club had an equal opportunity to sign any amateur free agent. *C'est la vie.*

If a scientist working in a lab with a computer and a batch of exotic chemicals sought to create a perfect pitching prospect, the result would resemble Strasburg. Perfectly proportioned at 6' 5" and 220 pounds, he is gifted with broad shoulders, long arms and enormous hands, in which an enveloped baseball almost disappears.

When the game began, Strasburg did not disappoint. His first six fastballs registered 98-99-98-98-99-98 mph. Strasburg mixed in his wicked 81–82 slurve, which when coupled with his fastball can be described as blatantly unfair. To his credit, Strasburg maintains his stuff as a game proceeds, touching 97–98 in the fifth inning while maintaining his 81–82 breaking ball.

For scouts, Mark Prior of USC remains the gold standard for right-handed college pitching prospects. Blessed with a perfect frame, excellent mechanics, pinpoint control, and a phenomenal arm, Prior was the second selection in the 2001 draft by the Chicago Cubs. Prior eventually signed a major league contract that guaranteed him 10.5 million dollars.

Comparisons between Strasburg and Prior are natural and inevitable. However, there are some subtle differences between the two. Both have ideal builds and once in a decade arms, but Prior's mechanics and command were noticeably more refined and polished at a similar stage.

For any pitcher at any level, command and mechanics are flip sides of the same coin. Prior's textbook mechanics gave him precise control. Strasburg's delivery fundamentals are not yet at a comparable level and his command suffers as a result.

As two examples, Prior's arm slot was high three-quarters; Strasburg's is three quarters to low three quarters and varies more than did Prior's. Prior's finish was perfectly balanced. Strasburg will occasionally land on a stiff front leg and tumble to his left or employ a quick hop at his delivery finish, both sure signs of a loss of balance.

Prior and Strasburg both possess explosive fastballs, but their curves differ. Prior's breaking ball was more of a true curve, with a distinct two plane break and a diagonal tilt. Strasburg's hammer is more of a slurve, starting at a hitter's thighs then swerving sharply down and sideways to shin level.

San Diego State won the game, 6–3, with Strasburg earning the win. Strasburg had a high pitch total, falling behind several hitters while running up numerous three ball counts. His pitching line was impressive, but does not fully reflect the moderate command problems he encountered: 5.2 IP, 3H, 1R, 1BB, 1 HBP, and 11 K.

• • •

UCLA right-hander Gerrit Cole, a leading candidate for the first overall pick in 2011, made his first college start Saturday in Westwood against UC Davis.

Cole brushed aside the Aggies in his six innings of work, allowing one hit, one run, walking two, and striking out seven. Cole's stuff was sensational. His fastball ranged from 94 to 97, peaking at 98. Cole used his 81 changeup more effectively than he did in high school and his hard 85–88 slider is simply brutal. UCLA won, 5–2, as Cole was credited with his first D-1 win.

Scouts agree that Cole's mechanics are showing steady improvement; however, some have voiced concern regarding his near maximum effort delivery. For that reason, big league organizations may be divided as to whether Cole profiles as a starter or a closer. There is little doubt that Cole's pure arm strength is matched at the college level only by Strasburg.

USC shortstop Grant Green was in action Sunday as his Trojans hosted Long Beach State at Dedeaux Field. Green had struggled in the first two games of the weekend series, going hitless in both contests.

Early arrivals to the game noticed an elaborate tape job on Green's left hand, raising concerns of a possible hamate bone problem—perhaps similar to the injury Troy Tulowitzki suffered in his junior season in 2005. The hamate bone is a small, hooked shaped bone in the wrist which, due to the stress of swinging a bat, is a common baseball related injury.

Not to worry, as a chat with Green's dad revealed that the hand wrap serves to protect his son's paw from painful blisters accumulated in batting practice.

The USC trainer worked on the Trojan star prior to the game. Green was put through a series of severe stretching exercises which are probably banned under the Geneva Convention. Fit and resilient, Green leapt to his feet when the trainer was done and bounced into the dugout.

Green found the swing that had been missing most of the weekend. He had two hits in three at-bats, drove in one, scored two and stole two bases as USC dropped a 5–4 decision to the Dirtbags. (Long Beach State's baseball team has been unofficially nicknamed the Dirtbags since 1989, but the school's official nickname is the 49ers.) Green's first hit of the 2009 season was a line drive home run, ripped into the netting beyond the left field fence.

Speed (6.55 seconds over 60 yards) and defense are Green's primary assets. He seemed tentative on his throws Sunday, bouncing one toss and making a throwing error later on. Green's glove work, on the other hand, is excellent. In all areas that defense encompasses—hands, range, arm, play making ability—Green is darn close to being major league ready right now. He also exhibits the smoothness, fluidity and ease of actions emblematic of all outstanding defensive players.

Green had ten assists in Sunday's game and he made a string of excellent plays: ranging to his left, coming in, short-hopping the ball, making off balance and on the run throws, etc. While Green's arm and defensive skills are not in the Tulowitzki stratosphere (whose are?), his ballet-like play at shortstop makes Green one of the finest defenders in the nation. Green is the rare college shortstop with five average to plus tool potential.

Stephen Strasburg was the first pick in the 2009 draft, selected by the Washington Nationals. He signed for $7,500,000. Strasburg made a sensational major league debut on June 8, 2010, striking out 14 Pirates in 7 innings.

In September, 2010, Strasburg underwent Tommy John surgery on his right elbow, returning to action in September of 2011.

Gerrit Cole was the first overall selection in the 2011 MLB draft, selected by the Pittsburgh Pirates. He made his big league debut in 2013.

The Oakland A's made Grant Green the 13th overall pick in the 2009 draft. He received a signing bonus of $2,750,000. Traded by Oakland to the Angels, Green made his major league debut with Los Angeles in 2013. Green began 2014 playing with the Angels AAA ballclub at Salt Lake City.

Barstow-ed

July 8, 2009

A handful of American cities are frequently subjected to good-natured ridicule. Cleveland is a common target, for instance, as is any city in Northern New Jersey. Gertrude Stein once famously trashed Oakland when she wrote, "There is no there, there."

Likewise, the small municipality of Barstow, California, has always been a dart board for barbs and wisecracks. Situated on Interstate 15, Barstow is renowned as the primary pit stop between Los Angeles and Las Vegas. Just like a stock car racer when visiting their pit crew, drivers attempt to flee Barstow in the shortest time possible.

A minute measure of solace among Barstownians can be extracted from the fact that their hometown is not quite as beleaguered as Lewiston, Maine. Unexpected home of the second Ali-Liston fight in 1965, Jim Murray wrote of the drab New England city: "As a town, Lewiston is so unknown the people who live there have never heard of it." (Actually, I have no idea if Murray ever wrote that line. I invented the quote since it sounds like something he would write.)

Home to withering 105 degree desert heat and sizeable tumbleweeds, Barstow has never been considered an oasis for amateur baseball prospects. In 2007, right-handed pitcher Matt Mitchell was drafted by the Royals in the 14th round. Only one other player has ever been drafted out of Barstow High School.

That scenario will no doubt change thanks to Aaron Sanchez, a 6' 3" 175 pound right-handed pitcher who will be a senior at Barstow High this fall. As the summer showcase season progresses, Sanchez is establishing himself as one of the premier hurlers in the 2010 draft class.

His latest tour de force occurred at Orange Coast College, site of the tryouts for the Milwaukee Brewers Area Code teams.

Tall, pencil thin, and extremely projectable, Sanchez was the star of the second day of the tryouts. Not so faintly resembling Orel Hershiser, Sanchez has a remarkably easy low three-quarters arm action which mimics a daydreamer skimming a stone across the surface of a calm mountain lake.

His 91–92 mph four-seam fastball is complemented by an 81 mph circle change and an exceptionally promising 75–78 curveball. The first two curves delivered by Sanchez simply moved up and down; he eventually sharpened that pitch until it exhibited a hint of depth along with a distinct tilt and tailing finish.

Sanchez's pitch release and body type promise additional future velocity. He adds advanced pitching smarts and an excellent feel for his secondary stuff. A virtual shoe-in to make the final Brewer Area Codes roster, Sanchez will participate in the Aflac All American game at Petco Park in San Diego.

Scouting directors, cross checkers, and area scouts, meanwhile, will have to gird themselves for the inevitable trip to Barstow in the spring of 2010. Wrapping oneself in ice beforehand may make the experience bearable.

Not that Barstow doesn't have some redeeming features: It boasts one of the busiest McDonald's franchises in the world.

"It has two drive through lanes," mused one prominent and well-respected agent. He paused and added, "I have no idea why I know that."

On April 15, 2010, I traveled to Ridgecrest, California, to watch Sanchez pitch for his high school team six weeks prior to the 2010 draft. I learned that Barstow and Ridgecrest share many common traits.

The scouting profession can take an individual to places he never planned—or particularly wanted—to visit. On Thursday, April 15, I traveled to the isolated hamlet of Ridgecrest, located in the high desert region of California. If you have never heard of Ridgecrest, don't be ashamed—neither has anyone else.

Located just outside the city limits is the US Navy's China Lake Weapons Station (why the Navy chose to place a base in the middle of the desert is anyone's guess). One scout asked aloud: "Why would someone put a town here? Did his burro die?"

Another scout informed me: "There has been a lot of UFO activity in this area—seriously." Of that I have no doubt. In all likelihood, the aliens landed, looked around—and decided they'd get more value for their vacation dollar by heading to Las Vegas, about 100 miles east.

Aaron Sanchez was selected by the Toronto Blue Jays in the 1st supplemental round of the 2010 June draft. The 34th overall pick, Sanchez received a signing bonus of $775,000. He began the 2014 season pitching for the Blue Jays AA ballclub at New Hampshire.

Nor-Easter

For scouts, Easter is a frantic time of year. Colleges at all levels are deep into their schedules and a wide variety of high school tournaments are held. In Southern California, the two most notable shindigs are the Anaheim Lions Tournament and the National Classic, both based in Orange County.

In March and April of 2010, I dropped in on several springtime games.

March 8, 2010

Right-hander Dylan Covey of Maranatha High in Pasadena, a 2009 Aflac All-American, enjoyed a sensational start to his 2010 season by recording 12 of 15 outs via strikeout in a game against Newbury Park High.

The contest was played at scenic but aged Jackie Robinson Field, nestled within Brookside Park in Pasadena, only a few hundred yards from the Rose Bowl. To state it bluntly, Robinson Field needs updating. Observed one scout, "They could use a few more bulbs in those lights."

Covey's pre-game bullpen warm-up session was a harbinger. Under a canopy of ancient, towering eucalyptus trees, sixty scouts watched as Covey pumped pitch after pitch into his catcher's well-worn mitt.

"Atta boy, get in a rhythm," advised Covey's pitching coach. "Drop it right in the hole."

Covey is one of the most distinctive pitching prospects seen in Southern California in many years. His flat billed cap is pulled well down on his forehead and his ill-fitting, low slung uniform pants are an odd sight in relation to his enormous boat paddle pair of feet.

Covey's stuff is eye-catching as well, but difficult to connect with. His four-seam fastball pounds the strike zone at 93–94 mph. Among the scouts sitting near me, I heard whispers of 96 on their radar guns. An 81–82 slider is Covey's best secondary offering, exhibiting sharp, late, veering movement.

A Maranatha parent engaged me in a brief conversation during the game. "That stuff is awfully hard for high schoolers to hit," he said. I replied, "It would be awfully tough for big leaguers to hit."

An American League cross checker summed up Covey's outing succinctly: "With all those scouts out there, he did exactly what he had to do. He showed his stuff, hit his spots and dominated. You can't ask for anything else."

Dylan Covey was selected by the Milwaukee Brewers as the 14th overall pick in the first round of the 2010 draft. A few days prior to the signing deadline, a physical exam revealed that Covey is diabetic.

He did not sign with Milwaukee. In 2013, Covey was selected by the Oakland A's in the fourth round of the draft. The A's assigned Covey to Beloit of the Low A Midwest League in 2014.

April 5, 2010

As usual, Easter week in Southern California has scouts scurrying from field to field to catch glimpses of top prospects participating in local round robin tournaments.

In an unusual twist from previous seasons, the National Classic is laden with underclassmen that are top prospects for future drafts; the Lions tournament is heavy with seniors who are elite prospects for the upcoming draft.

Such has not always been the case. When filing reports, scouts grade a player on a 20–80 scale. Rarely does any player receive an OFP (overall future potential) score above 60. A few years ago I spoke to a scout, since retired, who covered the 1993 National Classic and observed a senior shortstop from Westminster Christian High in Miami named Alex Rodriguez.

"He's the only prospect in my life that I've given a 75 OFP score to," the scout recalled.

The host ballpark for the Lions Tournament is Glover Stadium. Situated within La Palma park in Anaheim, Glover Stadium was opened in 1939, and served as the spring training home of the Philadelphia A's in 1940. That club was managed by Connie Mack and featured such stars as Sam Chapman and Bob Johnson.

The baseball field at Glover is named in honor of a man named Dee Fee, who at some point in his life no doubt endured the nickname "fiddle."

Attention in the Lions Tournament soon shifted to another locale: Boysen Park, also in Anaheim.

April 6, 2010

Dominic Ficociello's tape measure home run was the highlight of the second day of competition in the Anaheim Lions tournament. Forty scouts flocked to Boysen Park to watch the switch hitting Ficociello and his Fullerton Union High teammate Michael Lorenzen perform in a game won by Lakewood High, 9–6.

Scenic and exquisitely maintained, the field at Boysen Park boasts big league dimensions: 355 feet to left, 392 to left center, 400 to center, 393 to right center and 344 to right. In homage to Wrigley Field, foliage covers the outfield fence from corner to corner.

The ballpark is named for Rudolph Boysen, a gentleman who, among his many other accomplishments, is credited with being the first to cultivate boysenberries—much to the delight of toast lovers nationwide.

Ficociello landed on scouts' GPS during last summer's Area Code Games, when he knocked out five hits in a doubleheader. He followed that performance with a long wood bat home run in the Jesse Flores Memorial All Star Game in November at USC.

Tall and gangly, the University of Arkansas–bound shortstop has experienced a strangely uneven 2010 spring season. Ficociello began strongly, pounding four home runs in Fullerton's first six games. A bizarre incident then followed.

In a subsequent game, Ficociello was ruled to have ventured too far out of the dugout to celebrate a teammate's RBI. He was suspended for two games under a persnickety California Interscholastic Federation rule.

That silliness led to a prolonged slump by Ficociello in which he lost patience and selectivity at the plate, struggled with pitch recognition and flailed at every pitch with the intention of hitting two home runs with one swing. That slump ended emphatically on Monday.

Batting left-handed in the seventh inning, Ficociello blasted a letter-high fastball over the 393 sign in right center. The laser shot cleared the wall by approximately 40 feet, shearing off the branch of a tree stationed behind the fence.

It was perhaps the longest—and hardest hit—home run by a Southern California high schooler since Mike Moustakas (now in the Royals organization) unloaded a 500-foot shot for Chatsworth High at Granada Hills High in 2007. That particular monster cleared the right field fence and tall protective netting, crossed a residential street then landed on the roof of an apartment building.

Several scouts left the game early, prior to Ficociello's bomb. Their poor timing is reminiscent of the driver whose red tail lights can be seen leaving Dodger Stadium as Kirk Gibson hit his legendary walk off home run in the first game of the 1988 World Series.

Dominic Ficociello was chosen by the Detroit Tigers in the 23rd round of the 2010 Major League Baseball Draft. He did not sign with the Tigers and went on to play at the University of Arkansas. In 2013, Detroit again chose Ficociello, this time in the 12th round. He began 2014 playing with Western Michigan of the Midwest League.

April 8, 2010

Peter Tago, a right-handed pitcher, played his prep baseball at Dana Hills High School in South Orange County.

It can be stated with absolute certainty that Peter Tago is a dude.

In scouting vernacular, a dude is a definitive prospect. Based on his performance Wednesday in a Lions Tournament game at Boysen Park in Anaheim, Tago has ascended to the upper ranks of dude-eronomy.

In four innings of work in an 11–0 win over Thousand Oaks High, Tago struck out eight, allowing one hit and walking two.

Prior to the game, Dana Hills players trudged from their bus to the first base dugout. Tago coolly strolled by wearing a pair of designer wraparound shades. With earphones from his iPod securely in place, Tago listened to tunes while calmly bypassing—ignoring, actually—the sixty scouts in attendance.

Tago provides an ideal template for a right-handed pitching prospect. Tall, loose, lanky, and projectable at 6'3" and 180 pounds, his bullwhip arm action is easy and almost poetically smooth. He fires a four-seam fastball which ranges from 91 to 94 and will peak at 95–96. Tago's vicious two plane curve clocks in at 75–77.

Later in the season, I revisited Tago.

June 2, 2010

Nothing much seems to bother Peter Tago.

Like Harry Houdini escaping from a locked water tank, Tago wriggled out of jam after jam Tuesday at Blair Field in Long Beach, leading Dana Hills High to a 5–3 win over El Dorado High of Yorba Linda in a CIF Southern Section Division one semifinal playoff game.

Tago struck out thirteen in the seven inning game, but ran into trouble in the fifth. Unflustered by an El Dorado rally, Tago took a deep, chest-heaving breath—and then proceeded to retire the next seven hitters in a row, four by strikeouts.

With two outs in the sixth, Tago paused for a moment on the mound. He dropped his head, pinned his chin to his chest, and appeared to be practicing a form of Zen-like meditation.

Suddenly, Tago snapped to attention, went into his windup and delivered a curveball which veered around the on deck circle before dropping onto the outside corner at the hitter's knees.

Strike three, inning over.

Peter Tago was chosen by the Colorado Rockies in the first supplemental round (47th overall pick) of the 2010 draft. He received a signing bonus of $982,500.

Tago has struggled in his minor league career so far. He began 2014 at Modesto of the High A California League.

West Wooden

A few days after the death of incomparable UCLA basketball coach John Wooden, teams representing Cal State Fullerton and UCLA met at Jackie Robinson Stadium in Westwood, California, in an NCAA Division One Super Regional baseball playoff series.

Super was an apt description for the best 2 out of 3 set, as both teams did college baseball—and Coach Wooden's memory—proud.

Game One, Friday Night, June 11, 2010:

On a cool autumn day in November 2007, right-handed pitcher Noe Ramirez, then a senior at Alhambra High School in California, threw a bullpen session for the benefit of any interested scouts. Only two showed up: myself and Sergio Brown, assistant coach and intrepid recruiter for Cal State Fullerton.

For a rail thin and gangly youngster, Ramirez threw well but did not display early round draft stuff. Brown was crafty enough to offer Noe a scholarship on the spot.

Few if any pro scouts saw Ramirez pitch in his senior year. In fact, one laughed and told me, "I'm not going all the way out there to see a guy who throws 87!"

After his sensational performance Friday night in the opening game of the Los Angeles Super Regional, Ramirez, now a college sophomore, is guaranteed to draw considerably more respect and attention from scouts in 2011. He led the Titans to a thrilling 4–3 win over UCLA, outdueling the Bruins' own lavishly talented sophomore righty, Gerrit Cole.

On a field littered with high draft selections, future high draft selections and sons of former pros, Ramirez commanded center stage. He struck out 13 in seven innings of work, allowing two runs (one earned), two walks, and six hits. Ramirez, whose four-seam fastball sits at 91–92, constantly fooled the fastball-loving Bruins by utilizing his sweeping 77–79 slider and 84 change to record strikeout after crucial strikeout.

The packed house in Westwood provided an electric atmosphere to the evening. Hollywood celebs were not present, since that set prefers Lakers games. The closest thing to a celebrity sighting was Scott Boras, who arrived late and promptly sat down in the front row behind home plate. An usher ordered Boras out of the seat and instructed him to walk back to the top of the aisle.

A few innings later, Boras returned to the front row. No usher dared bother him again.

UCLA took a narrow 1–0 lead in the third inning. Fullerton rallied to snatch a 4–1 lead after five. Torturously, Bruin rallies in the bottom of the fifth, sixth, and seventh failed to net any runs, but plated two in the eighth to inch closer, 4–3.

Then came the critical and all-important ninth inning. With runners on first and third and no outs, UCLA called for a steal. Sensing a play was in the offing, Titan reliever Nick Ramirez picked Blair Dunlap off first. Fullerton handled the rundown perfectly, tagging out Dunlap while Beau Amaral was forced to remain anchored at third.

With a chance to win or tie the game, UCLA's Tyler Rahmatulla struck out and Chris Giovanazzo grounded out the end the game.

Friday night's game encompassed all that is great and not so great about upper echelon college baseball. It was filled with brilliant yet sloppy plays; was far too long; featured excitement and tension; left one team ecstatic and the other privately seething. In sum, it was a messy, unkempt masterpiece.

The two ball clubs outdid themselves the next evening.

Saturday, June 12, 2010

On Saturday night, Cal State Fullerton was one lonely out from a berth in the College World Series. The Titans led visiting UCLA, 6–5, with two outs and a runner on in the top of the ninth. Suddenly, Bruin second baseman Tyler Rahmatulla blasted the most important and dramatic home run in UCLA baseball history over the left field wall at Jackie Robinson Stadium.

Rahmatulla's drive gave the Bruins a shocking 7–6 lead. The Titans rallied in the bottom of the ninth as Gary Brown and Christian Colon, Fullerton's two first round draft picks, pulled off a scintillating double steal. Brown scored on the play to knot the score at seven and send the game into extra innings.

UCLA finally solved their inability to hit with runners on base by pushing across four runs in the top of the tenth to notch their final 11–7 advantage. Bruin shortstop Niko Gallego placed an exclamation point on UCLA's win in the bottom of the tenth, recording outs on two separate brilliant diving plays—one to his right and one to his left.

Saturday's game was physically exhausting and mentally draining. Players and coaches from both clubs trudged into the post game interview room in a daze, having survived college baseball's version of trench warfare.

Fullerton Coach Dave Serrano, while somber, was classy and unapologetic in defeat: "Just like UCLA had a tough loss last night, we had a tough loss tonight. It's a pretty tough loss when you're one out from Omaha [home of the College World Series]."

Serrano, who doubles as the Titan's pitching coach and calls his teams pitches, defended his decision to throw a 3–1 fastball to Rahmatulla, a dead fastball hitter. "I don't like walking guys, and he had count leverage," Serrano stated. "He does what good hitters do—he squared up the 3–1 fastball."

UCLA Coach John Savage looked like a condemned prisoner who had just gotten a reprieve call from the governor one minute before his sentence was to be carried out. "We have a lot of per-severance on this club," Savage said, voicing the obvious. In the understatement of his career, Savage added, "That was a hell of a college baseball game."

The third and deciding game of the series was anti-climactic. Then again, pretty much anything would have been anti-climactic after the first two games.

Sunday, June 13, 2010

Quite literally, Rob Rasmussen's career at UCLA got off on the wrong foot. In his first collegiate start in 2008, a screaming line drive through the box caught him squarely on his left foot, breaking it.

Rasmussen, a 5'11" 170 pound left-hander, valiantly returned to the mound later in the 2008 season. He started a Super Regional game against Cal State Fullerton, only to be yanked after surren-dering three runs and six hits in just three innings.

Now a junior, Rasmussen pitched brilliantly and gained a measure of redemption Sunday, as UCLA beat Fullerton, 8–1, in the third and deciding game of the 2010 Super Regional at Westwood. The decisive victory earned the Bruins a spot in the College World Series in Omaha.

Sunday's game had none of the impossible drama that games one and two possessed. After spotting the Titans an early 1-0 lead, UCLA marched to a methodical win, scoring three in the third, two in the sixth, one in the seventh, and two in the eighth.

In hurling his first complete game of the season, Rasmussen stifled Fullerton on two hits and one walk, while striking out nine.

In Omaha, UCLA may have an unseen advantage. The great UCLA basketball coach, John Wooden, recently passed away at the age of 99. In the post game interview press tent, current Bruin baseball coach John Savage acknowledged that the spirit of the inimitable Wooden is looking over his team.

Said Savage, "I'm very honored to be at the school where he coached. It's something we have talked about with our guys, about Coach Wooden."

"He is very much with us."

UCLA qualified for the championship finals of the 2010 College World Series in Omaha, losing to the University of South Carolina. The Bruins returned to the College World Series in 2012, winning their first National Championship.

Noe Ramirez was drafted by the Boston Red Sox in the fourth round of the 2011 draft. As of 2014, he was pitching at Portland of the AA Eastern League.

Gary Brown, selected by the Giants in the first round of the 2010 draft, began the 2012 season playing with Richmond of the Double A Eastern League. He spent 2013 playing for Fresno in the AAA Pacific Coast League and was assigned to Fresno to begin the 2014 season.

The 4th overall pick in the 2010 draft by Kansas City, Christian Colon was assigned to AAA Omaha in 2013 and 2014.

Lefty Rob Rasmussen was chosen by the Marlins in the second round of the 2010 draft. Since traded to the Dodgers, he pitched for Chattanooga in the AA Southern League in 2013. Now in the Toronto chain, Rasmussen began 2014 at AAA Buffalo.

People's Court

This article appeared at si.com, the Sports Illustrated website, on February 21, 2011:

Outwardly, baseball people always endeavor to be positive.

A .189 hitter isn't slumping, he "needs to make adjustments."

Pitchers with a penchant for surrendering upper deck souvenirs are not struggling, they "need to find a consistent release point."

Likewise, when the draft eligible high school talent in a specific region is scarce, area scouts invariably claim: "It may be a bit of a down year out here."

On Saturday, February 12, 2011, the Major League Scouting Bureau hosted their annual Southern California High School Pre-Season Showcase at MLB's Urban Youth Academy in Compton, California.

The overall talent decline this year is nowhere near as profound as, say, the dip in the stock market in October of 1929. Unfortunately, now, as then, the depression is rather obvious.

No doubt local scouts are spoiled. Southern California High Schools yielded Giancarlo Stanton, Freddie Freeman, and Mike Moustakas in the 2007 draft, all elite prospects. Aaron Hicks, Mike Montgomery, and John Lamb were selected in 2008. With Stephen Strasburg recovering from surgery, Orange County product Tyler Matzek may eventually become the top pitcher selected in the 2009 draft. (Boy, did I blow that prediction!) An array of splendidly talented right-handed pitchers were also nabbed in 2010 from the area.

Naturally, scouts were sanguine regarding Saturday's general level of talent. Said one, "It's a bit off this year . . . but 2012 is loaded."

Saturday's showcase was staged in perfect 80 degree weather. As is typical with events of this kind, the day began with wood bat batting practice then continued with 60-yard dashes and infield/outfield warm-ups. After a short break, a simulated game was played with each hurler pitching to five hitters.

A quick explanation: In baseball, the standard distance for timing a player's speed is 60 yards, not the familiar 40-yard standard used in football. A time of 7.0 seconds is generally considered "major league average," and will net the player a 50 rating on the traditional 20–80 scout grading scale.

The classic bromide "the pitchers are ahead of the hitters" applied perfectly to Saturday's showcase. In this instance, the hitters were in Compton and the pitchers were in Fresno. Swings and misses, topped dribblers, and weak pop-ups were the frustrating norm—for hitters and scouts.

The showcase was redeemed, partially, by the emergence of two previously unknown players. Amateur baseball is deluged by a horde of off-season events: scout ball, Area Code Games, the Aflac Game, sponsored showcases, etc.

Two players present Saturday have rarely if ever appeared on the "circuit," but their performances—and subsequent emergence as prospects—salvaged the day.

Kenneth Peoples is a 6'1" 170 pound middle infielder from Westchester High School in Los Angeles. Peoples ran a blazing 6.6 second 60-yard dash, the third fastest time of the day. In the field, he displayed decent fielding actions and an acceptable throwing arm. High school shortstops rarely remain at that spot in pro ball, but Peoples's athletic ability will permit him to play any number of alternate positions, with second base, left field or center field being the prime candidates.

During the simulated game, Peoples ripped a long triple into the gap in right center. The drive caught the attention of the two-hundred scouts in attendance and awoke a few who were napping. One scout was delighted that a participant had finally drilled a ball with authority. Dancing a jig, he sang, "was that finally a ball on the barrel?!"

Quincy Quintero, a 6'1" 185 pound right-handed pitcher from Valencia High School in California, will soon be deluged with calls and emails from pro scouts and college recruiters. Pitching from a stretch (which was his standard form), Quintero whips the ball plate ward with a smooth, easy arm action. His 90–91 mph fastball shows sinking and darting action to either side of the plate and his 78 mph curve is a quintessential knee buckler.

The performances of Peoples and Quintero redeemed a rather tedious showcase. Perpetually sunny, baseball folks always see a class as half full, not half empty.

"Look at it this way," one scout told me Saturday. "If we covered the New England area, this would be considered a loaded class."

Kenneth Peoples was selected by the St. Louis Cardinals in the fourth round (140th overall pick) of the 2011 MLB Draft. He began the 2014 season at Peoria in the Midwest League.

Quincy Quintero, in 2014, is playing at Butler University in Indiana.

Section Two:
Big Leaguers

7

Manny Mania

First round draft picks typically come from baseball areas in the so-called sunshine states: California, Arizona, Texas, Georgia, and Florida. Lately, Division-1 conferences such as the ACC and SEC have been well represented at the top of the draft pecking order. Las Vegas has also provided a rich trove of talent in recent years.

It is important to remember that great players can be found in any place at any time—even in locales traditionally thought to be football, basketball or hockey havens.

Joe Mauer, first selection in the 2001 draft, hailed from a high school in Minnesota. Jeff Francis, the ninth overall choice in 2002, was from British Columbia. The sixth overall pick in the 2000 draft, Rocco Baldelli, was plucked from a high school in Warwick, Rhode Island.

Most notably, the Angels selected Mike Trout as the twenty-fifth pick in the 2009 draft out of high school in an obscure town named Millville, New Jersey.

Manny Ramirez was discovered playing at George Washington High School in New York City. Film clips of Ramirez as an amateur show him taking pre-game outfield practice on an inner city asphalt playground—a far cry from well-groomed fields in affluent sun belt suburbs.

Ramirez was the thirteenth overall pick in the first round of the 1991 draft. Don Slaught, a former big league catcher who has long been recognized as one of the finest hitting coaches in all of baseball, studied Ramirez's swing when Manny was a big leaguer. Slaught found that 6 of every 10 swings Ramirez took were technically perfect, the highest percentage of any hitter he had ever studied.

A former big league hitting coach for the Tigers, Slaught has studied all great hitters of baseball's modern era, including Vladimir Guerrero, Ivan "Pudge" Rodriguez, Alex Rodriguez, Albert Pujols, and many others. He has discovered, shockingly, that Mickey Mantle's swing was almost identical to Ichiro's!

Despite his remarkable talent and mechanical proficiency, Manny Ramirez provides a cautionary tale for today's young draft prospects. Suspended for suspected PED usage, Ramirez irrevocably stained his career accomplishments and may have eliminated any chance for admission to the Hall of Fame.

Like so many others—Barry Bonds, Mark McGwire, Ryan Braun, etc.—Ramirez possessed exceptionally rare talent but felt the desire to augment those skills in order to elevate his play to an even higher level.

It was a Faustian bargain. Manny's temporary gain was quickly negated by a drug scandal which ruined his career and reputation, thereby seriously clouding all of his career achievements.

This story was published on the Baseball America website on June 30, 2009.

LEGENDARY BOXING TRAINER Angelo Dundee was once asked about the "Ali Circus," the tumultuous cadre of freaks and hangers-on who continually surrounded Muhammad Ali.

Dundee replied, "Nothing ever bothered Muhammad. After awhile, I got used to things being bizarre. . . . Bizarre was normal."

Bizarre was once again normal on Saturday at the Diamond, home of the San Diego Padres' High Class A minor league affiliate: the Lake Elsinore Storm of the California League. The Storm's opponent for the evening was the Dodger's California League club, the Inland Empire 66ers, accompanied by virtuoso soloist Manny Ramirez.

The sellout, and, one might argue, sell-out crowd of 8,099 was on hand for the sole purpose of Manny idolatry. Several fans were bedecked in Manny jerseys and faux Manny dreadlock wigs. The majority of the crowd seemed giddily unconcerned that Ramirez was nailed earlier this year by Major League Baseball for violation of its ban on performance-enhancing substances.

Ramirez is serving a 50 game suspension and, as his reinstatement to major league baseball looms, he has been "rehabbing" in the minor leagues. Manny's first stop on his tour was not the Betty Ford clinic but the Dodgers Triple-A affiliate in Albuquerque, New Mexico. Last weekend Ramirez descended on the California League, gradually working his way closer to Los Angeles.

Reporters from all levels of the journalistic caste system were present, including ESPN and prominent *Los Angeles Times* columnist Bill Plaschke, down to a rather talkative young man whose side job is running a lacrosse website.

The Dodgers are exceptionally PR and image conscious. Club Vice Presidents Kim Ng and Josh Rawitch were on hand, presumably to make sure that no one—public or press—asked Manny any questions. Heaven forbid Ramirez would actually have to account for his conduct.

A contortionist performed on the field between innings, once displaying the remarkable and somewhat gruesome ability to slide his entire body through an unstrung tennis racket. No word yet if the Dodgers have hired the contortionist to explain why Manny was busted for possessing a female fertility drug.

· · ·

Two hours prior to the game, Ramirez joined his temporary teammates in stretching exercises. He wore a white undershirt, standing out distinctly from his blue shirted cohorts. Of course, Ramirez need not wear a different shirt to stand out. His trademark dreads now reach the midpoint of his back, and he is the only hitter I have ever seen whose BP headgear is not a cap or helmet, but a bright blue do-rag.

I stood a few feet from Ramirez and marveled at his 220-pound physique. During games, Manny wears a baggy uniform which serves to hide his build from the TV cameras. The size, bulk, and definition in the muscles of his upper body are remarkable, reminiscent of a Michelangelo statue.

Ramirez is not a tall man—I'd guess he stands about 5 foot 10 (he is officially listed at 6 foot)—but as he stood on the first-base line during the national anthem alongside the youthful Inland Empire squad, he appeared twice as broad across the chest and back as any other player.

Ramirez took four rounds in the cage during batting practice and his timing was discernibly off. He squared up a few pitches, but for the most part was hitting lazy fly balls and top-spin grounders.

After Ramirez completed his pregame outfield sprints, dozens of fans pressed against the railing of the stands along the first base line begging for autographs. Manny started to head for the dugout but suddenly veered over to the fans—both Ramirez and the Dodgers realize a good PR gesture when they see one. Hordes of cameramen soon followed.

Ramirez batted leadoff in the Inland Empire lineup, penciled in as the DH. In his three plate appearances, he faced Nick Schmidt, a 6 foot 5, 240 pound lefty who was a first round pick out of the University of Arkansas in 2007.

Schmidt missed the entire 2008 season due to Tommy John elbow surgery and spent the first half of this season at Low Class A Fort Wayne in the Midwest League. Ramirez was the first batter Schmidt faced at High Class A. Welcome to the California League, kid.

I stood directly behind home plate with my radar gun trained on each pitch in all three Manny plate appearances:

1. Leadoff, top of first, no score. Schmidt backs Manny off the plate and gets a called strike on the inside corner with an 87 mph fastball. The next pitch is a changeup. Manny is slightly fooled and gets his weight out on his front foot by a fraction. He is still able to drive the ball deep into the left field corner, where it slips over the fence, despite some topspin, for a home run.

   It should be noted at this point that a column appeared in a local newspaper the next day. Chock full of righteous indignation, the column claimed that Manny heard "not one boo" during the evening. I was on the lower level for each Ramirez at bat, and while cheers were predominant there was no mistaking several loud boos every time

Manny strode into the batter's box. One fan, with no fear for his personal safety, stood up and yelled, "GO BACK TO BOSTON!"

2. Top of the third, no outs, man on first, score 1–0 Inland Empire. Manny takes an 88 mph fastball and a 76 mph curve for strikes, getting into a 0–2 hole. Schmidt then throws the mother of all waste pitches, sailing an 87 fastball off his catcher's mitt to the backstop, making the count 1–2 with a runner on second. Schmidt then delivers his best pitch of the night; a gorgeous back door 76 mph curve that appears to catch the outside corner and freezes Manny. Strike Three.

Except the umpire calls the pitch a ball, squaring the count at 2–2. Perhaps only a hitter like Ramirez gets that call in his favor. Next is an inside 90 mph fastball for a ball to run the count to 3–2. That pitch was thrown in order to set up the full count pitch, in which Schmidt attempted to back door the curve again. This time he clearly missed the plate, issuing Ramirez a walk.

Ramirez eventually scored a run in the inning; his base running escapades during the evening resembled a Mack Sennett slapstick comedy. Manny waddled from first to third on a double that any non-pitcher or non-catcher would have easily scored on; he later came home on a base hit.

On first base after his third at-bat, Ramirez misjudged a long drive that was snagged by Storm center fielder Brad Chalk. Running like a man late for a train, Manny stumbled over second base while retreating and was thrown out at first. It can be said with authority that at this stage of his rehab Ramirez's bat is well ahead of his base running.

3. Leading off, top of the fifth, score 4–0 Inland Empire. Schmidt misses inside with both a 73 mph curve and 85 mph fastball, falling behind 2–0. I have no idea what the next pitch was or how fast it came in, but I do know it went off the bat at 101 mph, a bullet that skipped off of the pitcher's mound into center for a single, forcing Schmidt to perform an impromptu tap dance.

Manny's exercise ended after his base running misadventures. Entourage in tow, he will play two more games at Inland Empire's home ballpark against Rancho Cucamonga and is scheduled to rejoin the Dodgers on July 3 at San Diego.

A noisy mob of fans congregated outside the entrance to the visitor's clubhouse. After emerging, Manny obliged a lucky few with autographs. Ramirez glumly worked his way through the roped off crowd and then entered a large white SUV, riding shotgun.

Manny did not answer any questions from anyone. The circus was over. It was time to move on to the next town.

8

Tommy Davis on Hitting

Once an amateur prospect is drafted and signed, he is assigned to one of his organization's minor league affiliates. As a pro, the player will have no shortage of coaching assistance. Every minor league club has a three man staff, including a manager, hitting coach and pitching coach.

Additionally, each organization has "roving" instructors; coaches who travel through all levels of the team's minor league system, dispensing instructions in his particular specialty. Many organizations have a pitching coordinator, who oversees all pitchers, coaches, and pitching instruction in his organization.

When I spoke to Tommy Davis in 2008, he was not an organizational hitting coach. However, this article reveals the type of precise and technical "insider" instruction that occurs in pro ball.

At that time, Davis was working as a private hitting coach, providing instruction above and beyond what youngsters could receive from their high school or travel ball coaches. Private baseball tutoring is a cottage industry that has exploded in the past ten years.

Tommy Davis was a two time National League batting champion, hitting .346 in 1962, and .326 in 1963, for the Los Angeles Dodgers.

July 25, 2008

A POPULAR (AND WIDELY satirized) television commercial of the 1970s depicted two silk tie Brooks Brothers suit-wearing businessmen lunching at a stately but packed midtown Manhattan restaurant. In the midst of the conversation, one sidles over and in a firm but level tone says, "My broker is E. F. Hutton . . . and E. F. Hutton says . . ."

Everyone in the eatery (waiters and patrons included) lean in, en masse, to hear the valuable insights.

Tommy Davis is the E. F. Hutton of hitting advice. Everyone—players, coaches, and scouts—listened intently as the former batting champion held court during lunch yesterday at the inaugural Breakthrough Series held at Major League Baseball's Urban Youth Academy in Compton, California.

Roger Angell, the great baseball writer of the *New Yorker*, once wrote that Davis "is a batter who studies each pitch with the eye of a jewelry appraiser." Such patience is to be expected of Davis, who in 1962 hit .346 with 230 hits and 153 RBI, which led all of baseball that year.

Davis was direct. "The most important thing in hitting is balance," he stated, adding "balance keeps you off of your heels and lets you get to the outside pitch."

As the assembled youngsters soaked up his wisdom, Davis continued. "Don't tilt your head! Keep your head level. A curve breaks twice as much if you tilt your head! See the ball with two eyes!"

Vision obviously is a crucial factor, according to Davis. "As a right-handed hitter, I want to intercept the ball with my left eye." He made the succinct point that once the hitter has picked up the ball with his lead eye, he needs to keep it trained on the ball.

"Swing your bat around your head," implored Davis, "and don't pull your front eye and head off the ball. The less you move your head, the more you see the ball."

Stride length was next on Davis's agenda. "Keep your stride as short as possible. Don't over stride. The ball gets to you quicker if you over stride. You see the ball much longer with a short stride."

Once his chat had concluded, I approached Davis and asked him his preferences regarding grip and grip pressure. He handed me a bat and told me to grip it as tight as I could in my palms. "You see!" he exclaimed. "Your hands become too tight, and the muscles in your forearm tighten up."

Davis then exhibited the correct grip—loose and relaxed, with the bat handle placed in the fingers, not the palm. He took his stance. I could imagine him in the batter's box staring down Whitey Ford or Warren Spahn.

It dawned on me that listening to Tommy Davis, Frank Robinson, Rod Carew, and Maury Wills speak at the Academy over the past several days was akin to hearing Ernest Hemingway speak on writing, Claude Monet on painting, or Enrico Caruso on singing.

Instruction and guidance was the primary goal of the three-day Breakthrough Series, and given the quality of the speakers it was a smash success on that point.

Tommy Davis benefited from the intervention of his elders when he was a youngster. "I was scouted by the Yankees, Phillies, Dodgers, and Indians," he said. "This was in the mid-1950s."

"In fact, I worked out so often with the Yankees at the stadium they gave me a locker by the trainer's room. I'd see Ford, Berra, Bauer, Skowron, and Mantle walk in all the time. I even got up the courage to say 'Hi Mickey!' when he walked in."

Davis informed all interested scouts that he was set to sign with the Yankees on a Tuesday evening. Alarmed, Al Campanis of the Dodgers (yes, *that* Al Campanis) had Jackie Robinson call Davis directly. Tommy couldn't hide his excitement.

After picking up the phone and recognizing the voice on the other end of the line, Davis yelled to his mom, "It's Jackie on the phone!"

Davis signed with the Dodgers Tuesday afternoon.

The Bronx Bombers were shut out.

Almost sixty years after Tommy Davis had a locker in Yankee Stadium and worked out with the big club as a high schooler, major league teams still permit prospects to work out with big leaguers as a ploy to lure draftees into signing.

A few years back, the Yankees drafted a youngster out of a Southern California high school. A college education was important to both the player and his family, and the young man had a generous scholarship offer to play baseball at the University of California—a locale which would be a major advantage to both his baseball and academic aspirations.

During the time gap between draft day and the signing deadline, the Yankees flew the player to New York and for several days gave him a locker in the clubhouse at Yankee Stadium near those of both Derek Jeter and Alex Rodriguez. The draftee was generously allowed to take batting practice on the field at Yankee Stadium in the presence of the big league stars and Monument Park.

The player politely turned down Cal and signed with the Yankees.

9

Baseball Is a Human Game

Frank Robinson was elected to the National Baseball Hall of Fame in 1982. Robinson was baseball's first AfricanAmerican manager, piloting the Cleveland Indians in 1976. He later managed the San Francisco Giants, Baltimore Orioles, Montreal Expos, and Washington Nationals.

In his brilliant playing career—spent mostly with the Reds and Orioles—Robinson slugged 586 home runs. He won the Triple Crown in 1966 and is still the only player in history to have been named MVP in both leagues—in the NL with Cincinnati in 1961, and the AL with Baltimore in 1966.

In our conversation, which took place in 2008, Robinson discussed the issue of instant replay in baseball—perhaps the most controversial "hot button" topic in Major League baseball in 2014.

I encountered Robby during a game in the inaugural Breakthrough Series, an MLB sponsored showcase which features high school players from across the nation.

July 26, 2008

I WAS SITTING IN the shady comfort of the press box at
Major League Baseball's Urban Youth Academy in Compton,
California, on Wednesday. Lost in a daydream, I was jolted
back to reality when the entrance door, located back and to my
left, opened.

In walked Frank Robinson, who quietly and without ceremony
sat down next to me. I concluded he was either taking pity on me
or no other chair was available. Slightly flummoxed, a thought
quickly ran through my head:

"What in the hell do I say to Frank Robinson?"

The legendary slugger and managerial pioneer could not have
been nicer. As it turns out, conversation was not lacking. A lively
but friendly discussion erupted among the press box occupants
concerning the issue of instant replay in baseball.

An important piece of baseball etiquette occurred as Robinson
spoke. When Frank Robinson speaks, no one else speaks. No one
else makes a noise. In fact, you breathe at your own risk.

Robinson may have mellowed in his seventy-second year, but
he still holds sharp opinions and has no reservations expressing
them. His massive hands jabbing the air for emphasis, Robinson
argued his case.

"Instant replay should never be used in our game," he said.
"Baseball is a human game."

No one present was inclined to disagree with him.

A few minutes later, I gently—very gently—reminded the
Hall of Famer that in Game Five of the 1969 World Series, an
inside fastball skipped off his uniform belt. The umpire errone-
ously ruled that the ball had been fouled off the knob of his bat.

"I had to go into the dugout for treatment from the trainer," Robinson recalled.

He smiled slightly, sensing the subtle point I was making regarding instant replay.

I didn't budge his opinion one millimeter.

At this point I needed a safety valve. "You hit one off of Koosman in that game which I think is still traveling," I said. Robinson smiled at the memory.

If any of the youngsters participating in the Breakthrough series sign professional contracts, they figure to be savvier about the process than was Frank Robinson's mom.

In 1953, a Cincinnati Reds scout descended on the Robinson household. He solemnly informed Mrs. Robinson: "I want your son to play professional baseball with us. I'd like to sign him to a contract for $3,500."

"That's wonderful!" Mrs. Robinson replied. "But there's one problem."

Confused and puzzled, the scout asked, "Uh . . . what's the problem?"

Mrs. Robinson's answer was honest and direct:

"I don't have $3,500."

Note that Robinson signed for $3,500. As I'll discuss in an upcoming chapter, from 1953 to 1957, any players signed for $4,000 or more were subject to the "Bonus Baby" rule. That meant the signee was mandated to stay on a big league roster for two years before being shipped out to the minors for seasoning. No African American prospect during that time was signed for a bonus at or above $4,000. Robinson's figure was conveniently $500 below the limit.

Not that some scouts and organizations were reticent to flout the rules. In the early 1960s, the Giants were keen on a left-handed pitching prospect from the same Oakland neighborhood that produced Frank Robinson, Vada Pinson, and Curt Flood. The prospect was permitted by the Giants to shop at a local sporting goods store on their tab. He loaded up generously not only on clothes and equipment for himself, but felt obligated to "take care of everyone in my neighborhood." The bill came to $400 ($3,000 in today's currency).

Unfortunately for the Giants, the youngster signed with another club. This drew the ire of the team's scouting director, who, via telephone, screamed at his area scout: "YOU MEAN TO TELL ME HE SPENT $400 OF OUR MONEY AND YOU DIDN'T FUCKING SIGN HIM?"

After the lefty signed his contract, the signing club's area scout politely asked the kid and his mom if the three of them could go to the upstairs portion of the family home. The scout slipped the youngster $1,000 in ten $100 bills.

Said the scout, "I just want to show you how much I appreciate you signing with us."

10

The Gret Wayne Gretzky

Under the current rules, citizens of only two countries are eligible for the annual Major League Baseball Free Agent Draft held each June. Those countries are the United States and Canada. Prospects in Puerto Rico, a US Commonwealth, are also subject to the draft.

Major League Baseball for many years has openly discussed the possibility of an all-encompassing international draft but has yet to implement that procedure.

To be considered for the draft, a prospect in one of those countries must be:
1. *A high school senior;*
2. *A junior college player who has completed his first and/or second year of eligibility;*
3. *A player at a four-year college or university who has spent three years at that institution.*

There are some arcane exceptions but the majority of draftees fit into one of these categories.

Prospects in all other countries are not currently subject to these quali-fications. A major league organization can sign a player from another country as early as age sixteen. This tactic is routinely employed in the signing of youngsters from Latin America nations, particularly the Dominican Republic.

In the late 1970s, prior to the implementation of the current stan-dards, Canadian citizens were not subject to MLB's draft and could be signed by an organization as early as age sixteen.

One such prospect was a skinny youth from Ontario named Wayne Gretzky. Enamored of his skills as a middle infielder, the Toronto Blue Jays made a lucrative contract offer to Gretzky, who, respectfully but wisely, turned the offer down.

It is not uncommon for baseball scouts to pursue athletes whose skills— and future—lies in another sport. In the pre-draft days, Joe Namath was offered $50,000 to play the outfield for the Chicago Cubs.

In 1979, Dan Marino was the fourth round selection of the Kansas City Royals. John Elway was first drafted in 1979 by the Royals and again in 1981 by the Yankees. Elway played briefly in the New York organization. Ken Berry, a former major league OF who was Elway's minor league manager, noted in a report to his front office that Elway had "a way, way above average arm."

Wayne Gretzky, along with Bobby Orr, is considered to be the great-est player in the history of the National Hockey League.

Elected to the Hockey Hall of Fame in 1999, Gretzky is the NHL's all-time leader in goals, assists, and points. He was awarded the Hart Trophy as NHL MVP nine times and played on four Stanley Cup championship teams.

I spoke with Gretzky at the annual Area Code Games in Long Beach, one of the nation's premier high school baseball showcases.

August 9, 2010

HEAD DOWN AND immersed in thought, I strolled through a grassy public park toward the entrance of Blair Field, home of the Area Code Games. For some unknown reason, I happened to look up and noticed Wayne Gretzky walking toward the parking lot in the opposite direction.

At the risk of getting body checked into a pine tree, I was determined to kindly introduce myself and ask Gretzky a few questions. I concluded I was safe—he wasn't carrying a hockey stick so my chances of getting slashed or poke checked were virtually nil. Turns out I had nothing to be concerned about, as Gretzky was one of the most pleasant interviewees I have ever encountered.

Gretzky told me that he grew up in Ontario, Canada. Unlike many of today's young athletes, he was not programmed exclusively into one sport as an embryo.

"As a youngster," Gretzky said, "I played not just hockey but baseball, lacrosse, and ran track. After April 10, I put my ice skates away and didn't touch them again for six months."

Gretzky is an ardent believer in the idea that kids should play multiple sports in their formative years, and then begin to focus on one sport around the age of fourteen to fifteen.

His son, Trevor, is an Area Code Games participant and a pretty fair left-handed hitting prospect. Trevor's first sport was not hockey . . . nor was it soccer, but baseball. Exhibiting a touch of his father's athletic versatility, the younger Gretzky also spends his autumns as a top-notch high school quarterback.

As a seventeen-year-old amateur shortstop in 1978, Wayne Gretzky received substantial attention from the Toronto Blue

Jays. At that time, Canadians were not subject to the Major League Draft as they are now.

The Blue Jays offered Gretzky $100,000 to sign, which in 1978 was equivalent to signing bonuses given to first round draft selections. He smiled at the memory and added, "I decided against it." A scant four years later Gretzky set the all-time NHL record for goals scored with 92.

In 1988, Gretzky was traded from the Edmonton Oilers to the Los Angeles Kings in the most spectacular swap in NHL history. On Saturday, October 15, 1988, Gretzky played his second game as a King at the Forum in Inglewood.

Across town at Dodger Stadium, the Dodgers and A's were battling in the first game of the World Series. Thousands of fans in the Forum had brought transistor radios, listening to the ballgame via thin white earplugs while watching the hockey game unfold in front of them.

At the very instant Gretzky's skate touched the ice, a thunderous, ear rattling roar went up from the crowd. Unbeknownst to Gretzky, Kirk Gibson had chosen that moment to loft a Dennis Eckersly slider into the right field bleachers for a game-winning home run—providing one of the most thrilling and iconic moments in baseball history.

When Gretzky heard the shattering noise and raucous cheering he was convinced his mere presence had suddenly converted the blasé LA fans into hard core hockey nuts. Gretzky recalled, "I thought: 'Wow! These people really love me and they really love hockey!'"

Trevor Gretzky was chosen by the Chicago Cubs in the seventh round of the 2011 Major League Baseball Draft. In 2014, he was traded from the Cubs to the Los Angeles Angels—for the son of Angels manager Mike Scioscia.

11

The Giants Win the Pennant!

Former New York Giants third baseman Bobby Thomson's "Shot heard 'round the World" in 1951 is generally considered to be the greatest moment in baseball history.

From a scouting and player development standpoint, the story of the 1951 National League Pennant Race gives us a sharp distinction with modern Major League Baseball.

In the third and final game of the 1951 NL pennant playoff, six of the nine players in the starting lineup for Brooklyn began their big league careers with the Dodgers. For New York, seven of the nine starters began their big league careers with the Giants.

By contrast, only three of the ten players in the starting lineup for the World Champion Red Sox in the sixth and final game of the 2013 World Series began their major league careers with Boston.

With rare exceptions (Tony Gwynn, Cal Ripken Jr., Derek Jeter), players drafted and signed today almost never spend their entire career with one organization. Free agency has altered baseball's landscape in ways unimaginable sixty-three years ago.

Modern teams are an amalgam of players acquired through the draft, trades, and free agency. Ball clubs of the pre-free agency era were often composed of players who began their minor league careers together and stayed together throughout lengthy big league tenures.

Yankee stalwarts Mickey Mantle, Whitey Ford, and Yogi Berra played together from 1951 to 1963, after which Yogi became the manager of the team. The Los Angeles Dodgers infield of Steve Garvey, Davey Lopes, Bill Russell, and Ron Cey played together for nearly a decade from the early seventies into the early eighties.

One of the fascinating offshoots of free agency today is that a few ball-clubs have locked up their best young players, signing them to lucrative, long-term deals well before they are free agent eligible. Recently, the Atlanta Braves have smartly used this strategy.

This tactic ensures the club retains top-notch talent it has spent valuable time developing. It also gives the signing team long-term stability and prevents rich clubs (Yankees, Red Sox, Dodgers) from swooping down like vultures and picking off the best talent from small-market teams.

None of these factors was a concern to organizations in 1951. At that time, the standard Major League Baseball player's contract contained a "Reserve Clause," which bound a player to the club he signed with for life—unless and until that club traded or released him.

Coupled with a highly controversial Supreme Court decision in the twenties which granted Major League Baseball an exemption from Anti-Trust laws, the Reserve Clause limited player movement and depressed salaries until the seventies. Lawsuits filed by star outfielder Curt Flood and the increased power of the Player's Union, led by Marvin Miller, paved a path to the repeal of the Reserve Clause.

In a separate vein, as proof of the cold nature of constant player turnover in baseball, only two years after his heroics which brought the New York Giants the 1951 NL pennant, Bobby Thomson was traded to the Milwaukee Braves.

Johnny Antonelli, a pitcher received by the Giants in the deal, helped New York to the World Series championship in 1954 by posting a 21–7 record with a league leading 2.30 ERA.

Set to be the Braves starting LF in 1954, Thomson broke his ankle in spring training and missed most of the season. He was replaced by a twenty-year-old from Mobile, Alabama, with an unusual double vowel last name: Hank Aaron.

Then, as now, baseball marches on.

August 17, 2010

B OBBY THOMSON, WHOSE National League pennant-winning home run in 1951 provided perhaps the most thrilling and dramatic moment in baseball history, died Monday in Savannah, Georgia, due to complications of Alzheimer's disease.

A talented OF/3B, Thomson, 86, was nicknamed "The Staten Island Scot." He played 15 major league seasons from 1946 to 1960 with the Giants, Braves, Cubs, Red Sox and Orioles, finishing his career with 264 home runs and a .270 batting average.

Deadly rivals, the New York Giants and Brooklyn Dodgers engaged in an epic National League pennant race in 1951, which culminated in Thomson's scintillating home run. The story of Thomson's home run—and indeed the entire 1951 season—provides one of the most fascinating tales in all of American sports history.

The 1951 season served as a kind of cosmic baseball conver-
gence. Yankee center fielder Joe DiMaggio, riddled with nagging
injuries, suffered through his final campaign. As DiMaggio
faded out, Willie Mays and Mickey Mantle made their major
league debuts.

A self-described hick from Oklahoma (nicknamed the
"Commerce Comet" after his hometown), Mantle arrived at
Yankee spring training camp in Phoenix wearing an $8 suit and
carrying a cardboard suitcase. The speedy and powerful teenage
switch hitter enjoyed a phenomenal spring, hitting .402 while
blasting a series of monumental home runs.

Hitting left-handed during an exhibition game at USC,
Mantle drove a pitch over the right field fence which also cleared
the width of an adjoining football practice field—a drive esti-
mated at 550–600 feet.

Herb Fields, now President of Bedford Freight Lines in Los
Angeles, was in attendance. "Mantle hit a ball that went out of
sight, it just disappeared. No one said anything, there was silence.
All the fans were shocked. No one had seen anything like it. We
didn't know what to say."

Meanwhile, Giants manager Leo Durocher was enduring spring training at St. Petersburg, Florida. (The Giants and
Yankees had switched training sites that year.) With his team
unable to play one day due to rain, Durocher and one of his
coaches invaded downtown to partake of the local night life. A
noted bon vivant, Durocher found the social scene in St. Pete,
then a retirement community, to be less than captivating—no
match for his customary haunts in New York or Hollywood.

Finding nothing better to do, Durocher stumbled into the
parlor of a psychic/tarot card reader. After a protracted wait, the
female seer emerged from behind a curtain dressed in flowing
robes and adorned with elaborate jewelry. Gazing into a crystal

ball, she informed Durocher that his ballclub would start the season poorly, rally late in the year, and win the pennant in a flourish with a dramatic home run.

Durocher was unimpressed. Leaving the building, he exclaimed, "What a crock of *#!&! That lady is nuts!"

The Giants opened the 1951 regular season by winning two out of three games from the Boston Braves. Disastrously, the New Yorkers then lost 11 straight. As his club continued to struggle, Durocher instinctively understood that wholesale changes needed to be made.

The Giant skipper moved right-handed curveballer Sal Maglie out of the bullpen and into the starting rotation (Maglie would win 23 games in 1951). Thomson was moved from center field to third base, and Mays was promoted from AAA Minneapolis to take over in center.

On July 1, Thomson was mired in a dreadful slump, hitting only .220. Thomson's spread, stand up batting stance was a clone of his idol, DiMaggio. Durocher, infuriated, strode over to Thomson one day and ordered a change. "Move your feet closer together!" Durocher barked. "Crouch down! Shorten your stride!" Thomson complied. He went on a tear the remainder of the season, finishing with 32 homers, 101 RBI and a .293 batting average.

Mays was hitting .477 at AAA Minneapolis when promoted. He joined the Giants in Philadelphia, where he put on a stunning batting practice display at old Shibe Park. Hall of Fame pitcher Robin Roberts watched from the Phillies bench, curious to see what a .477 hitter looked like. Mays hammered the ball all over the yard, ripping shots into the bleachers, onto the left field roof, into the rafters.

Unfortunately for Mays, he was not as productive in the games. Hitless in his first 12 at-bats, he drove a Warren Spahn pitch over the roof at the Polo Grounds for his first big league hit. Mays was hitless in his next 13 at bats. At the depth of his slump, Mays broke down in tears and had to be consoled with a pep talk by Durocher. The "Say Hey" kid soon raised his average to .322 before settling down to a .274 mark with 20 homers by season's end.

Durocher's alterations energized the Giants. By July 3, they had moved into second place, only 4.5 games behind the Dodgers. Crushingly, the Giants lost three games to the Dodgers at Ebbets Field, including an excruciating 6–5 setback in the first game of a July 4 doubleheader. With the Giants leading 5–4 entering the bottom of the 11th, the Dodgers scored twice. After doubling in the tying run, Jackie Robinson was picked off second. He miraculously escaped a rundown and wound up on third. Pitcher Preacher Roe—well known as a terrible hitter— then squeezed Robinson home for the winning tally.

Legend has it that after the third game of the series, Dodger manager Charlie Dressen and a few of his players sidled up to the thin wooden door that separated the home and visiting locker rooms at Ebbets Field. Dressen led his charges in a rousing version of "Roll out the barrel," adding the verse "we've got the Giants on the run." Durocher and several of his players responded loudly and profanely. National League authorities later ordered the door to be reinforced, locked, and bolted.

The Giants stumbled aimlessly after the Ebbets Field debacle. In the next month, the Polo Grounders faded to 13 games behind Brooklyn after another three-game sweep at Ebbets Field and a listless 4–0 loss on August 11 against the Phillies.

Suddenly and unexpectedly, the Giants reeled off 16 consecutive victories to slice the Dodger margin to 5 games. The key win in the streak was a 3–1 decision at the Polo Grounds on August 15.

With the score tied 1–1 in the top of the eighth, Dodger third baseman Billy Cox was on third with one out. Carl Furillo belted a long drive into the gap in right center. Mays raced over, speared the ball, spun around, and fired a 300-foot strike to home plate, nailing Cox for an inning-ending double play. Wes Westrum homered in the bottom half of the eighth, to give the Giants a 3–1 victory.

It was not the only spectacular play Mays made in 1951. In a game at Forbes Field in Pittsburgh, Pirates slugger Ralph Kiner pounded a long drive in the spacious gap in left center. Mays ran over, stuck out his right hand, and, to his and everyone's astonishment, caught the ball barehanded. Pirates general manager Branch Rickey sent a handwritten note to Mays in the Giant dugout: "That is the finest play I have ever seen, and the finest play I ever hope to see."

Overall, New York won 37 of their final 44 games to finish in a deadlock with Brooklyn. The Dodgers did not collapse, winning 26 of their last 48 contests. Three critical games helped decide the outcome.

· · ·

On September 9, Maglie had Brooklyn shutout 2–0 through 7 innings at Ebbets Field. With a run in, one out, and Robinson dancing off of third, Andy Pafko hit a screaming ground ball at Thomson. Snaring the shot with a backhanded lunge, Thomson tagged a retreating Robinson and threw over to first to complete a rally-killing double play. The Giants won, 2–1.

At Boston on September 27, the Braves edged the Dodgers, 4–3, on a hotly disputed play. With the score tied in the bottom of the eighth, Boston's Bob Addis was ruled safe at home by umpire Frank Dascoli. Brooklyn catcher Roy Campanella argued vehemently that he had tagged Addis out. An ugly exchange ensued, and after the game the door to the umpire's room was kicked into splinters. In the aftermath, NL President Ford Frick fined Roe, Robinson, and Campanella.

Entering the final day of the regular season on Sunday, September 30, the Dodgers and Giants were tied atop the NL standings. Incredibly, New York had closed a staggering 13 game (13 1/2 in some accounts) gap. The Giants slipped past the Braves, 3–2, in Boston, forcing the Dodgers to beat the Phillies in Philadelphia in order to remain alive.

Thanks to Jackie Robinson, the Dodgers prevailed. Rallying from deficits of 6–1 and 8–5, Brooklyn tied the game at 8–8, sending it into extra innings. With the bases loaded and two out in the bottom of the 12th, Phillie Eddie Waitkus smacked a low liner to Robinson's right near second. Robinson dove and caught the ball centimeters off the ground, saving the game and season for Brooklyn and temporarily knocking himself out in the process.

In the 14th, Robinson drove a solo home run into the bleachers to give Brooklyn an improbable and almost operatic 9–8 win. New York and Brooklyn finished the 1951 regular season in a tie, both with records of 96–58. (Major League Baseball schedules were 154 games long until the start of the 1961 season.) A best two out of three playoff was necessary to determine the NL champion.

Assisted by home runs from Thomson and Monte Irvin (both off of Ralph Branca), the Giants took the first game at Ebbets Field, 3–1. Behind a shutout hurled by rookie Clem Labine, the Dodgers evened the series at the Polo Grounds, winning Game Two, 10–0.

Game Three was held at the Polo Grounds on a damp and overcast Wednesday, October 3, 1951. Dodger ace Don Newcombe and Maglie were locked in a 1–1 tie until the Dodgers rallied to score three in the top of the eighth. Thomson had misplayed a grounder at third base during the Dodger uprising. Downcast, he would soon turn from goat to hero.

• • •

The New York Yankees had survived a tough race of their own to win the American League pennant. Several Yankees were present at Game Three, including Yogi Berra. Convinced the game had been effectively decided and that Brooklyn would be their World Series opponent, the Yanks left early to beat the subway rush.

The "Miracle at Coogan's Bluff," a.k.a. "The Shot Heard 'Round the World" was in the offing. Trailing 4–1 in the bottom of the ninth, the Giants scored one run on singles by Al Dark and Don Mueller, plus a double by Whitey Lockman. Mueller slid awkwardly into third on Lockman's hit and suffered a broken ankle. After a long and agonizing delay in which Mueller was carried off to the center field clubhouse, Clint Hartung came in to run for Mueller.

Thomson strode to the plate with one out and a nervous—and slumping—Willie Mays on deck and the Giants trailing, 4–2. Lockman represented the tying run, with Thomson's bat carrying the potential winning run.

Dressen decided to make a pitching change, lifting Newcombe. He called the Dodger bullpen, located in deep left center. Clyde Sukeforth, the Dodger bullpen coach, answered. Observing Branca and Carl Erskine warming up, Sukeforth (who had been instrumental in signing Robinson) informed Dressen: "Erskine just bounced a curve. Branca looks ready." Dressen's order was terse: "Give me Branca."

Branca ambled in from the bullpen, exchanged back pats and pleasantries with Newcombe, and received encouragement from Dodger center fielder Duke Snider: "Go get 'em, Honk." Concurrently, an announcement was heard in the press box: "Attention, press. World Series credentials for Ebbets Field can be picked up at six o'clock tonight at the Biltmore Hotel."

Branca's first pitch was a fastball straight down the middle of the plate. Thomson took it for strike one. Attempting to jam Thomson up and in, Branca's next offering was a high inside fastball.

Thomson whipped his bat around and sent a long, sinking drive toward the 315-foot mark down the left field line. Despite severe topspin, the ball slipped over the tall fence for a walk off, pennant-winning three-run home run.

A Dodger fan taped Giant Broadcaster Russ Hodges's radio call of the bottom of the ninth, confident he could use the tape recording of a Dodger victory to embarrass his Giant loving friends. The plan backfired.

Hysterically, Hodges yelled into his microphone: ". . . there's a long drive, it's gonna be I believe . . . THE GIANTS WIN THE PENNANT! THE GIANTS WIN THE PENNANT!" Hodges's call remains the most famous play by play description in baseball history. In a fascinating aside, during the entire span of his call Hodges never uttered the words "home run."

Pandemonium erupted. As Thomson was mobbed by his teammates at home plate, black jacketed Giant second baseman Eddie Stanky raced across the diamond and accosted Durocher, who was coaching third (a common practice by managers then). Stanky leapt on Durocher's back, happily pummeling his manager who was trying to break free to join his ballclub at home plate.

The Dodgers, meanwhile, sullenly marched off the field. Champagne and electronic equipment set up in the Dodgers locker room to record a celebration had to be hurriedly transferred to the Giants locker room. Dressen entered the clubhouse, ripping the buttons off his uniform. An understandably dejected Branca sat on the clubhouse steps, head in hands. After removing his jersey, Branca laid—face down—across the same steps. The scene was captured in prize-winning photos by Dodger photographer Barney Stein.

Only one Dodger remained behind to watch: Jackie Robinson, the pioneer who had integrated baseball and whose heroics in Philadelphia had forced the playoff, stood motionless and watched Thomson complete his home run trot.

Wanting to ensure that Thomson touched all the bases, Robinson observed closely as Thomson toed each bag and then leapt onto home plate in glee.

Robinson turned and slowly walked toward the center field clubhouse.

The New York Yankees defeated the New York Giants in the 1951 World Series, 4 games to 2. It was the first World Series for Mickey Mantle and Willie Mays, and the last for Joe DiMaggio.

12

From the Cellar to the Penthouse

Bill Mazeroski's World Series-winning home run in 1960 joins Bobby Thomson's dramatics as one of the signature moments in baseball history.

As you read this account of Game Seven of the 1960 series, keep in mind the importance of the job of general manager in Major League Baseball. A GM places his fingerprints on all aspects of the baseball side of his organization: scouting, drafting, player development, and the major league team, referred to in industry circles as "The Big Club."

Modern GMs have an additional array of duties: free agent signings, trades, composition of the major league team, releasing players, hiring and firing managers and coaches, juggling enormous big league payrolls, legal issues, media interaction. In 2014, a GM's job is impossibly demanding and is often referred to as a 24/7/365 occupation.

Despite this relentless burden, the primary job of a GM in 2014 is the same as it was in 1960: Assembling a major league roster that is capable of winning a World Series.

Ben Cherington, GM of the Boston Red Sox, performed a near miracle in 2013. In 2011, with a playoff berth nearly assured, the Sox suffered a late collapse and missed the postseason. A disastrous losing season followed in 2012. Wielding a deft touch, Cherington rebuilt the Red Sox and hired a new field manager, John Farrell, who led the club to the title.

Branch Rickey performed a similar feat over a half century ago with the Pirates. Pittsburgh had been the worst team in the NL in the early fifties. After losing a fight with Walter O'Malley for control of the Brooklyn Dodgers, Rickey was hired as Pittsburgh GM and set out to revamp the Bucs.

Savvy scouting brought prospects Dick Groat, Bill Mazeroski, Vern Law, and Roberto Clemente to Pittsburgh; brilliant trades provided other key contributors. A scant six years after suffering three consecutive 100-loss, last place seasons, the Pirates were World Champs.

As they do today, the Yankees of 1960 dealt from a position of strength. Their farm system was unequalled, providing key replacements as older stars faded. Trades—often with the unusually compliant Kansas City A's—brought necessary additions.

In his twelve years as Yankee Manager from 1949 through 1960, Casey Stengel guided New York to ten AL pennants and seven World Series titles. The true architect behind the Yankee success in this era was their GM, George Weiss.

Curmudgeonly and penurious, Weiss was an unparalleled judge of talent. His ability to recognize, sign, develop, and trade for top echelon players was stunning. After molding the Yankees into the premier dynasty in the history of the game, Weiss constructed the ballclub which became known as the 1969 "Miracle" New York Mets.

Never accused of being a "people" person, Weiss frequently developed adversarial relationships with his players; Billy Martin in particular. Weiss traded Martin to Kansas City after a 1957 nightclub fight in which witnesses claim Martin was not involved. Later, Weiss hired detectives to follow players he suspected of misbehaving on road trips.

Viewed from the perspective of scouting and player development, it is crucial to remember that behind every successful franchise is a capable GM. He serves as baseball's equivalent of an orchestra conductor, a maestro. This tenet was true in 1960; it is just as true in 2014.

Along with Game Six of the 1975 World Series, Game Seven of the 1960 World Series is considered the greatest game in baseball history.

October 2010

UNSEEN FOR FIFTY years, a film of the live TV broadcast of Bill Mazeroski's walk off home run in the bottom of the ninth inning of Game Seven of the 1960 World Series was discovered late last year.

Recently transferred from film to DVD, the game broadcast will be shown on MLB Network in December. Major League Baseball has exclusive rights to the property, which will be made available for individual purchase by the public later this year. Originally, the film was shot in kinescope form—which simply means the live broadcast was filmed off a television monitor.

Mazeroski's Pittsburgh Pirates defeated the New York Yankees in that deciding game, 10–9. Despite getting outscored 55 to 27 in the series, the Bucs edged the Yanks to capture the title.

Considered one of the greatest games in baseball history, as well as a historical milestone, Game Seven of the 1960 Series has previously been preserved only in photographs and the official MLB World Series highlight film. No other recording of the game's TV broadcast—in whole or in part—is believed to exist.

To the delight of professional and amateur baseball historians, films of classic moments have randomly surfaced. In 1988, a grainy film was discovered of Game Three of the 1932 World Series, showing Babe Ruth's alleged "called shot." Earlier this year, MLB Network debuted by showing Don Larsen's perfect game in the 1956 World Series—another classic TV broadcast thought to be irretrievably lost.

The 1960 telecast was discovered in Bing Crosby's longtime Northern California home. Crosby, velvet throated crooner and motion picture star, died in 1977 at the age of 74. A lifelong baseball fan, Crosby was a part owner of the Pirates for many years.

Reportedly, Crosby couldn't bear to watch the game on TV or in person, so he and his wife Kathryn headed to Paris. The Crosbys listened to the game with their friends Charles and Nonie de Limur.

"We were in this beautiful apartment, listening on shortwave, and when it got close Bing opened a bottle of scotch and was tapping it against the mantel," recalled Kathryn Crosby. "When Mazeroski hit the home run he tapped it hard; the scotch flew into the fireplace and started a conflagration. I was screaming and Nonie said, 'It's very nice to celebrate things, but couldn't we be more restrained?'"

Crosby hired a film company to make the kinescope, which he watched upon his return. The landmark film was then stored—unnoticed—in Crosby's Hillsborough, California, home for a half century. Robert Bader, VP of Bing Crosby Entertainment, found the film canisters while searching through the singer's personal memorabilia collection. The tins were innocently marked "1960 World Series."

I spoke to Nick Trotta, senior manager of library licensing for Major League Baseball. According to Trotta, the film—which had been stored in Crosby's wine cellar—was in pristine condition. Upon transfer, the resulting quality of the DVD is remarkable, given the film's age.

First, a quick baseball history lesson. In 1960, major league baseball had only 16 teams—8 in each league. All clubs played a 154-game schedule. There were no divisions or layers of playoffs in 1960—the league champions advanced directly to the World Series.[1]

In the American League, the dynastic Yankees broke open a tight pennant race by winning their final 15 games. New York boasted a lineup full of All Stars and Hall of Famers, including Mickey Mantle, Whitey Ford, Roger Maris, Yogi Berra, Elston Howard, and Bill Skowron.

In the early fifties, Pittsburgh was one of the worst teams in baseball history. The Pirates had finished in last place (coincidentally known as "the cellar" in baseball lingo) from 1952 through 1955. As the decade progressed, the Bucs improved their fortunes.

Their 1960 pennant was the organizations' first in thirty-three years. Pittsburgh featured Cy Young Award winner Vernon Law, National League MVP and batting champion Dick Groat, budding superstar Roberto Clemente, and defensive stalwarts Bill Virdon and Mazeroski.

The Yankees blasted the Pirates in games two, three, and six by scores of 16–3, 10–0, and 12–0. Pittsburgh scored more modest wins in games one, four, and five by scores of 6–4, 3–2 and 5–2. The seventh and deciding game of the series was played at Forbes Field in Pittsburgh, on Thursday, October 13, 1960.

---

1 The AL expanded to ten teams and a 162 game schedule in 1961, and the NL followed suit in 1962. Major League Baseball first introduced pre-World Series playoffs in 1969. Playoffs prior to that date occurred only after teams finished in a regular season tie. Those playoff games were counted as part of the regular season—in 1946, 1948, 1951, 1959, and 1962.

The contest was broadcast live across the nation via NBC-TV. At that time, all Series games were played in the daytime, never at night.[2]

Pirate play by play man Bob Prince handled the first half of the game solo and legendary Yankee announcer Mel Allen covered the final innings.

The kinescope is in black and white despite the fact that the actual live broadcast was in color. NBC used a then unusual technique which is now a common practice—a center field camera aimed over the pitchers shoulder in toward home plate. Prior to 1960, most major league telecasts used a main camera positioned above and behind home plate, giving TV watchers a kind of "press box" view.

The Pirates, aided by a Rocky Nelson home run, jumped out to a 4–0 lead. New York, boosted by home runs from Bill Skowron and Yogi Berra, rallied to take a 7–4 edge going into the bottom of the eighth. With a runner on and no outs, Bill Virdon rapped a certain double play ball at Yankee shortstop Tony Kubek. Suddenly, the ball took a bad hop and struck Kubek in the throat. Both runners were safe. Injured, Kubek was forced to leave the game. Pittsburgh, behind Hal Smith's home run, rallied to take a 9–7 lead.

After Virdon's ground ball, Casey Stengel can be seen ambling out of the Yankee dugout to check on Kubek. Allen stated that Smith's home run would be "remembered for a long time."

It was, until the top of the ninth. With the score 9–8 and runners on first and third and one out, Yogi Berra hit a ground ball down the first base line. Nelson, the Pirate first baseman, snagged the drive and toed the bag for the second out. That move by Nelson removed the force play on Mickey Mantle, the Yankee runner at first. Nelson needed only to tag Mantle to record the final out.

---

2 In 1960, all big league stadiums, with the exception of Wrigley Field, had lights. Tradition— quaint to some, outdated to others—dictated that Series games be played during the day. The first World Series night game occurred in 1971, thirty-six years after the first regular season night game.

The Mick wriggled away from Nelson's attempted tag and safely returned to first as the tying run scored.

Allen very succinctly explained the unusual play to viewers, while Mantle stood on first with his hands on his hips, looking calm and confident. Tied 9–9, the game moved into the bottom of the ninth.

Mazeroski led off for the Pirates. He took Ralph Terry's first pitch for a ball. After that pitch, Yankee catcher Johnny Blanchard jogged to the mound for a quick chat with Terry. With Blanchard back behind the plate, the center field camera was zeroed in on the action as Terry went into a full windup.

Mazeroski swung at Terry's offering and sent a long drive toward the 406-foot sign in left center. Yogi Berra, playing in left for the Yanks, drifted back as if he had a play on the ball. Quickly realizing his only chance was to play a possible carom, Berra reversed course and headed back toward the infield. No matter.

Mazeroski's drive cleared the left field fence, winning the game and the Series for Pittsburgh. To this day, it remains the only walk off home run to win the seventh game of a World Series.

Allen can be heard describing the moment perfectly: "There's a drive to deep left field . . . look out now . . . that ball is going, going, gone! The World Series is over!"

After the ball cleared the fence, a camera located on the third base side captured a tight shot of Mazeroski's reaction. He bounced up and down, pinwheeling his arms in celebration as he held his batting helmet in his right hand. A mob of fans and teammates greeted Mazeroski at home plate.

The Yankees, somber in defeat, marched from their third base dugout. The tunnel to the visiting dressing room at Forbes Field was located next to the Pirates first base dugout. This forced the Yankees to awkwardly walk around the delirious mob at home plate to get to their clubhouse.

Bob Prince, wearing a loud checkered sport coat, conducted a string of interviews in the clubhouse after the game. He then tossed the show back to Allen in the press box, who did a brief wrap-up and signoff, ending the telecast.

Viewing the game film today exposes both subtle and obvious differences that have evolved in the game of baseball and the televising of baseball in the past fifty years:

- Not a single hitter wore a batting glove.
- Batting helmets were a fairly new invention in 1960, but no helmet had ear flaps.
- All uniforms, of course, were made of flannel.
- Plain black spikes, with no flashy corporate logos, were worn by all ballplayers.
- The seventh game in 1960 was played in bright sunshine, but I detected no eye black being used by any player.
- Baseball in 1960 was played at a much quicker pace than today. Pirate pitchers Vern Law and Elroy Face worked very rapidly and would probably draw "quick pitch" warnings in 2014.
- Hitters did not wander and dawdle outside the batter's box in 1960. Today, even a fine player like Dustin Pedroia exits the box after every pitch, seeming to suffer a nervous breakdown as he endlessly fiddles with his batting gloves.

Game Seven of the 1960 World Series was played in 2 hours and 36 minutes. This despite all the pitching changes, runs scored, and Kubek's injury. Postseason games today average between 3.5 and 4 hours. Average game time in the 1957 Series was two hours and twenty-seven minutes. The fourth and final game of the 1963 Series took 1 hour and 50 minutes. If Bud Selig wants to learn why baseball has trouble attracting young fans, perhaps he should start studying postseason game times.

The Forbes Field crowd was particularly interesting. Almost every adult male wore a suit and tie. All six umpires wore suits and ties. One fan can be heard constantly chirping encouragement to his Pirates: "Just a little bingo!" he is heard saying during a Buc rally, and "Let's get two!" as Elroy Face faces a New York rally in the ninth. Prior to Mazeroski's homer, he can be heard advising "Just get on Billy! We'll figure out a way to get you around!"

Little quirks were fascinating. Ballparks fifty years ago had unusually large mound circles, much larger than today. The check swing rule was not in effect. Several hitters took half swings that unquestionably would be called strikes today. Catchers and home plate umpires did not check with first or third base umps to confirm half swing strikes in 1960.

In the bottom of the eighth, Hal Smith faced a two-strike count. He took a half swing on a high fastball which undoubtedly would be called a strikeout today. In 1960, there was no strike call, not even an appeal. Smith homered on the next pitch.

During one of his frequent mound visits, Stengel chats with his pitcher while standing on the mound. He then descends off the mound onto the grass, turns, and walks back onto the hill to render some more advice. In 2014, Stengel's actions would be ruled to be a second mound visit and the pitcher would be forced to leave the game.

From studying the telecast, my guess is that NBC used only four cameras: Center field, press box, first base, third base. Not a single play in the contest—critical or trivial—could be viewed a second time, as there was no instant replay. If a viewer missed the play, tough luck.

Replay was first used during a college football telecast in 1963. In 1960, TV viewers were not bombarded with blaring music, endless high-tech graphics, needless intrusions, promotional cutaways, or smart aleck commentators. The only graphics used displayed a hitter's name across the bottom of the screen as he came up to bat.

Perhaps the best postscript to the classic game involves comedian Lenny Bruce. A friend of sportswriter Dick Schaap, Bruce attended the seventh game as Schaap's guest. It was the first and only game Bruce saw in person.

Bruce was stunned. "Geez, that was incredible," gushed the comic. "Are all baseball games like that?"

Shortly after the 1960 World Series, the New York Yankees fired Casey Stengel and George Weiss.

13

The Three Dog

In scouting jargon, "hiding someone out" means to draft and/or sign a player who no other club has filed a report on or even scouted.

Today's techno information world makes hiding a prospect out a near impossibility, but stories of past hide outs are legendary. In 1968, the great Giant scout George Genovese "hid out" Gary Matthews Sr. and signed him after San Francisco made the Sarge a first round draft pick.

Mike Cameron, whose son Daz is a first round candidate for the 2015 draft, drew interest from only two ball clubs as a high school senior in the backwoods of Georgia. He was picked off in the eighteenth round of the 1991 draft by the White Sox. Cameron played seventeen years in the majors, hitting 278 career home runs while stealing 297 bases. As a member of the Seattle Mariners, Cameron came back to haunt the White Sox by blasting four home runs against them in a game in 2002.

Naturally, in order to hide a player out, clubs need to be highly secretive. In making small talk during games, a scout needs to avoid asking the common question, "so—have you seen so and so?" to prevent a tip-off.

There are two ways for an organization to determine if they have successfully hidden a prospect out. First is to check if the Major League Scouting Bureau has filed a report on the player. The Bureau has an NSA-like knack for compiling information and their blanket coverage is remarkable.

Second, each draft prospect must be assigned a draft number by the Bureau in order to be selected. Clubs attempting to hide a player out wait until the last possible moment prior to the submission deadline. If their prospect is assigned a fresh, previously unissued number, the club knows that no one else is "on" the player.

In the pre-draft era, former Dodger star Willie Davis was a "hide out." No other ballclub was remotely interested in Davis. The late Dodger scout Kenny Myers was blessed with an incredible eye for spotting raw, submersed talent. Myers's skill and diligence in developing Davis, along with Willie's strong work ethic, made him a big league star.

Extravagantly talented but personally troubled, Willie Davis patrolled center field for the Los Angeles Dodgers from 1960 to 1973. A left-handed hitter blessed with remarkable speed, Davis finished his career by playing short stints with the Montreal Expos, Texas Rangers, and California Angels.

Nicknamed "The Three Dog" in honor of his uniform number, Davis was an integral part of the Dodgers 1963 and 1965 World Championship ball clubs.

Davis died of natural causes on March 9, 2010.

P HIL POTE, THE self-described "Ancient Mariner," has been involved in baseball for fifty-five years. Affectionately nicknamed "The Mayor" by his fellow scouts, Pote has scouted for the Oakland A's, Los Angeles Dodgers, and, most recently, the Seattle Mariners.

A distinguished high school and junior college coach, Pote piloted Fremont High School to the 1963 Los Angeles City baseball championship—the last inner city school to win the title. That Fremont team featured future big league stars Bob Watson, Bobby Tolan and Willie Crawford.

In the mid to late fifties, Pote was a student-teacher at Roosevelt High, another inner city school in Los Angeles. During his time at Roosevelt, Pote encountered Willie Davis, whose recent passing has distinctly saddened the baseball fraternity.

Pote recalls, "Willie was a tremendous athlete. He played basketball, baseball, and ran track. As a sprinter, he ran a 9.5 second 100-yard dash (at a time when the world record was 9.3) and long jumped 25' 5"."

"As a baseball player," Pote recalls, "he was a very ordinary high school player. He could steal and go and get the ball, but he batted right-handed, wasn't much of a hitter, and had a weak arm."

Davis graduated from Roosevelt in 1958. Pote said, "Very few scouts were aware of Davis, and no one approached to sign him."

Except Kenny Myers. A part-time scout for the Los Angeles Dodgers, Myers had been an outstanding minor league hitter. "Kenny signed Willie for the Dodgers because he sensed Willie's athleticism," Pote stated, and added, "but he signed for a very small amount of money."

Davis signed in the summer of 1958, but was not farmed out to play minor league ball until 1959. In the intervening time, Myers and Davis went to work.

"They made each other," according to Pote. "Myers worked in a meat packing plant in Vernon, and he and Willie would get

up early and go to the field . . . and they also worked out on
weekends." Pote says Myers utilized several ingenious coaching
tactics on his star pupil, turning Davis into a sort of baseball lab
experiment.

To improve his throwing arm, Pote says Myers had Willie
"lie flat on his back and stretch his left arm over his head,
holding a basketball." Davis would then throw the basketball
using a straight overhand motion, an action known in baseball
as "coming over the top."

Davis was a pathetic hitter, but Pote recalls that Myers developed a series of novel and unique drills to reinvent Willie.

One such technique involved a fish net which had a baseball
bat handle. "Willie was using his hands wrong, so he couldn't
catch the ball in the net" remembers Pote, adding "Myers also
had Willie hit with a square-barreled bat—to teach him to center
the ball."

A unique pop-up batting tee was also employed, which Myers
operated by stepping on a foot pedal which softly tossed the ball
straight upwards. Pote says Davis couldn't touch the ball at first
but eventually "got the hang of it."

After several months of hard, frustrating, and difficult work,
Davis began his pro career at Reno of the Class C California
League in the spring of 1959. Myers's idiosyncratic coaching
style paid immediate and spectacular dividends.

Davis hit .365 at Reno. Promoted to Class AAA Spokane in
1960, Willie hit .346. He was called up to the Dodgers to stay
in late 1960.

I would be delighted to report that the remainder of Willie
Davis's career had a warm, fuzzy, toasty, Disney cartoon sto-
rybook ending, but it did not. Struggles and disappointments
typified his first eight full seasons with the Dodgers, from 1961
through 1968. Davis bore the weight of being a "promise unful-
filled" player.

In the second game of the 1966 World Series against the Baltimore Orioles at Dodger Stadium, Davis dropped two consecutive pop-ups. After the second flub, he angrily picked the ball up and fired it into the stands behind third base. That was the last game Sandy Koufax would ever pitch. Baltimore swept the Series.

In a later game of that Series, which had shifted to Baltimore, Davis camped out under an easy fly ball. Willie had his jaw set in determination and his glove extended as the ball approached. Lou Johnson raced over from left field and snatched the ball away at the last instant. Davis screamed at Johnson as Lou, laughing all the way, sailed past.

Almost completely forgotten nowadays was Willie's incredible, gravity defying catch of a ball hit by Baltimore's Boog Powell in Game Four. Powell drove a towering smash over the six-foot-high chain link fence in straightway center field. Willie scaled the barrier, reached far back with his right arm, and impossibly snagged the ball in the webbing of his glove.

Maury Wills was appointed Dodger team captain in the mid-sixties. His first move was to fine Davis for not hustling. Manager Walt Alston intervened. "You can't fine Willie for not hustling," Alston told Wills. "Why not?" said Maury, "You just made me team captain!" Alston replied, "Because if you fine Willie every time he doesn't hustle, he'll run out of money by mid season."

Finally, around 1969, Davis began to, as baseball people say, "figure it out." He stopped trying to be Willie Mays and instead became Willie Davis. His thin frame was never suited for home run hitting, so Davis began to shorten his stroke, use the entire field and let his speed provide infield hits.

It worked. Davis hit .311 in 1969 with a 31 game hitting streak. I was in attendance at one of the games during the streak as Davis ripped a sharp base hit up the middle which deflected off the second base bag. (I was also in the crowd when Don Drysdale pitched his record-setting sixth consecutive shutout in 1968, which occurred the night Bobby Kennedy was assassinated. It was Lomita Little League night.)

Davis followed his fine '69 campaign by hitting .309 in 1970, and .305 in 1971. He belted a home run in the 1973 All Star Game—off of Nolan Ryan no less, who that year pitched two no hitters and set a still standing record with 383 strikeouts. Willie collected 2,591 lifetime hits, led the NL in triples twice, and stole 20 or more bases in thirteen seasons.

Not that Davis didn't have, let's say, some "personality." He dabbled in Buddhism and was known to recite chants to himself in his locker before games. As the Cincinnati Reds were taking batting practice before a Sunday doubleheader in 1970, Davis, in full uniform but wearing shower clogs (flip-flops), walked across the outfield and into the visitors bullpen. Davis got a squad full of "what the hell are you doing?" looks from his opponents.

• • •

Post-baseball retirement was difficult for Davis, often tragic. He struggled with substance abuse and was once accused of attempting to attack his parents at their home with a samurai sword. During a hiking trip, his wife fell off a cliff to her death as Willie desperately extended his hand to save her.

I saw Davis at an autograph signing convention in downtown Los Angeles in the early nineties. Bob Gibson was the featured attraction, while Davis sat off to Gibson's left and signed autographs for free. Willie had a dozen markers of various colors laid out on his table.

During the prime of his playing career, Davis was 6' 3" and 180 pounds. As he signed autographs, Davis was shockingly gaunt, probably weighing only 120 pounds. The sight of Willie and his long, skeletal fingers stunned those in attendance, many whispering under their breath, "My god! What happened to him?"

Davis did eventually receive assistance, both financial and personal, but he was never able to totally eliminate his demons.

I prefer to remember Willie Davis as he was in the sixties. Phil Pote told me, and many old-time baseball people agree that no one was better at going from first to third or second to home than Willie Davis. In the outfield, his graceful and gliding running style allowed him to chase down drives in the gaps and snare bloopers off the top of the grass. Once he settled into his natural hitting style, Davis was a dangerous and productive offensive threat.

To his credit, Davis did not take the game too seriously and possessed a sly, clever sense of humor.

My favorite Willie Davis anecdote occurred during a television pre-game show over forty years ago. Prior to each local Dodger telecast, Bill Welch of KTTV in Los Angeles would bring two little leaguers on camera, where they would receive advice and inside tips from a selected Dodger player.

Davis was the featured Dodger one day. Welch, being pleasant and making small talk, asked one of the youngsters what his batting average was. "Well, I'm batting over .400!" the kid enthused.

Davis's response was deadpan and perfectly timed:

"Maybe you should give *me* the tips."

14

Sandy Is Dandy

Prior to the installation of the draft in 1965, Major League Baseball utilized what was known as the "Bonus Baby" rule from 1953 to 1957. Ridiculous in retrospect, the rule mandated that any club signing an amateur free agent for a bonus at or above $4,000 ($35,000 in today's money) was required to keep that player on its Major League roster for two years before he could be shipped out to the minor leagues for seasoning.

In that brief four-year span, fifty-seven players became Bonus Babies. A tiny number of Bonus Babies were unaffected by the restrictive rules. Al Kaline, for instance, never spent a day in the minors and won the American League batting title at the age of twenty in 1955. However, the majority of Bonus Babies were failures, no doubt due to the loss of precious development time in their late teens and early twenties.

Two Bonus Baby trivia items to note: One of the Bonus Babies was Vic Janowicz of the Pirates, who had won the Heisman Trophy as an Ohio State running back in 1950. Janowicz's career was cut short when he suffered a serious head injury in a car accident. Also, none of the Bonus Babies signed to lucrative contracts were African American.

Sandy Koufax was a Bonus Baby, signed by the Brooklyn Dodgers for $25,000 in 1955. (That's $218,000 in today's money.) Sandy pitched sporadically and inconsistently in his first six years in the majors, stunted by a lack of minor league development. As the following article points out, once Koufax, as baseball people say "figured it out," he became darn near unhittable.

Interesting anecdote: Before being signed by the Dodgers, Koufax worked out for the New York Giants at the Polo Grounds. The Giants were unimpressed and declined to offer Sandy a contract. If the Giants had signed Koufax . . . imagine a sixties Giants ballclub with a rotation headed by Koufax and Juan Marichal, with Willie Mays, Willie McCovey and Orlando Cepeda in the everyday lineup. Unquestionably, that team would have dominated the National League throughout the sixties and would have obliterated the American League competition in the World Series.

March 3, 2010

O N THE NIGHT of Friday, June 18, 1966, my mother piled me and my two older brothers into the family car, a white Dodge Dart. Our destination was Dodger Stadium and our objective was to watch Sandy Koufax pitch against the San Francisco Giants of Willie Mays and Willie McCovey.

Koufax did not disappoint. He and the Dodgers beat the Giants that evening, 3–2. Sandy allowed 4 hits and 3 walks while striking out 10 in a complete game. Los Angeles would win the National League pennant in 1966 edging the Giants by 1.5 games. It was the Dodgers' third pennant in four seasons.

I was eight years old in 1966, and I sat with my family in the Loge section (second deck) of the stadium, down the right field line near the foul pole. Forty-four years passed before my next live, in-person encounter with Koufax. That occurred Saturday night at the Nokia Theater in downtown Los Angeles.

While I was seated closer to Koufax in 2010 than I was in 1966, one constant remained: Sandy was my all-time sports hero in 1966. He still is.

The occasion for Koufax's reappearance was a charity event hosted by Joe Torre and his "Safe at Home" foundation, which aims to assist victims of all forms of domestic violence. Saturday's event raised $700,000 for the worthy cause.

Koufax and Torre fielded questions, chatting and reminiscing for ninety minutes. The session was shown live on cable TV. Torre, about to embark on his third year as Dodgers manager, was his usual articulate and entertaining self. However, the focus of the evening was on Koufax, the Hall of Fame left-hander who began his career with the Brooklyn Dodgers in 1955, came west with the team from his hometown to Los Angeles in 1958, and retired after the 1966 campaign due to assorted arm and shoulder injuries.

In his final four seasons (1963 through 1966), Koufax was the greatest pitcher in baseball history. He won three Cy Young Awards ('63, '65, '66) when only one award was given for both leagues.

Even in the pitcher's era of the sixties, Sandy's stats were remarkable. Viewed today, they appear to be fantastic, almost surreal. The following is a chart of Koufax's performance from 1963 to 1966:

Year	W–L	ERA	IP	K	CG	SHO
1963	25–5	1.88	311	306	20	11
1964	19–5	1.74	223	223	15	7
1965	26–8	2.04	335 2/3	382	27	8
1966	27–9	1.73	323	317	27	5

Koufax threw four no-hitters in consecutive years (1962–1965), including a perfect game against the Cubs on September 9,

1965. Sandy was the NL MVP in 1963 and was World Series MVP in 1963 and 1965, as the Dodgers defeated the Yankees and Twins, respectively.

Vin Scully, the voice of the Dodgers, has often likened a Koufax performance to that of a maestro conducting a grand orchestra. Indeed, Koufax on the mound projected a regal presence, and his pitching motion was not only distinct, but magnificent. Sandy did not throw or pitch a ball, he launched it. He began by slowly drawing his hands from his waist above his head to the back of his neck. Driving off the edge of the rubber, he bent his left leg like a kangaroo's hind leg, with the toe of his right foot pointed toward first base. Koufax strode plate ward, then catapulted the ball from a release point located almost directly above his head.

His stuff was phenomenal. I once asked former big leaguer Jacke Davis about Koufax's fastball: "He threw 100, easy." Bobby Richardson was shocked by the velocity of the fastball and its sudden late rising life, saying, "It was like a rocket taking off."

Tim McCarver has always gushed about Sandy's curve, as did John Roseboro, a longtime catcher for Koufax. The breaking ball started above Sandy's head and then, as Roseboro described, "dropped straight down out of the sky." After striking out against Koufax in the 1963 World Series, a befuddled Mickey Mantle turned to Roseboro and asked, "How you supposed to hit that stuff?"

On Saturday night, in front of a crowd partially composed of sports and entertainment celebrities, Koufax, 74, regaled those present with several anecdotal stories.

Frustrated by a lack of success in his first six years in the big leagues, Koufax decided to quit after the 1960 season. He took the extreme measure of placing his glove and spikes in a clubhouse trash can after the final game of the year.

"I was making only $14,000, so it wasn't like I was giving up a multi-million dollar job," he said. "I took a real job in the off-season and figured I'd better go back to baseball." In early 1961, clubhouse manager Nobe Kawano handed back to Koufax his discarded equipment. "I thought you might need these," said Kawano.

The turnaround in Koufax's fortunes occurred in spring training of 1961. On a flight across Florida to play the Twins in a "B" exhibition game, Gil Hodges pointed to Koufax and told him he was to pitch the entire game. Seated next to Koufax was backup catcher Norm Sherry, who advised Sandy to pace himself, concentrate on strikes, and to not throw so hard.

After walking the first three batters, Koufax worked his way out of the jam and threw a no-hitter for eight innings. That day began the process of transforming Koufax from promising prospect into an icon and legend.

Today's players are still in awe. Clayton Kershaw ambled up from the audience and placed his hand palm to palm with Koufax's hand. Sandy's paw, with his remarkably long fingers, was almost twice the size of Kershaw's. Koufax also gave the young Dodger lefty a pointer on how to throw a curve: "Grip it on the seams with your middle finger, no pressure on the index finger, and don't push it with the thumb." Koufax will soon be instructing pitchers at the Dodgers spring training camp in Arizona.

Not everyone appreciated Koufax in his day. In 1966, he held out in tandem with Don Drysdale, demanding an increased salary. Koufax, whose salary today would exceed $20 million per year, settled for $125,000.

In 2001, I spoke to Buzzie Bavasi, who was the Dodgers general manager in 1966. Bavasi said, "We could have ended the holdout anytime, we just kept it going for publicity purposes." He added that TV actor Chuck Connors—a former major league player—intervened to halt the holdout. Said Bavasi, "The four of us got together in an Italian restaurant in downtown LA and worked it out."

After signing, Koufax and Drysdale reported to Dodgertown in Vero Beach, Florida, for spring training. Intentionally or not, the two had begun the process of destroying the so called reserve clause, which contractually bound a player to one club with no options. Free agency would later ensue.

Sandy Koufax merits respect and, dare it be said, reverence.

Sandy's presence reminds me of a scene in the film *To Kill a Mockingbird*. Scout is gently ordered to stand up by Reverend Sykes as her father, Atticus Finch, leaves the courtroom.

"Jean Louise . . . Jean Louise, stand up," the Reverend says. "Your father's passing."

Baseball fans and all those who work in the baseball industry share the same type of respect for the brilliant left-hander:

Stand up, everyone . . . Sandy Koufax is passing.

15

The Duke Was Robbed

As a sixteen-year-old, Duke Snider was first noticed by the Brooklyn Dodgers at a tryout camp in Southern California. Over seventy years later, almost all ball clubs still hold tryout camps or pre-draft workouts. In early March of 2014, the Los Angeles Dodgers held an open tryout camp at their spring training complex at Camelback Ranch in Arizona. Two players were signed out of that camp.

Almost every major league ball club conducts pre-draft workouts, in which prospects are invited to display their talents in front of scouts and front office personnel. Often, these workouts are held at the club's major league ballpark; if that field is unavailable a local college or junior college field is rented for the day.

For decades, the workouts have followed a time honored routine. In the morning, position players run the 60-yard dash. Next is an extended infield-outfield session, in which players from all positions on the field display their fielding skills and—most importantly—their throwing arms. Wood bat batting practice finishes the morning workout, with all hopefuls getting two full rounds of eight or ten swings each.

After a lunch break, a simulated game is played. Each pitcher throws to three (sometimes five) batters, and hitters not cut after the morning session take several at bats. In some workouts, pitchers throw a limited number of pitches to a catcher with no hitter present, simply to display his stuff and repertoire to the scouts. At the conclusion of the tryout, the staff discusses and debates the merits of each player.

At pro workouts, the organization decides who will be offered a contract. After amateur pre-draft workouts, the staff has a clearer picture of the tools and abilities of potential draftees.

Of course, rarely—if ever—do scouts find a player at a tryout/workout camp as gifted as Duke Snider.

T HE 1950s ARE viewed by many as a Golden Age in baseball history, with ample justification.

Several of the game's iconic, signature moments occurred in that decade: Bobby Thomson's home run; "The Catch" by Willie Mays; Brooklyn's only World Series triumph; Don Larsen's perfect game; West Coast baseball; Harvey Haddix's pitching masterpiece.

Integration significantly elevated the overall level of talent and athleticism in the big leagues as well as the quality of play. Active in the fifties were all-time greats such as Willie Mays, Mickey Mantle, Stan Musial, Ted Williams, Jackie Robinson, Warren Spahn, Frank Robinson, and Ernie Banks, just to identify a sampling.

The two dominant teams of the decade were the New York Yankees (8 AL pennants, 6 World Series titles) and the Brooklyn/ Los Angeles Dodgers (5 NL pennants, 2 World titles). In 1955, the Brooklyn Dodgers vanquished years of bitter disappointment by knocking off the Yankees in an epic seven-game Series.

That Dodger team was lead by catcher Roy Campanella, a two time NL MVP. Campy batted .318 with 32 homers and 107 RBI. Center fielder Duke Snider belted 42 homers, adding a .309 average and 136 RBI.

Naturally, both Campy and Snider were leading candidates for the National League's Most Valuable Player Award, voted on and bestowed by members of the Baseball Writers Association of America (BBWAA).

The BBWAA's 1955 NL MVP vote provided one of the most unusual and bizarre episodes in baseball history.

Under BBWAA rules, the MVP award winner is the player who receives the highest number of total points, not the player with the largest number of first place votes. There have been at least two instances in which the player getting the most first place votes did not win the MVP award.

In 1960, Roger Maris won the AL MVP award with 8 first place votes and 225 total points. Mickey Mantle finished second with 10 firsts and 222 total. Then in 1966, Roberto Clemente beat out Sandy Koufax in the balloting with 8 firsts and 218 points to Sandy's 9 firsts and 208 points to win the NL MVP.

Now let's return to 1955. At that time, Major League Baseball had only 16 teams—8 in the AL, 8 in the NL. In each league, 3 BBWAA member writers representing each of that circuit's eight franchises were chosen to vote. Twenty-four total ballots were tallied for each league's MVP award.

All voters listed their selections from 1 through 10, and the following point system was used:
1st Place: 14 points
2nd Place: 9 points
3rd Place: 8 points
4th Place: 7 points

5th Place: 6 points
6th Place: 5 points
7th Place: 4 points
8th Place: 3 points
9th Place: 2 points
10th Place: 1 point

Each ballot contained a value of 59 points with 1,416 total points available. Keep in mind that no writer was permitted to vote twice for one player.

In 1955, no fax, email, texts, or Internet existed, of course. Completed ballots were required to be submitted via US Mail after the conclusion of the regular season (Sunday, September 25) and before the beginning of the World Series (Wednesday, September 28).

That gave the voters a two day "window" on Monday and Tuesday, September 26 and 27. After all ballots were collected, the votes would be counted after the conclusion of the World Series (Tuesday, October 4) with the results announced in early December.

Now it gets complicated. Former major league pitcher Stan Baumgartner was then a baseball writer for the *Philadelphia Inquirer.* Near the end of the season, Baumgartner fell ill and was hospitalized in Philadelphia.

Despite his illness, Baumgartner was a trooper. He completed and mailed in his BBWAA NL MVP ballot on schedule. Unfortunately, Baumgartner died on October 4, 1955, after his ballot was mailed but before the MVP votes were tallied. Brooklyn's Johnny Podres pitched a 2–0 shutout that same day in the seventh game of the World Series to secure the Dodgers first Championship.

Baumgartner listed Roy Campanella in first and in fifth place. Snider was entirely omitted from Baumgartner's ballot.

As they examined the ballots and counted the votes, BBWAA officials were faced with a massive, complicated problem: What to do with Baumgartner's ballot? There was, of course, no way of going back and finding out what his intent actually was.

The BBWAA had several options, including:

1. Throw Baumgartner's ballot out.

   Technically, this seems to be the most sensible option since the rules did not allow a writer to vote for one player twice.

   If the BBWAA had used this option, Snider would have won 8-221 to 7-212.

2. Throw the ballot out and have another Philadelphia BBWAA member submit a ballot.

   Since the ballots were mailed in after September 26, and the result was not announced until early December, there was more than enough time to utilize this option.

In this scenario, if Campy got the first place vote, Snider would still win if he was listed as fifth or above. Duke would have tied for the MVP with Campy if he had been listed sixth. Snider would have lost only if he had been listed seventh or below, an extremely remote possibility.

There is one notable hiccup in this option. The primary reason ballots are submitted after the regular season but before the beginning of the postseason is to prevent a writer from being unduly influenced by a player's great, good, fair or awful postseason play.

This choice would have favored Snider unfairly, since Duke hit .320 against the Yankees and tied his own National League record for home runs in a single World Series with four. That record stood until 2009.

A recent biography of Roy Campanella claims that Baumgartner's voting chores were indeed assumed by a substitute

Philadelphia writer. There is no indication in the book if this switch was made prior to or after Baumgartner's passing. In this version of the tale, it was the replacement writer who supposedly submitted the erroneous ballot.

If true, the BBWAA's final decision is doubly nonsensical. BBWAA officials could have simply asked the new voter to clarify his error, correct his voting card or submit another ballot. Problem solved.

3. Count Snider first and Campy fifth.
   If so, Snider wins 9-235 to 7-212.
4. Count Campy first and Snider fifth.
   Snider wins narrowly if counted fifth: 8-227 to 8-226.

The BBWAA instead made a bewildering decision. On Baumgartner's ballot, they counted Campanella's first place vote but vacated the fifth place vote. That meant that no one, Snider included, received Baumgartner's fifth place vote.

Therefore, Roy Campanella was awarded the 1955 NL MVP award over Duke Snider by a final official count of 8-226 to 8-221.

Joe Posnanski, a former *Sports Illustrated* writer, authored a web blog about this controversy entitled, "1955 MVP: A Detective Story." Posnanski cites modern Saber stats, hints at shadowy motives and points out fascinating hijinks in the voting and tabulations.

Posnanski's take is entertaining but moot. The fact remains that one writer voted for Campanella twice and was not allowed to do so; Snider's name was not on that ballot in any spot and should have been; the BBWAA resolved the matter in a grossly incorrect fashion.

Viewed today, the BBWAA's decision, while not an outright travesty, appears to be a rather serious error in judgment. It is impossible to believe that Baumgartner intended to leave Snider off his ballot, plus, well, *somebody* deserved that fifth place vote. Since the announcement of the NL MVP award in December of 1955, the BBWAA has never issued a public explanation regarding their handling of the disputed ballot.

I am no fan of conspiracy theories and I am certain one does not exist in this saga. My guess is that the BBWAA did not want to throw out the ballot of a recently deceased writer who was liked, admired, and respected. In addition, as mentioned above, after the World Series a new vote may have favored Snider unduly. So, the BBWAA faced an awkward, uncomfortable problem that contained no perfect remedy.

Common sense and the passage of time strongly suggest that the BBWAA chose the least sensible solution. Roy Campanella was a great player and an exemplary human being and (almost) every honor he has been granted is richly deserved. However, Duke Snider should have been awarded the 1955 National League Most Valuable Player Award. At the time, Campanella himself was quoted as saying, "I wish Duke had won this one."

Of course, the possibility that the BBWAA would reverse its decision, take the plaque away from Campanella and award it to Snider at this late date is incredibly remote. Nor would it be fair to Campanella, his memory or his family to strip him of the 1955 NL MVP award.

Still, Snider deserves that award. Perhaps a co-1955 NL MVP award could be presented to Snider's family in Duke's memory. US Military medals and other types of honors handed out by the federal government are frequently awarded posthumously or on a delayed basis, often decades afterwards.

I cling to the exceptionally remote hope that the BBWAA will admit their error and clarify the voting inconsistencies regarding the 1955 NL MVP vote. It is time that some small measure of justice is done for Duke Snider.

Despite the Pete Rose gambling scandal and the more recent steroid era, Major League Baseball has rarely retroactively eliminated records from the record books and has never changed the winners of major awards.

When Jose Canseco's confessional tell-all book, Juiced, *was published (a vitally important public service by Canseco for which many in baseball excoriated him), Mike Greenwell insisted that he should be awarded the 1988 AL MVP award. Greenwell had finished a distant second in the voting, but his sentiment had many supporters. No reversal was forthcoming; Canseco still has the award.*

A reevaluation of the record books occurred over twenty years ago. Ernie Shore and Harvey Haddix were denied perfect games and the asterisk was removed from the home run record of 61 set in 1961 by Roger Maris. Maris died several years before and did not live to see his accomplishment vindicated.

Duke Snider passed away on February 27, 2011.

16

Mantle from All Sides

A famous black and white photo from the forties shows Wilt Chamberlain standing with his grade school classmates in Philadelphia. The Stilt towers two or three feet above all other kids in his grade.

In scouting amateur prospects—particularly ones in high school—the tools and abilities of top players tower above all others on the field, precisely like Wilt Chamberlain soared above his grade school pals.

When I first began scouting, an old-time scout gave me a valuable bit of advice: When you go to a game in which you have not seen the teams play and are unfamiliar with their personnel, watch each club as they play catch prior to the game. Ninety percent of the time, the player who is most impressive playing catch is his team's best player.

I scoffed at the old-timer's advice at first, but, of course, he was exactly right. In the summer of 2002, I watched two travel ball teams warm up prior to a tournament game. A tall, thin youngster for a San Diego area team was making throws—on a clothesline—from the right field foul line to the fence in deepest left center. I was flabbergasted.

Because I could not see the player's number from where I was sitting, I asked a team parent for the name of this player. Said the parent, "His name is Adam Jones."

Tom Greenwade was the New York Yankee scout who signed Mickey Mantle. Shockingly, Greenwade was not impressed with Mantle the first few times he saw Mickey play in North Eastern Oklahoma.

In a year's time, Mickey grew a few inches and gained twenty pounds of muscle. Greenwade saw Mickey enjoy some big days at bat, but he was still not moved. One day, Mantle faced a left-handed pitcher. Greenwade was not aware, until that moment, that Mantle was a switch hitter. After observing Mantle hit from the right side, Greenwade was convinced of Mickey's potential.

Sixty-five years after Greenwade signed him, Mickey Mantle remains baseball's ultimate prospect. Along with Bo Jackson, no single prospects in baseball history have combined speed and power to such a fantastic extent. Perhaps only Mickey, Bo, Willie Mays, and Kirk Gibson were "80/80" prospects—players with 80 speed and 80 power.

All baseball fans are familiar with the litany of Mantle's tape measure home runs: At USC in 1951; at Washington, DC in 1953; at Yankee Stadium in 1956 and 1963; etc. Prior to a knee injury in the 1951 World Series, Mantle was the fastest player in baseball history, with speed comparable to Willie Davis, Bo Jackson, and Billy Hamilton of today's Cincinnati Reds.

I have no idea if the stories of Mantle as a rookie racing down the line in 3.1 seconds on a drag bunt from the left side are true. I suspect those tales are exaggerated. However, I do possess a video of the 1958 World Series.

A portion of the film shows Mantle tagging up at third base on a sacrifice fly to the outfield and racing all the way to home plate. I have timed Mickey's dash and I find he covers the 90 feet in 3.51 seconds.

My guess is that only Billy Hamilton and Mike Trout can cover that distance that quickly in Major League Baseball in 2014.

As a youngster growing up in Southern California, I saw Mickey Mantle play in person. In a game at Anaheim Stadium, on April 18, 1968, Mickey, batting left-handed, blasted a 430-foot home run over the center field fence. He also walked once and struck out three times.

This article offers my perspective on Mantle as a player in his era, and speculates how a young Mantle would fare in modern Major League Baseball.

October 15, 2010

ONE OF THE opening scenes of the movie *61** shows a cranky old sportswriter walking down the first base concourse at Yankee Stadium arguing with team officials. Mickey Mantle had a lousy season in 1960, the scribe contends, since he hit a paltry .275 after winning the Triple Crown only four years earlier.

Nonsense, insists one team official. Mickey led the league in homers and finished second in the MVP balloting, and who wouldn't love to have that type of "bad year"?

Actually, both men are correct. Mantle had both a crummy and a terrific season in 1960. Why the massive, glaring contradiction? The answer is simple, and it goes to the heart of understanding Mickey Mantle as a player and as a hitter.

Mantle was a vastly superior hitter from the right side of the plate. For many of his eighteen big league seasons the gap was staggering.

Let's take 1960. Mantle hit only .246 batting left-handed that year. He hit .344 with 16 homers in 160 at bats swinging right-handed. Extend that pace to a full 600 at-bat season and Mickey would have collected 60 home runs.

Other years produce similar discrepancies. Thanks to stats available at retrosheet.org, this chart provides a quick sample:

Year	Righty	Lefty	Total
1953	.337	.235	.295
1954	.317	.292	.300
1955	.364	.281	.306
1958	.377	.282	.304
1961	.371	.291	.317
1963	.409	.255	.314
1964	.424	.241	.303

In fact, Mantle batted .300 or better from the right side in twelve of his eighteen seasons, but hit .300 or better from the left side only three times. Those three seasons happened to be his MVP years—1956, 1957 and 1962. In his entire career, Mantle hit .329 right-handed and .282 left-handed—a whopping 47 point differential.

Bob Costas and Billy Crystal have made a sort of cottage industry out of Mantle worship, and it is easy to understand why—we all have soft spots for our childhood idols. For a moment, let's put aside the understandable sentimentality and evaluate Mantle as a player.

Mickey was, no doubt, a great player. Along with Bo Jackson, Mantle was the most spectacularly talented young prospect baseball has ever seen, combining incredible speed with remarkable raw power.

Mantle was not, however, the greatest player of all time or even the greatest player of his *own* time. Willie Mays was the best player of Mantle's generation and, in my view, the greatest all-around player in baseball history.

Mantle had awesome raw power, but Willie Mays, Hank Aaron, and Harmon Killebrew were more consistent home run hitters from year to year. Stan Musial, Ted Williams, Hank Aaron, and Roberto Clemente were better hitters, in total, than Mickey. By his own admission, Mantle was not a great defensive outfielder. Many of his peers were superior in the field, including Willie Mays, Richie Ashburn, Curt Flood, Vada Pinson, and Jimmy Piersall, to name a few.

Despite the fine career numbers he posted, why did Mantle fail to totally fulfill his great talent? Most would point to his numerous injuries, which was an obvious factor. Others would refer to his well-known carousing and late night partying. Those who recall the bizarre left and center field dimensions in old Yankee Stadium correctly note that it was a graveyard for right-handed power hitters—301 down the line but 402 to the bullpen, 457 to left center, and 461 to straight away center.

All of these are legitimate factors, but my answer is more direct: Mantle never should have hit left-handed—he should have hit right-handed exclusively. Even with his home park's odd measurements, Mantle would have been far more productive overall as a right-handed hitter.

Thankfully, World Series highlight films and kinescopes of old TV broadcasts can enable us to break down and evaluate Mantle's swing. From the left side (and this is starkly visible in the 1958 film version of *Damn Yankees*), Mickey hit from a pronounced crouch. Closing off his front side, he would then load up by drawing his hands and weight backward. Taking a long forward stride, Mantle swung with a severe uppercut which produced a grand, wraparound finish.

From the left side, it's plain to see that Mantle did not have the ease in his swing that he had from the right side and nowhere near the plate or strike zone coverage. Lefty, Mickey was exceptionally vulnerable to hard stuff in and soft stuff away.

Mantle had no such difficulties as a righty. He used a stand-up stance, knees slightly flexed, feet spread but front foot closed. Utilizing no load but a slight amount of pre-swing hand movement to get himself started, Mickey shows a gorgeous, fluid, and sweeping right-handed swing. From the right side, Mantle was able to handle any type of pitch in any location and hammer it hard to all portions of the field.

By far the best sample of Mantle's perfect right-handed swing can be viewed in the old "Home Run Derby" TV programs on Hulu. The shows were hosted by Mark Scott and filmed at the Los Angeles version of Wrigley Field in the 1959–1960 off-season. Replay Mickey's second contest against Jackie Jensen, in which Mantle out-homers the Boston star, 13–10. Watch Mantle's shot hit at the 8:25 mark. You'll never see a longer home run or a harder hit ball.

All of which leaves a burning question: How would Mantle perform today?

In this fantasy, let's transport the Mantle of his glory years, 1956 and 1957, into the modern game. Also, let's assume that today's advanced medical technology either prevents many of his injuries or reduces their severity. Furthermore, let's speculate that modern Mantle's agent, team conditioning coach, or personal motivational karmic guru has forced him to keep reasonable hours and take better care of himself.

Finally, let's posit that Mantle is a right-handed hitter only and is playing his home games in a stadium with reasonable, average dimensions and not the unfair "Death Valley" of old Yankee Stadium.

Given all of those preconditions, Mantle would be, far and away, the best player in baseball. Imagine one player with Mike

Trout speed, Giancarlo Stanton raw power, and Miguel Cabrera's hitting ability.

In fact, in this admittedly elaborate scenario, Mantle would be one of the very, very few players who would have been better today than he was in his own time. That can be said of almost no other player in baseball history.

Recollections of Mantle in books, films, and interviews almost always attempt to portray him as a kind of epic Greek hero, full of glory and power but fraught with tragic demons and personal flaws.

Having seen him play and after studying his career, my conclusion is far less operatic or dramatic. Mantle was an incredible—if not unprecedented—baseball talent. Some of his fate was bad luck (injuries) and some of it his own doing (carousing). To quote a line in *61**, "he's still pretty good."

Dreaming and speculation regarding Mantle is fun, in fact it has become a business unto itself. Personally, I am certain of one thing. Baseball history and baseball's record books would be significantly different if Mickey Mantle had, somehow, been able to stay healthy, play in a normal-sized park and, most importantly—bat right-handed exclusively.

17

All Rolled into One

Every performing art has one individual who serves as that industry's "Gold Standard."

Literature has Shakespeare; Music has Mozart; Sculpture has Michelangelo; Dance has Nijinsky; Singing has Caruso; Painting has Rembrandt.

Baseball has Willie Mays.

Baseball scouts speak and write in a code of their own.

If a parent hears a scout describe his ballplayer son as "average," often the parent is depressed or angry. Should a scout bestow the word "average" on a young player, it is actually lofty praise. The scout is stating he believes the youngster will develop into an average Major League ballplayer. That's quite a compliment—and an honor.

Scouts are equally cautious in comparing players. Some of that caution is innate; some of it is born from fear of getting a scalding phone call from a superior. Ninety-nine percent of scout comparisons are rather mundane—ordinary players being compared to other ordinary players.

On occasion, scouts compare a modern player to a great player of the past. For instance, many scouts compare Mike Trout to Mickey Mantle and for an extremely good reason.

Within the baseball industry, scouts never compare anyone to Willie Mays.

Yasiel Puig would be the one modern player who might draw a Mays comparison; however, even casual fans recognize that Puig is light years away from approaching that standard.

Media members—even the dopes—are loath to compare any player to Willie. They realize such a comparison is a credibility destroyer.

When Bryce Harper made his big league debut, Baseball America's website reprinted an article I had written on Mr. Phenom. BA's intro claimed I had compared Harper to Mays.

I instantly wrote a comment explaining that I had not compared Harper to Mays—there is no such comparison to be made. Instead, I had written that Mays was discovered by a Giant scout when that scout had attended a game to view another player. Similarly, I had witnessed Harper at a showcase in which scouts were focused on older, draft eligible players.

Baseball people understand that Mays was incomparable; there will never be another. Beyond being baseball's "Gold Standard," Willie Mays was the ultimate player—the one all others inevitably fall short in equaling.

Willie Mays played center field for the New York and San Francisco Giants from 1951 to 1972; he finished his career with the New York Mets in 1972–1973.

I N THE SUMMER of 1988, I worked at a private investigation firm on the outskirts of downtown Los Angeles. One day, I noticed a large ad smack in the middle of the sports section of the *Los Angeles Times*.

Willie Mays, the ad insisted, would appear at a downtown bookstore to sign copies of his new book, *Say Hey*. During my lunch hour on the appointed day, I quickly drove downtown to snatch his autograph.

I can quickly "run in and run out" I thought, figuring that only a tiny number of hardcore baseball nostalgia buffs would show up. Fifteen years after his retirement, I reasoned, the world had forgotten Mays. People had moved on to worship modern sports stars or idolize talent-bereft, publicity-machine-manufactured "flavor of the month" entertainers.

As I walked toward the bookstore I was stunned: the line snaked through the store, out the door, down the hallway of the mall, and out onto the street. Privately, I was delighted.

"Thank heavens," I thought. "These people remember. They understand."

I will concentrate on the prime of Willie's career: a thirteen-year stretch from 1954 through 1966. In that era, Mays was to baseball what Michael Jordan was to the NBA from 1984 to 1998: Not just the best player in the game, but the most exciting, dynamic, and charismatic player.

My favorite Mays factoid is, I think, the best avenue to understand Willie as a player. In 1962, Mays led the major leagues in home runs with 49. He also led all big league outfielders in putouts with 429. In fact, his 429 putouts in 1962 was the largest number of putouts registered by any outfielder in either league in a single season in the entire decade of the sixties.

Absorb that for a moment.

A single player hitting the most home runs *and* chasing down the most line drives and fly balls in the outfield in one season? (In the live ball era, my research shows that the only other players to accomplish this feat were Hack Wilson in 1926 and Ralph Kiner in 1947.)

In the sixties, league home run leaders were usually cumbersome, hulking sluggers such as Willie McCovey, Frank Howard, or Harmon Killebrew. All-time greats, no doubt, but none of them would have the remotest chance to lead the league in outfield putouts.

Fast forward to our modern era. Home run leaders are typically players like Albert Pujols, Prince Fielder, Miguel Cabrera, or Ryan Howard. All are superlative players, but would any of them ever lead the big leagues in outfield putouts? No way.

Let's reverse this concept. Outfield putouts leaders fifty years ago were typically players like Richie Ashburn, Jimmie Piersall, or Curt Flood. Wonderful players, but did any of them hit 49 home runs in a season? Nope.

The 2012 leader in outfield putouts was Adam Jones of the Baltimore Orioles with 422. Jones is a favorite of mine, for I once helped him gain entry to the Area Code Games showcase when he was a high school player in San Diego. Jones is a sensationally gifted young man with a bright future, as is evidenced by the generous, long-term contract he signed with the O's in 2012. His single season high in homers, accomplished in 2013, is 33. Not bad, but not quite Willie.

Mays was not just versatile, it was the remarkably high level of his versatility that indicated his greatness.

- In the sixties, no player in the National League had a single season in which he hit more than 46 home runs. Except Mays. Willie topped 46 three times in the '60s: 47 in 1964, 49 in 1962, and 52 in 1965.

- In the fifties, no National League player stole more than 35 bases in one season. Except Mays, who did it twice: 40 in 1956 and 38 in 1957. In those years Mays was the first National Leaguer to turn the 30 home run, 30 steals trick, and the first player in baseball history to do it twice and in consecutive seasons.

- Willie hit 51 homers in 1955, the highest single season mark in that decade for a National Leaguer. Soak that one in. Mays had the highest single season home run *and* stolen base mark in one decade.

Ralph Kiner hit 54 homers in 1949, top NL record for that decade. Think he ever led the league in steals? Not a chance. Ruth hit 60 in 1927, Foxx 58 in 1932, Greenberg 58 in 1938. Any of those guys lead the league in outfield putouts? Steals? Forget it.

You'll get the same results with modern players. Speedy All-Star Carl Crawford can lead the league in stolen bases, but in home runs? I don't think so. Albert Pujols may be the greatest right-handed hitter of all time and has led the NL in homers twice, as has Ryan Howard. Not to disparage those two stars, but have they ever lead the league in steals? Nope. Mays led in homers four times and in steals four times.

Now you're getting the picture. It's difficult enough for any major leaguer to average 20 home runs and 15 steals per year and hit .275 for a ten-year period. That imaginary guy would be an outstanding player. From 1954 through 1966, Mays averaged 40 home runs per season, 109 RBI, 117 runs, 21 steals, 396 putouts, and all while hitting .315.

Not a one- or two-year wonder, Mays was great for an extended period of time. Willie is the only player to have 50 home run seasons ten years apart. His eleven years between MVP awards—1954 and 1965—is also unprecedented.

Mays recorded 7,095 outfield putouts in his career. That's the all-time record. The next guy on the list, Hall of Famer Tris Speaker, trails by 307.

Few modern players could compare to Mays. Ken Griffey Jr. was similar in the nineties. When he played for the Braves, Andruw Jones came closest to emulating Mays for a stretch of seasons in the 2000s. If he learns how to play the game and behave like a pro, Yasiel Puig, the shockingly talented Dodger rookie flash of 2013, could be the next Mays. But that's a *big* stretch.

In his pre-flaxseed oil days, Barry Bonds was a candidate. Bonds could hit and run with Mays, but his glove and arm were clearly inferior to Willie's. (I strongly contend baseball fans must disregard Bonds's numbers when he was a BALCO client. There's no doubt whatsoever in my mind that Bonds was a steroids cheater beginning around 2000 and the records he set afterward should be completely discounted.)

To this day, Willie Mays remains the gold standard against which all prospects and players are judged. As described in the preface, scouts rank position players in five skill areas, called "tools": hit, power, run, throw, and field. Many ballplayers could match Mays in one or two areas, maybe three. A handful could equal Willie in four tools. But no one—absolutely no one—in baseball history did everything as well, for as long, or at as high a level as did Willie Mays.

From a scouting standpoint, Mays briefly may have been the only "80" player in baseball history. Returning from a hitch in the army, Willie played four final seasons (1954 through 1957) in New York before the Giants moved to San Francisco.

At that time, Mays rated an 80 in all five categories on the 20 to 80 scout grading scale for position players. Take 1955. Willie led the majors with 51 home runs (80 power); notched 24 steals and 123 runs, both second in the NL (80 speed);

hit .319, second in the league (80 hit); recorded 422 putouts, second in the circuit (80 field); and led the majors with 23 outfield assists (80 arm).

Oh, I must mention Mays now gets love from the Saber geeks as well. His career 156.1 WAR is second all-time among position players. Willie's WAR of 11.2 in 1965 is the highest single season position player post war WAR (I couldn't resist) in the National League. (If you want to file a protest regarding the above paragraph, please note that I delete Barry Bonds from the record books, even if Bud Selig won't.)

Watching Willie Mays play was infinitely more enjoyable than talking about him or reciting numbers.

Mays was a showman without being a showoff. Willie's cap inevitably flew off when chasing a fly ball or racing around the bases. He was not the originator of the basket catch, but he was the master of it.

My favorite Mays feature was his swing. Prior to every at bat, Willie dug a deep hole in the batter's box with his right foot. He used a slight crouch, held the bat low behind his back shoulder. Waiting for the pitch, Mays would turn his head directly at the pitcher and shift his weight to his back leg.

Dead still as the pitch arrived, Willie would suddenly and violently lash out at the ball, whipping the bat barrel through the strike zone, driving his weight forward and then spinning around his axis, flaring his hands high above his head as he finished.

Numbers are a poor way of describing Mays; words are worse. You had to see him play in person. I pity those who didn't. Unlike another idol of mine, Muhammad Ali, Mays didn't need to call himself the greatest.

If you saw, you knew.

Leo Durocher, Willie's favorite manager, said it best: "Willie Mays is Joe Louis, Jascha Heifetz, Sammy Davis, and Nashua all rolled into one."

Section Three: Clearing the Bases

18

The Job

From 2011 to 2013, I conducted a series of interviews with area scouts from around the nation. Each scout was promised complete anonymity.

My goal in these interviews was not to fit each discussion into a pre-determined pattern or theme; instead I asked each scout to express his honest, unrestricted feelings about the scouting profession and the business of baseball.

O NE SCOUT I interviewed, who has since moved on to another profession, was remarkably candid.

I loved the game. I loved evaluating players and forecasting talent. Too many scouts are in the game for the wrong reason. I was shocked how few loved the game and many had horrible attitudes.

Several scouts falsified mileage, falsified expense reports. Many don't even scout but spend their time down the line socializing. Often scouts advance not because they are good scouts but because they are good politicians and have the ability to bring others down. Several are insecure; they don't want to hear differing opinions.

This scout admits he was naïve when he got his first full-time area scouting job several years ago and his enthusiasm was abundant, at least at the outset: "It was really exciting. I had a blast watching the games."

Soon, one of his organization's national cross checkers made the scout's life miserable: "He was a complete moron, never had an original thought in his life. He had never been an area scout; in fact, he had gotten his start as a member of the grounds crew at a spring training facility."

The scout continued, "He couldn't scout to save his life, he was arrogant and didn't handle disagreements well. His grades always mimicked those of the scouting director and were always within a point of the boss."

"He was clueless," the scout added, and the cross checker "often asked others what they thought," since he essentially had no idea what he was looking at.

As an example, the scout stated that the cross checker "Didn't like Justin Verlander and didn't consider Verlander a candidate to be a high draft pick. He didn't think Verlander could get anyone out!"

When the scout I spoke with sought support from a regional supervisor who had been a former major league player, he found no assistance. The ex big leaguer, said the scout, "had no courage, was a yes man who never stood up for anything."

After that year's draft had been conducted, the scout's standing within the organization began to deteriorate. He took a vacation, flying to Boston to visit a close friend. While in New England, the scout decided to attend the Cape Cod League All Star Game.

The national cross checker, says the scout, spotted him at the game. "He was enraged. I wasn't assigned to scout the game, I just wanted to watch it for fun, but the guy saw me as a threat."

Later that summer, the scout was assigned to observe an event in Wilmington, North Carolina. The scout claims the cross checker "had a fit and accused me of not being a team player when I went to lunch with a friend who was a college coach and an ex big leaguer." Matters were made worse when the scout politely refused to go "out with the guys" for a midnight beer when he had a 7 a.m. wakeup call.

During the annual Area Code Games event in August of that year, the scout asserts that the cross checker was "constantly on my case." Utilizing some free time after the conclusion of the ACG, the scout then drove up the California coast toward Oregon for a bit of R & R.

Then came "The Call." Almost every scout has gotten it at some point in his career. On the line was the organization's scouting director. "I was informed that my contract was not being renewed. Naturally, I asked why; the scouting director said he was concerned that I was too interested in finding major leaguers!"

Within a few months the scout was hired by another major league organization. The move, the scout said, "was like getting out of jail." He continued, "I had a good impression of the main people but that soured over time."

"I disagreed with the scouting director on baseball matters, but I did not dislike him personally. Later the director became a Saber guy. He had been open-minded but that changed; he stopped listening and shut other guys out. Promotions were not based on merit, they were based on politics."

The scout found three superiors to be particularly offensive: "One supervisor had an oversized ego—he over graded players in his area and under graded guys in other areas. That hurt the team."

Another supervisor, insists the scout, was "a blatant racist. He used the N-word, he was lazy, and had a sense of entitlement. He was also one of the most ignorant people I've ever known.

This guy would never admit when he was wrong but always took credit when things went right."

A contributing factor, the scout believes, was his feeling that this supervisor "was an alcoholic. He treated me terribly but I was disturbed by the fact that others liked the guy."

A third supervisor forced the scout to drive hundreds, often thousands, of miles to games while the supervisor flew to the same locales. Over time, the scout challenged the supervisor to explain why the supervisor was usurping his travel budget.

"He promised to be open on expenses, to show me the books, so to speak, but he never did." Additional problems developed. "At scouting meetings, he would deliberately trump my opinions on players we had both seen, just out of spite."

Later, the scout said the supervisor "hired a young scout with no experience whatsoever. The new guy was subservient to the scouting director and the supervisor . . . essentially a puppet." The "puppet" is now a scouting director.

This scout summed up his feelings about the scouting profession: "I don't miss it. What I'm doing now is much more fulfilling than baseball. I want to make more of my life than that."

He added: "Due to the corruption within organizations, I've got a distaste for baseball. In fact, if I were growing up today, I wouldn't even like the game."

This scout's final comments were adamant: "Baseball used to be the only sport I watched. Now it's the only sport I don't watch."

. . .

The next scout I spoke with informed me that he thoroughly enjoys his job: "I love evaluating, seeing into a crystal ball, and predicting players in the future."

He continued, "Others in the profession are irritated when they are not promoted to cross checker or scouting director, but not me. If it happens, it happens."

"I listen to that stuff from others but it doesn't bother me; if I'm an area scout for fifteen to twenty years, I'd be happy."

The scout then discussed his relationships with prospects:

I love going to watch players but also getting to know the kids . . . kids need to realize that this is a job interview. They should fill out paperwork themselves, not have Mom do it. I can always tell when a Mom fills out paperwork!

I like to get to know the kids, to build and develop a relationship with them. I like to start early, but I also like to "lay it out for them." As time goes on, I develop a gut feeling about the kid and I develop a sense if I like the kid.

I want to break through and see the real kid. All I care about is: Is he a good kid or a bad kid? When I do a home visit, 95 percent of the time the kid answers the door. If not, that's not a good sign.

The best thing a kid can do is ask questions. Kids shouldn't be afraid; they need to shake hands and look me in the eyes. It's a two way street—I need to get to know them, they need to get to know me . . . kids need to learn to communicate and how to have a conversation.

He added, "Prospects need to respond quickly with paperwork and emails, etc. That goes a long way with scouts."

The scout expounded on the fundamentals of a scout's job:

Our job is to evaluate tools. We don't have a system or a formula that everything fits into. That takes away from a scout. We have the freedom to go against the grain.

In our organization, our scouting director lets us work and gives us the freedom to work. I only hear from him if I do something wrong. There's no hovering, no pestering.

The number of visits to see a kid play is up to me as a scout. I start to get a sense of the player in the showcase season. I try to understand what type of player he will be. For instance, does he have an advanced feel for hitting? Does he stay inside the ball?

One aspect of amateur baseball troubles this scout: "It bothers me when high school freshmen commit to a four-year college. I think it's an injustice and bad business on the part of the colleges to get a verbal commitment that early. That part is wrong."

Ball clubs often change scouting and drafting philosophies over time. The scout explained, "Our club has recently done a turnaround in our drafting style. We were drafting college guys we thought were close to the big leagues, but when they didn't pan out, we had no foundation. Now we are developing a foundation."

This scout concluded, "As a scout in your reports, you have to fly on your own. Your opinion must have some conviction when reporting a player."

"You have to scout, you have to do some investigation. Just sitting in the stands isn't good enough."

• • •

A veteran scout I spoke to expansively discussed issues within scouting and player development. He began by stating that Major League ball clubs are "Pulling people into the profession who are young guys with no baseball background. I sometimes think this is done so superiors can feel smarter. The bosses are afraid of exposing themselves and what they don't know. One reason so many young guys are being hired is that ball clubs can pay them less."

In hiring, this scout insisted:

There is frequent age discrimination and "bo-bo-ism" [nep-
otism]. Today's scouts are often part of a [baseball] political
group; a pack always materializes of guys who want to promote
each other. Meanwhile, veteran guys are out here scuffling.

Scouting is a great job but doesn't pay well, and things are
getting worse. Front office types say "Scouting is the lifeblood
of an organization" but they don't back that up. Benefits are
not good, especially for retirees. There have been attempts to
unionize, but scouts didn't do so for fear of being blackballed.
A scout's tenure is absolutely at the mercy of the front office.

So many GMs now are not baseball people, they're the most
insecure group out there. Front offices now are too political
and just don't have enough people who are knowledgeable.
Few front office types have a baseball foundation; they have
no clue regarding scouting.

Each fall, the Major League Scouting Bureau conducts a "Scout
School." The thirty big league clubs enroll two students into the
program, giving each class sixty members. This scout once discussed, with a former major league star, the wisdom of sending
front office types to scout school. Said the former player: "Scout
school isn't worth a damn. It's not worth the time. You can't learn
scouting in two weeks."

He continued with his opinions on the modern state of scouting:

Scout salaries vary around the country, there is a lot of discrepancy. You can make more if you teach in many parts of the
country. The front office can get rid of you and it often makes
no difference if you are a good or bad scout.

Scouting is much different today. Pre-1965 [when the draft
was instituted], all scouts were retired players, older guys.
Many of them could never adjust to the draft. Now, with every

club guaranteed a first rounder and forty picks, lazy clubs and scouts can pick off a good player just by sitting there. When all sixteen or twenty clubs had a shot at a kid, the scout had to really get to know the kid and his family and do his homework to get the kid to sign.

Nowadays, I see some guys who are out there as cross checkers who are somebody's bo-bo, for heaven's sake. Some are legit, no doubt.

Years ago at a spring training game, this scout watched as a retired Hall of Fame player sat behind home plate. A general manager strolled past. The GM had once been a scouting director and had received a generous amount of laudatory media coverage. So as he walked by, the Hall of Fame player exclaimed loud enough for all nearby to hear, "There goes the dumbest guy in baseball!"

Next, this scout discussed player development:

Often it's a mess out here today; there's anarchy going on with pitching.

Good player development makes scouting. Proper funda-mentals should extend from the lowest level of the minors to the big league club. Often within an organization, if a couple of guys have success, everyone copies it even if they're doing it wrong! That's why some big name draftees have broken down— they put up big numbers in the low minors and the player devel-opment people don't realize their mechanics are bad. I see too many pitchers who spread too soon, too many guys who are too quick to the plate and develop arm trouble, etc.

Teams have to be careful with player development. It's tricky. You try not to immediately put your mark on a guy and change him around, then again, if you try to make him a clone of your other players, you can ruin him. It's hard to try not to confuse a player or get him to adjust without telling him to change completely.

Many of the injury and prevention guys are on the wrong track. Some take the attitude that if a pitcher, for instance, has made it to the big leagues he is perfect mechanically. Not so, he can still blow himself out.

Player development varies widely in quality. Some players need to get out of an organization to perform well. Occasionally, recognition is poor. Many years ago I was at a game where the starting pitcher was great in the bullpen before the game but had nothing when he crossed the white line. "He has no Balls!" many of the other scouts said. Turns out his problem was a weak rotator cuff. He was diagnosed, rehabbed and then made the majors. You can't write a guy off. His problem may be physical or it may be that he's not being taught properly, his mechanics need altering.

He then returned to the topic of scouting:

The top guys, the general manager and the scouting director, have to control things, keep people from getting into adversarial positions, not at each other's throats. That rarely happens since it's hard to find quality people.

Too many scouts advance when they're not ready. Scouts should be out five years before they advance to cross checker, now many get promoted when they've only been out two or three! Now, many front office types scout on a computer. Many of them have never played, have never crossed a white line. Nothing can replace experience—playing, scouting, development. Numbers can't substitute for that.

Pro coverage is a great tool to grow as an area scout. In fact, when an area scout starts out, it's a good idea to pair him up with a pro scout when he does his pro coverage.

Some scouts can be territorial in nature, hardheaded. Also, some supervisors didn't want anyone to ask questions because they thought they had it all figured out.

A lot of people who come into the industry don't want to work at it or don't know how to work at it. Some scouts always want to be at the big game to show off and network themselves and they take the attitude, "Everybody likes this player so he must be good!"

Sometimes you have to be off the beaten path. Many scouts lean on other scouts and can't or won't make decisions themselves. Many don't know what they are looking at and aren't able to identify a prospect if he is not well known or hasn't been a regular on the showcase circuit. Lots of guys run their mouths, too many parrot other scouts' opinions.

Many guys are kiss-ups. Some area scouts will do an end run around the cross checker and complain to the scouting director if the checker has submitted a negative report on a player the area guy likes.

He also provided examples of what he believes is poor scouting:

One well-known scout would pressure the organization to draft a large number of players from his area, sort of "Throwing everything on the wall and hoping for something to stick." He'd rob other scouts of draftees in their areas. He'd tout himself if one of his picks was successful, ignoring all his other picks that failed.

Despite his public reputation and notoriety, this scout "was not a good talent evaluator. He wrecked every organization he was at. If he had been a team player, he would have wanted the best players nationwide for his club, not just players he could use to promote himself."

As another example of bad scouting, the scout pointed to a circumstance which occurred many years ago: "Two prominent scouts engaged in overkill. They'd see the top guy in their area every time he played, ignoring the rest of the territory. One college coach told me he had no idea who that club had covering his territory since he had not seen the guy all year. After the season the scout was reassigned since the director realized, 'We're getting killed there!'"

He concluded by stating, "Video and sabermetrics are tremendous tools, but decisions should not be based solely on those. You need knowledge of the game and how it should be played. Many of these young guys are know-it-alls who don't know what they're looking at and don't have knowledge of the fundamentals. That's why so many things are done wrong."

• • •

The next scout I spoke to has experience as a full-time pro scout and a full-time amateur area scout.

> There is so much to love as an area scout. The biggest thing is the thrill of discovering THAT guy. There's a big difference between being a pro scout and an area scout. It's unusual to see a young guy as a pro scout; most are older guys.
>
> In pro scouting, you don't get to know anyone. There's not as much small talk and camaraderie as in amateur scouting. When I moved from amateur scouting to pro scouting, I missed that. Also, as an amateur scout you have more flexibility, more freedom, you can set your own schedule. In most territories you often scout in your own backyard and can go home at night.

Not that amateur scouting does not have some drawbacks, the scout added:

> A new scouting director can come in and you can get let go for no reason. You can have a great work ethic, great communication skills, a great personality. It doesn't matter how organized you are, how on top of your paperwork and reports you are. It's not fair.

As an amateur scout within your organization, it takes 3 to 4 years to build up trust; when you're let go, you have to start all over again with a new organization. Still, you can't burn bridges, you can't be a negative scout. You have to be a positive guy and objective.

Your relationship with your supervisors impacts so much. Some guys you respect, some you don't. Some guys you have to work hard to prove yourself. Trust is critical. Some clubs, you trust their system and their supervisors, some you don't. The best organizations have an established scouting system and established guys; they know exactly what they're getting.

Respect within an organization is vital also. Some supervisors didn't or haven't earned respect. You can't do that in a short time. Some front office guys get supervisor positions after two to three years; you can't earn respect in such a short time.

Change is inevitable and is always going to happen. The worst part of the business is getting let go for no real reason. How do you fix that?

Next, the scout explained his views on new wave versus old school scouting:

I'm a traditionalist. I believe in true scouting, in looking for tools.

New scouts, kids, have a lot to bring to the table. They're sharp, smart, they know what the front office wants. But it's tough for [Ivy League/Saber scouts] to earn respect. They have to get experience and respect only comes with years of experience.

It takes two to three years to figure things out. Many of them are going to whiff their first year. The front office may have a long-term plan for those guys, but they have to prove themselves.

If an area scout has associate scouts, he needs to take care of them. Many supervisors don't appreciate associate scouts. Associates applying for regular area scout positions often get passed over nowadays in favor of young [Ivy/Saber] scouts. The associates who get passed over know the area and work hard, they deserve the job. I value those types of associates a 100 times more than other guys.

He then focused on scouting reports:

In our industry, we're forced by the front office to be conservative. Anytime you go over a six OFP on a prospect you get a phone call. That makes you afraid to drop a seven or eight on someone. Yet, when you see a big league game, there are players with one or more seven to eight tools all over the place!

As a scout, you should take pride in your reports; you should take a lot of time [in preparing reports]. Conformity on grades in the industry prevents us from really projecting on guys. We're programmed to have middle grades—fives—most of the time.

We don't pay much attention to the Major League Scouting Bureau reports. They are really good guys and they work very hard, but most clubs either use them sparingly or not at all. Some even have no access to the Bureau.

Agents were the next topic we discussed:

An area scout should have a relationship on a personal level with agents. Some area scouts hate agents, but dealing with agents is part of the job. A couple of agents will "big league" you, but I get along with most of them. I've never butted heads with them, things have never gotten so bad I couldn't communicate with them.

Often agents overprice their clients. If they took fair slot money for their clients, the kids would be better off. If a kid is overpriced and the word gets out, not only can a kid slip in the draft but you can't get your cross checker out to see the kid! Also—many agents can't scout; they call area guys and "gauge" the value of their client. Give me a break! Figure it out for yourselves or get out of the industry!

Regarding prospects, the scout said:

> If a kid is a prospect, others are envious of him. He should be excited but he has much to do. Some kids see psych tests, paperwork, eye tests, etc. as a bother but it has to be done. Some players and their parents will love you or hate you, but there really isn't anything we can do about that.
>
> There is much to love in amateur scouting. But, there is a lot of uncertainty. It's tough to have a family; if you have one already it's very tough on the family.
>
> But, in the end, it's the best job in the world. You smile every time you're asked, *What do you do for a living?* because you take extreme pride in what you do and understand how lucky you are to be doing it. I understand how lucky I am and I hope that I can be a scout for the rest of my life.

"Baseball is my escape," said another scout I spoke with. "I use the game the same way as a player and as a scout—a tool to take me out of worry, fret, or family situations."

Getting to know the player is crucial, said this scout.

> I enjoy relationships with young players and I try to get to know them at the early stages. I try to get to know their faults as well as their strengths. You get to know a kid when he's playing, but you also want to get to know the family, the girlfriend, who he hangs out with. I try to find out if he's hiding anything.

He added, "Relationships early don't always lead to relationships later. A kid can be close to an area scout when he is sixteen or seventeen, but once a kid gets an advisor and signs, the player all of a sudden becomes Elvis."

In some instances, the arrival of an agent changes a scout's relationship with the prospect. Said this scout: "The agents want something, but it's not [the same reason] why I was interested in the kid. It can be emotional since, in some cases, I've known the kid for ten years. I try to build trust with agents but sometimes it's hard. Some are positive but some are negative and deceiving. All in all, I try to treat agents well, but some agents don't speak to area scouts, they 'big league' us. That will come around to get them in the ass.

"Some agents tell the kid how to act, how to speak, and not to return medical forms or organizational paperwork. It can be difficult. In a few cases I've known a kid three or four years before the draft process starts.

"Before the new CBA, agents had a lot of power. Morals were set aside. Agents do what they do best: manipulate the system. Things were way out of control, but the new CBA settled things down. In the new CBA, agents have to be held accountable."

The scout then described his outlook on the business of baseball.

The game has never changed, the business has. It does in every sport. You have to make adjustments. Personally, as an area scout, I like pressure. It makes me go above and beyond to beat my competitors. It's going to help us create a deeper system if done right and if they're listening to their trusted area scouts.

With higher end picks, in rounds 1 to 3, the majority has to be on board with the player—general manager, scouting director, etc., because the money is so great. There's a little more latitude later in the draft.

He next discussed scouting politics.

It frustrates me, seeing some guys getting promotions. Young kids, saber guys who never put on a jockstrap before now get promoted. Saber scouts now seem to have formed a clique, a buddy system. They promote their guys and shut others out. How can they get promoted when they haven't even had the time to learn the territory or the job? It's frustrating when you don't get an opportunity for progression.

Regarding prospects and the draft, this scout pointed out:

A kid has to be an individual. Sabers must pay attention to the human element. I think they understand it; they just don't want to implement it. We're all speaking baseball, just using a different language. The sabers talk total bases, walks and WAR, but they're talking about the individual's stats, not the individual himself.

Shifting topics, the scout next discussed showcases, which have produced a new set of worries for major league organizations. "Showcases don't groom kids for the long haul of 100-plus games. Pitcher's mentalities are to be one- or two-inning pitchers, worried about lighting up radar guns."

This scout believes that showcases can have a negative effect on young pitchers: "Pitchers used to have to work on all aspects of their game: arm maintenance, conditioning, arm strength. Pitchers used to run, run, run. I don't see that as much anymore.

Author's Note: Controversy rages in baseball today as to why so many pitchers require Tommy John surgery. Suspected culprits are numerous; answers and solutions practically non-existent. This scout, I believe, has touched on the main reason for the avalanche of TJ procedures: Lack of proper conditioning, mechanics, and preparation.

In my view, young pitchers are not provided with the proper
foundation as little leaguers. The key to a pitcher's arm health
and stamina is a proper arm action combined with correct usage
of his lower half in the delivery. I don't see that as much anymore!

Travel ball is also prevalent among young players. This scout
stated, "Travel ball has now become a country club sport. It
weeds many kids out. Some parents have to pay $1,500 to par-
ticipate in travel ball. That makes their kids feel privileged, even
if their talent doesn't match. I ask, 'Has this player dealt with
serious adversity?'

"The best players are still coming from the same places. Most
toolsy impact players are still coming from the same background
. . . such as a dirt lot in the Dominican Republic."

This scout expounded on his approach to scouting:

I'm a tools scout. I believe in tools and athleticism. I want the
entire package. I'm not looking for average players; I'm looking
for superstars who have a lot of athletic baseball player in them.

Makeup is the sixth tool. I try to find out about the kid—I
talk to parents, friends, enemies. I'm not into signing milk
drinkers or the uber-nice guy; I want the guy who has an edge
to him. If I had to choose between a private school guy and a
sandlot guy, who would I pick? I want the guy that I can go to
battle with every day and fight bad guys with.

All great players have impact tools. I believe in athletes, but
you must have the right teachers to teach. You must believe in
your development system. Younger guys take time to develop,
but it's all about impact. Any club can pick a low upside college
guy as a safe pick. If you draft an athletic multisport guy out of
high school, you have to treat him like a sixteen-year-old out of
the Dominican Republic. Most high-upside athletes have some

swing and miss in them, but where I become interested is when this player can recognize secondary pitches. When they learn to either lay off the pitch or learn how to hit them.

I look for kids with live hips, good feet, and who can throw. When I see looseness and flexibility that sparks my interest. When a kid has a plus tool, he likes to show it off. If he has a big arm, he will air it out.

When I see a kid walk, if he has a spring in his step or a little hop or a bounce, I can tell he can run. If he has a high ass, high back pockets, a small waist, and an arch in his back, I can tell he has a strong core.

As a prospect prepares to hit, this scout observes "what he does before he gets in the box. How much time does he invest in seeing what the pitcher has to offer? I look at the way he takes pitches.

"I pay attention to the hitter's hand and swing path. I don't like to see a kid try to create power by manipulating his body and not the bat head. I want to see the hitter maintain the same swing path and make adjustments by manipulating the barrel. Adjustments are small in most cases, and I like to see repeatable swing balance and a repeatable bat path."

Confidence is a crucial factor in hitting, insisted the scout: "You have to get some confidence in the kid first. Pro baseball has the best instructors, but not so much in all colleges. We need to solidify our approach. Some kids fizzle because of bad coaching and can't get their confidence back."

From a tools and makeup standpoint, the key question this scout asks himself is, "Does he have enough to make it to the big leagues?"

Players—and scouting—has changed over the years, said the scout: "Players are given things, such as invitations to showcases where they used to have to go out and earn them. It feels better when they earn it, they think they deserve it."

"Today, it's often too tough for kids to figure it out, or they don't want to figure it out. Well, you can't play certain positions—and be a pussy—you can't be a pussy in the big leagues! You can't play third or catcher and be soft. The only position that I've seen players who are soft in is on the mound.

"Kids who sign today often do not have to deal with adversity. They haven't had to learn perseverance and how to be away from their homes and their parents. Everyone has modern technology, iPhones, Skype, so they never have to 'really' be away from home.

"We almost never had to go to the emergency room. Nowadays they go to the emergency room after a slide or getting hit by a pitch."

The scout then attempts to identify tougher players, ones that can cope with adversity: "I look for a kind of emotional muscle which corresponds to a place from within. I try to recognize that. I want to see a kid that can deal with what happens to him. That turns promising players into clutch players."

I also asked what he likes best about the profession:

As an area guy, I get my biggest thrill out of being the first scout to discover a top prospect. I also enjoy being able to see players as young men and watch them develop.

The things I enjoy most are going to the yard, the smell of the grass, and the purity of the game of baseball. I like the freedom of setting my own schedule and I enjoy being an expert on the game.

As a scout, we really don't pay attention to who wins or loses, because we focus on the player(s) we are scouting. I enjoy helping kids fulfill their dreams and I enjoy meeting people from different walks of life. I love interacting with other scouts, as it lets me relive the clubhouse camaraderie and brings back that locker room feel.

He then discussed portions of the scouting industry that he feels should be changed:

In certain positions, I'd like to see more baseball people as scouts, cross checkers, and as scouting directors. As a whole, I'd like to see young area scouts be taught the proper way, because that way we can bring in better players. It's hard to have a conversation with a guy who never played or put on a jockstrap. They're never right or wrong!

It's important to keep an open mind. You have to ask, *What kind of creativity can we offer?* I think an organization has got to take a chance on tools. They have to trust the area scouts and listen to them, for instance, when they discuss undrafted free agents. Organizations need to listen to guys who know what it takes to get to the big leagues.

You want to be a scout, you need to respect scouting. There's a lack of loyalty in some parts of the game, and that bothers me. When an area scout does things right, the organization should pay attention. Appreciation goes a long way.

The scout then asserts that people inside and outside of baseball need to understand that "Numbers don't constitute makeup. In the game that's played, there is a human element that numbers can't cover.

"I'd like to see more former baseball players in upper management and front office positions. If those guys are taught the proper way, we would have a greater insight on players we sign and what it takes to compete at the major league level. I believe we need to put trust in baseball experience and implement saber numbers together . . . but you can't go wrong with the human element."

In closing, he left me with a reflection on the community of scouts: "I'd make a note to young scouts, especially young scouts who did not play the game—pay respects to the older scouts. Say hello. When you do that, you pay respect to the game. You need to pay respects to guys who played before and guys who scouted before you came along.

"It makes our fraternity better and stronger."

19

Agents: Whoever Does the Deal, Gets the Money

I N DECEMBER OF 2013, Internet news outlets reported that at the Major League Baseball winter meetings in Orlando, Florida, two baseball agents engaged in a loud, nasty argument in a hotel parking lot.

Reportedly, several punches were thrown. Because the combatants were agents, only 5 percent of the punches landed.

All joking aside, the business of baseball agents is often vicious and nasty, an endeavor most definitely not suited for the sensitive or weakhearted. It's one of the few aspects of baseball in which public perception and stereotype fits actual reality.

I interviewed a prominent agent and received his take on the industry, one culled from his many years of combat experience.

He began with a description of the nuts and bolts of being a baseball agent:

"To become an agent is fairly easy," he stated. "To be certified by the Major League Baseball Player's Union, an agent must have at least one player/client on a major league 40-man roster. There is a small fee and an application must be filled out. Certification is good for two years."

The Major League Baseball Draft is conducted in early June. Today the draft is spread over three days, with day one (1st round, 1st supplemental round, and 2nd round) conducted on live television. Rounds 3 through 10 continue via the Internet on day two, with the final portion (Rounds 11 to 40) performed on day three.

If a player is drafted, he has until July 15 to sign a Standard Minor League Contract. The contract normally contains two addendums: One specifying the amount of bonus to be paid and how the money is to be distributed. In the second addendum, details of the player's College Savings Plan are laid out. (Not all players ask for or receive the College Savings Plan.)

The College Savings Plan designates money to be set aside for the player's college education, should he decide to pursue one. Loaded with details and requirements, agents must ensure their clients understand the details of the CSP so as not to unwittingly forfeit benefits. Money for the CSP is separate from the signing bonus; the amount is not deducted from the bonus.

When a player signs a minor league contract he is not, of course, a member of the Major League Players Union. That being the case, many organizations issue a list of strict guidelines to their minor leaguers. The guidelines are essentially restrictions relating to propriety and personal behavior and many prevent the players from getting piercings or tattoos, growing facial hair, obtaining bizarre multicolored or Mohawk-style haircuts, etc.

If a player becomes a major leaguer, the guidelines cease to exist. One scout once told me, "When they become big leaguers, they can do whatever the hell they want."

The agent continued:

If a client is drafted and signs the standard minor league contract with the team that drafted him, there are various ways a bonus can be paid. Payment splits are negotiable, but one half of the bonus must be paid within six months.

Some clients take the entire bonus in one payment. Most, for tax purposes, split the payments between calendar years. Commonly, if a player signs on or before the mid-July deadline, he'll take one half of his bonus within 30-45-60 days after the commissioner's office approves the contract. He'll take the remaining half from January 15 to January 30 of the subsequent calendar year. Passing a physical exam makes the deal final.

The ball clubs deduct the taxes and tax rates vary from state to state and in Canada.

The unintended consequence of tax inequity means retention percentages after taxes can vary significantly for signees. Often, this leads to strained feelings among youngsters who sign for generally the same bonus amount.

"If a ball club, for instance, agrees to pay half of the bonus within 45 days of contract approval, most teams actually pay early before the negotiated deadline," the agent said.

I should point out that not all teams are quite as prompt. One ball club, whose identity I won't reveal, is notorious for waiting until the last moment to pay up.

The agent informed me: "Agent percentages on bonuses vary. Most charge a standard 4 percent." I know from my own experience that a large, well-known agency in the late 1990s charged 5 percent of the first $500,000 and 3 percent of all money above that figure.

Larger agencies also charge for additional services. These include preparing a client's taxes, handling his day to day finances, assisting with long-term financial planning, and resolving any legal issues that may arise. Agents also aid the player in forming corporations and charities.

One goal of a full service agency is to assist the player, but, as the agent noted, this tactic also "piles percentage onto percentage, making it harder for a player to leave an agency."

The primary drawback in this arrangement is that if something goes catastrophically wrong, the agency gets blamed—causing a loss of prestige and clients. One prominent player went bankrupt as a result of mismanagement by his agency.

Poaching spurred the altercation mentioned at the beginning of this chapter and is rampant in the agent business. Amateur players awaiting the draft are poaching targets as are minor and major league players.

A few agencies employ individuals whose sole job is to poach minor league or major league players.

This agent expounded on poaching: "Agents often stalk players in order to steal them. Poachers in the minors often follow the team bus from town to town."

The approach is simple and direct, said the agent. "If a problem doesn't exist between the player and his agent, the poacher attempts to create one. Your agent only gave you two pairs of shoes?! I'll give you four!

"The union should monitor agent's poaching tactics. Poachers try to brainwash kids. They bribe a kid by finding out what he is 'into' and then they provide him with that commodity.

"Smaller agencies are particular targets. Bigger agencies attack their clients relentlessly. They try to eat the smaller guys and drive them out of business. Poachers try to steal kids 24/7, there's almost no loyalty. A kid can get plucked away at the last moment."

There are three primary, but not exclusive, instances when rival agents endeavor to poach clients. First, when the player is close to the draft; second, when the player nears arbitration; third, when the player approaches free agency.

When an amateur player is drafted and signs the standard minor league contract on or before the designated signing deadline, that player is now a professional and is ineligible to play baseball at an NCAA institution. (He is allowed, however, to participate in other NCAA sports if he so chooses.)

The player's agent at this stage asks him to sign an Agent Designation Form. This form tells the union who is representing the player and that the agent is acting in the player's interest and on his behalf. The ADF is a year to year contract, the agent told me, and a player can leave at any time after its expiration.

Keep in mind that prior to signing a contract, the agent is called an "advisor." In that role, he can provide advice *only* and nothing of value. Providing any items of value is ethically impermissible and, if discovered, would lead to the player being disqualified from NCAA participation if he is drafted and does not sign. None of this, of course, prevents some agents from distributing booty like shopping mall Santa Clauses handing out candy canes.

A possible poaching scenario was outlined by the agent: "A player can be with an agent for ten years, let's say, beginning when he is drafted and signs at the age of eighteen until age twenty-eight when the player is poised to sign a free agent deal. Two weeks before signing, the player fires his agent of ten years and hires a new agent.

"The player signs a contract for 100 million dollars. The new agent, *not* the ten-year agent, gets the entire agent's percentage—which, in this case, would be four million dollars.

"Whoever does the deal gets the money."

Our next subject was the recruitment of clients. The agent informed me that he typically hunts for clients utilizing four methods. First, naturally, is by attending games and showcases. Agents develop a network of scouts and coaches who often pass along tips on prospects. Cold calling is another tactic and in our modern Internet age, social media and websites provide another avenue for agents to discover players. (One well-known baseball website is notorious for being chummy with agents.)

In talking with prospects, the agent told me, "Some scouts try to direct kids to certain agents." It should be noted that there is no evidence currently available that indicates scouts are getting kickbacks from agents, but scouts do often prefer "friendly" agents—ones they are familiar with and who scouts know will be easy to work with at negotiation time.

College coaches, as I was told, have also been known to direct players to particular agents. Again, it must be noted that rumors of coach-agent bribes or kickbacks have been rampant in the baseball industry for many years, but no reliable confirmation has yet surfaced.

Competition for players among agents is fierce, said the agent. "If multiple agents are 'on' a player, agents will talk trash about the rival agencies."

> Another tactic is "big timing." Large, so called umbrella agencies often have superstar clients. Often, an agent for that company will drop the superstar's name when recruiting the prospect. This occurs even in circumstances where that agent has had zero contact with the superstar.
>
> In large companies that have multiple divisions, including other sports and an entertainment division, it is common for an agent to take a meeting in his office with a prospective client and his family. Prior to the meeting, the agent will send around an interoffice memo to determine if any big name star—sports or entertainment—will be in the building and available for a drop-in.

Several years ago, I spoke to a prospect who told me about an experience he had with an agent. (He signed with a different agent.) The youngster and his mother went to the agent's lavish office in a glittering skyscraper and were dazzled by the opulent surroundings. Laying the sales pitch on thick, the agent not only promised potential millions for the ballplayer, but informed him and his mom that a singing career could be arranged for him after his playing days were over.

When the meeting concluded, the player and mom drove home, flush with excitement and the "buzz" of the experience. An hour into the drive, reality set in. Loudly, the mom asked, "Wait a god damn minute! How many ex-players have singing careers? Unless Taylor Swift played in the big leagues and I missed it, I can't think of any!"

Some agents are office agents, while others are home agents. The office agent is uncomfortable in a player's home, therefore seeks to get the potential client in his "ballpark," that is, his fancy office. These agents are usually "slicksters." Home agents are typically far less superficial and more down to earth, being substantially more at ease in speaking to the player and his folks at the ballpark or in their home.

A few years ago, an African American prospect took a meeting in his home with an agent, hiring him on the spot as the meeting concluded. The player's home was in a depressed, crime-ridden section of the inner city. As he was leaving, the agent asked, "By the way—why did you choose me?"

Said the player's mother, "Because you're the only dumb ass fool brave enough to come down here!"

"Hovering" is also a common recruiting ploy. Agents endeavoring to secure amateur clients frequently hover around the player's parents during a game in a near-Siamese type of attachment. Used as a device to prevent rival agents from approaching the parents, this tactic often backfires. On many occasions, I've witnessed annoyed looks on the faces of perturbed parents whose main wish is to simply watch their son play. Two prominent West Coast based agencies are notorious for hovering.

"Running the Gauntlet" is another bizarre agent ritual. At large showcase events, agents line up in an area where players exit the dugout. Agents greet their clients as they exit, showering praise on them. If a desirable player has no advisor, agents descend upon him en masse but will approach the youngster one by one. It's baseball's version of speed dating.

"In the past," the agent continued, "agents were almost always lawyers. Now there are many non-lawyers in the business, particularly in the recruiting aspect. (Recruiters for agents are called 'runners.') Many runners are ex-players who rag on competing agents who are lawyers but not ex-players. They'll say, 'What does that guy know? He never played!'

"It's not our job to be ex-players! It's our job to give legal advice and to represent the player's legal interests. It's important that an agent be educated not just on the specifics of his job, his duties and the law, but on the tactics used in the baseball business."

Next, the agent focused on negotiations with colleges and big league organizations:

Scouts are attempting to sign a player for as little as possible. College coaches try to steer a kid toward the school he has committed to. Advisors need to coach their clients in the tactics used by both scouts and college coaches.

Some agents deny scouts and college coaches all contact with their clients; most allow contact but still coach clients on how to deal with both coaches and agents. If a kid and his parents are not prepared, they will get run over.

Intent on fixing signability, scouts often pressure players, said the agent. "Scouts can be aggressive, saying to the kid, 'If I don't get signability then I won't scout you and I won't have my cross checker come out!'" Another ruse, says the agent, is for the scout to insist, "All the other kids in my area have given me a number, but you haven't!"

Unanimously, scouts are insistent that all paperwork they give a prospect be filled out promptly and completely. This can be problematic for a high schooler, for not only can he be besieged by thirty major league organizations, he must contend with school-work, friends, his own team's games, and an often active social life.

Scouts conduct home visits with players and distribute paper-work to them several months prior to the annual June draft, often during the preceding summer or fall. Agents commonly advise their clients to leave the signability section of the paper-work form blank, in order to avoid getting locked into a particular figure far in advance of the draft.

This strategy unleashes a torrent of indignation from scouts, most of it poorly feigned: "I need signability! I can't hand this in to my office without signability! My (pick one): career/your career/my life will be ruined without signability!" Scouts and agents are fully cognizant of this ritual nonsense. It's the agent's job to make his client understand this bizarre verbal jousting match as well.

I am reminded of a situation which occurred a few years back. It's a scenario which, as odd as it may seem to a layperson, occurs quite frequently in baseball. A player was selected in the June draft but decided to "hold out." Our friend played sum-mer league baseball from mid-June up to the (at that time) mid-August signing deadline.

Heated negotiations took place between the player, his agent, and the area scout from mid-June to mid-July. The scout made his "absolute final offer" in mid-July; it was rejected by the player. Angrily, the scout shot back, "That's it! I'm done scouting you! My organization is done with you!"

After a monthlong communications blackout, the player received a phone call on August 14, the day before the signing deadline. To the player's utter lack of surprise, the scout was on the other end of the line, dripping with sincere insincerity: "So . . . how 'ya doin'?"

Miraculously, the organization discovered it had money available it didn't realize it had one month before. They must have checked under the office couch cushions.

The player didn't sign.

As we concluded our conversation, the agent riffed on the business of baseball agent representation as a whole:

Often agents are intent on beating other agents rather than servicing their clients.

Many agents will hold out a kid for a large sum of money when the kid himself will gladly take a lower amount. This results in some kids going to school who don't truly want to go to school.

This business should not be about what the agent wants, it should be about what the clients want. All agents have their own angles, of course, but a few take things too far. In rare instances, parents get jobs from an agent who wants to get a kid or will provide stuff to the parent and/or kid to secure that player. Often that stuff is quite valuable. That's not right.

Many agents are poseurs, with more bark than bite. With some agents, if a kid fails to perform, they'll drop him and won't even return his phone calls.

College coaches can also be front runners or fair weather friends, said the agent. "Nowadays, colleges can get a commitment from a kid as a high school freshman. The college can drop him if he doesn't pan out as his high school career progresses but the kid can't talk to other schools."

"Here's how the system is," the agent continued. "When a kid and his family are choosing an agent, they need to ask themselves: Who do you like? Who do you trust?"

Large, well-known agencies are an ideal fit for some prospects and a bad fit for others. A player has to find the one he is comfortable with. With some agents being "sharpies" if not downright con men, that can be a difficult decision.

Concluding, the agent noted, "An agent will represent the kid's legal interests and attempt to secure as much money for him as is possible. But the player must understand reality. It's not the agent's job to produce on the field or to make money for the player."

The agent tells each player: "It's *your* job to perform well. It's *your* job to make yourself the money."

20

Five-Plus Tools

In this chapter, I've chosen seven players—three active, four retired—and will evaluate them based on my observations. In my lifetime, I have seen five of the seven players perform in person. I'll evaluate the other two based on video, statistics, and historical accounts.

FOR BASEBALL FANS and active or retired professional scouts, it is easy to identify the two premier prospects in baseball history: Mickey Mantle and Bo Jackson.

Bo Jackson, pre-injury, may have been the greatest athlete in American history.

No two players in their pre–big league days combined speed and power at such cosmic levels as Mantle and Jackson. That is no revelation. Every fan knows that.

Mantle and Jackson are the standards, but, of course, there have been other phenoms. Drafted out of Michigan State in 1978, Kirk Gibson was a rare 80 speed/80 power prospect. Darryl Strawberry, Ken Griffey Jr., Josh Hamilton, and Alex Rodriguez received OFP scores in the 70s coming out of high school.

I am going to toss another name into this mixture. You may think I am crazy, but if you have read this far into my book, you've no doubt reached a conclusion on that point anyway.

From a tools standpoint, the most gifted player in baseball history on a "pound for pound" basis was: Jimmy Wynn.

No, I am not kidding. If you are under forty-five, you're probably asking, "Who the hell was Jimmy Wynn?"

But I contend, relative to physical size, Wynn was the game's most talented ballplayer.

Wynn had incredible power. His tape measure shot at Cincinnati's Crosley Field on June 10, 1967, was as long as any blast by Mickey Mantle, Richie Allen, or Frank Howard. All of those men outweighed Wynn by 25 to 100 pounds. (Per the book *Baseball's Ultimate Power*, that home run by Wynn was measured at 507 ft.)

A textbook base runner, Wynn had terrific speed and knew how to use it. He stole 43 bases in 1965 and was caught only 4 times. Wynn stole 225 bags in his career and scored over 100 runs four times.

In a game at Candlestick Park in 1965, Wynn threw out Jesus Alou at home plate from center field. Willie Mays—an authority on fantastic throws—wrote that Wynn's throw was the best he had ever seen.

Wynn led the National League in outfield putouts in 1965 and 1967. Keep in mind that superlative defensive center fielders such as Curt Flood, Willie Mays, Willie Davis, Bill Virdon, and Vada Pinson were active in those years.

Perhaps Wynn's only drawback was that he never hit for a particularly high average. A big swing and big miss type hitter, Wynn's career mark was .250. In Wynn's defense, he drew a

bushel basket full of walks in his career, and his saber friendly
.366 on-base percentage ain't too shabby.

Despite his low batting average, I believe that Jimmy Wynn
packed more tools into his frame than any player baseball has
ever seen.

• • •

Now let's evaluate a selected menu of preeminent five-tool players. I have chosen Mike Trout, Yasiel Puig, and Bryce Harper
among active players, and Willie Mays, Hank Aaron, Babe Ruth,
and Joe DiMaggio among former players.

Mike Trout

Mike Trout is the finest all-around player in baseball today.
I first laid eyes on Trout in August of 2008, when he participated in
the annual Area Code Games event in Long Beach, California. At
that time, Trout had just finished his junior year at Millville High
School in New Jersey, and was preparing to begin his senior year.

As I recall, Trout played on the New York Yankees scout team,
representing the Northeastern section of the country. Prior to the
Yankees' first game in the tournament, I was outside the ballpark
talking to someone on the concourse as Trout's club took pre-
game warm-ups. I had never heard of or seen Trout before, and
because I missed warm-ups I had no idea what position he played.

As the Yankees came to bat in the first inning, I took a seat
in the ballpark. Trout came to bat and I scanned my magazine-
style program to find his name. Naturally, I was impressed by
Trout's strong and athletic build but since he was a not a long,
lean, and lanky type, I understood immediately that Trout had
no physical "projection." After watching him play I realized how
utterly meaningless projection can be in certain cases.

With his stocky build, I assumed Trout was a catcher. If I remember correctly, he rapped a ground ball to the left side of the infield—short or third. I watched as Trout tore off toward first and was stunned by his incredible speed. *THAT AIN'T NO CATCHER!* I screamed to myself inside my head.

In my program, I underlined his name twice and put a star next to it. I was determined to keep a very close eye on Trout.

My next encounter with Trout occurred in July of 2010. He was named to participate in the Futures Game prior to the MLB All Star Game, scheduled to be held that year in Anaheim Stadium, Trout's future office space.

Trout's audition that day was stunning. He rapped out several hits, tore around the bases, and was clearly the best player on the field. I noted that he seemed to have some trouble in the outfield on fly balls; my guess is that he was not accustomed to multi-tiered big league stadiums, having played only in single-tiered minor league parks. That problem, of course, has since been resoundingly solved.

My notes also indicate that I was concerned with the pre-swing position of Trout's hands. I jotted down that Trout was close to wrapping the bat behind his neck, adding unwanted length to his backswing. Also, I felt his hands were gripping the bat too tightly. Trout would not reach his full power potential, I felt, until he loosened his top hand and let it fly when he swung, generating bat speed in the bat barrel.

In peeking at some YouTube footage of Trout's minor league swing and comparing it to his current major league swing, I can clearly see that he has adjusted and solved both of those issues.

Nowadays, Trout is a major leaguer. In his first two full big league years, he has posted numbers rivaling the freshman and sophomore years of all-time immortals such as Joe DiMaggio, Ted Williams, and Albert Pujols.

Trout's 2012 season was spectacular, filled with acrobatic catches, tape measure home runs, multi-hit games, and daring base running; sort of a yearlong highlight film. The numbers posted by Trout in 2013 were again sensational, but his season was far more workmanlike.

In 2012, Trout was a death defying circus act; in 2013 Trout was a lunch pail toting, work boot and hard hat wearing, grind-it-out blue collar construction worker. In 2013, Trout 1 for 3'd his opponents repeatedly.

How does he do it, what type of player is Trout, and how would he be graded? Let's go through each of the five tools and examine Trout.

Run

I have never recorded a 60-yard dash time for Trout. My guess is his time would be comfortably under 6.4. I have, however, timed Trout in 3.89 seconds as he thunders down the line from home to first.

Just as velocity is useless for a pitcher without command, speed is useless for a ballplayer without the knack to use it properly. Example: Herb Washington.

Trout rarely gets thrown out and almost always get an ideal jump on the bases and in the field. He's the rare player with great natural speed and the ability to use it to near perfection.

Field

Trout has not had the opportunity to make as many acrobatic plays in 2013 as he did in 2012, but he has established himself as one of baseball's top defensive outfielders. Trout's breaks, jumps, and routes are excellent and he can run down any ball hit laterally, in front, or behind him. He made only two errors in 2013 and posted a sparkling .994 fielding percentage.

Throw

Trout's arm is his only tool that does not rate at the top of the scale. It's not a bad arm . . . it's just not a colossal arm. His throwing motion is a bit stiff, not the sort of free and easy arm stroke scouts prefer to see. To Trout's credit, his arm has improved since his graduation to the majors. His release is decent and he consistently nails his cutoff man. Interestingly, Trout recorded zero outfield assists in 2013.

Power

Trout's raw power is stunning, as evidenced by his frequent appearances on the ESPN Home Run Tracker, which measures baseball's longest home runs each season. Two shots in 2013 come to mind—one in Kansas City and one in Oakland. Two 2012 blasts, one in Toronto and one in Detroit, were mammoth. All traveled around 450 feet.

His power frequency isn't quite as high, simply because he doesn't try to hit home runs in every at bat. Trout attempts to pick out a hittable pitch and hit it hard somewhere between the left field foul line and the right field foul line. If it goes out, fine. That is, in my view, a more intelligent approach than the "grip it and rip it" approach many hitters use.

Hit

I've always wondered what Trout's vision score is. My guess is that Trout's eyesight is 20/10. His combination of vision, strike zone knowledge, pre–at-bat plan, or "approach" is the best I have seen in baseball since Wade Boggs.

Trout appears to know if a pitch is a strike or a ball 10 to 20 feet before it reaches home plate. Many hitters have no idea if a pitch is a ball or a strike even when it reaches the catcher. Trout almost always takes the first pitch, and then waits for a pitch in an area where he can attack it. With a non two-strike count, he rarely chases a pitch out of the zone.

Trout's swing reminds me of Rocky Marciano's punching style. It's not graceful, easy, or fluid, not the smooth type of swing scouts dream about. Trout's mechanics are technically sound but not aesthetically pleasing. Like Marciano, he delivers massive power in short, compact, often perfectly timed fashion.

These are the current grades I would give Mike Trout:
Run: 80
Throw: 55
Field: 70
Hit: 80
Power, raw: 80
Power, frequency: 70
Overall Grade: 72.5

Approximately 18,000 men have played major league baseball. Probably only twenty position players have ever merited a grade of 72.5 or higher. If Trout continues to perform at his current level, he will be one the greatest players in baseball history. For his sake—and for the sake of the game—I pray that happens.

Trout is what Mickey Mantle would have been if the Mick had batted right-handed exclusively and stayed healthy.

There are some differences: The style of play in Mantle's time and the poor physical state of his legs dictated that Mantle would never steal a large number of bags. Trout is a better defensive outfielder than Mickey, but Mantle, prior to a 1957 shoulder injury, had a better arm than Trout.

Yet in a general sense the two players, Trout and Mantle, are fascinatingly similar. Both are/were great hitters, possessed remarkable power, had similar body types and incredible speed.

As Mickey Mantle was from 1952 to 1964, Mike Trout is the finest player in the American League and should become the face of Major League Baseball for the next several years.

• • •

Yasiel Puig

In art, animation, or film, it's a common ploy to show a dying flower, wilted and bent over against a dry, desolate background. From one side of the frame comes a water can, applying several drops to the bud. Symbolizing rebirth, the flower first straightens then grows and blooms brilliantly.

In 2013, Yasiel Puig was the water can that brought the Los Angeles Dodgers back to life.

The once great franchise had been slogging through a string of nondescript seasons. LA was saddled with inadequate, distracted owners, vicious internal front office politics, and dreadful player personnel moves. The Dodgers appeared to be more concerned with the writings of a local sports columnist than they were with the product on the field.

Puig's brilliant talent, good looks, smile, infectious personality, and electrifying play suddenly transformed a drab, listless, last place Dodger ballclub into a division champion. Blasé LA fans, rendered into a near comatose state before Puig's arrival, began to cheer wildly on their own initiative, not just when prodded by the stadium scoreboard.

What is Puig, exactly, and what will he become? As the old saying goes, the possibilities are endless. Puig may be a sudden, temporary "flash in the pan" who quickly fades into mediocrity, a la Bob "Hurricane" Hazle. Perhaps Puig will be a lavishly talented sort who never fulfills his celestial abilities. Think of a Ruben Rivera. Or Puig could be a phenomenal talent whose career is cut short by injuries and/or misfortune—a Bo Jackson type.

Yet another scenario may see Puig having an outstanding career but not quite reaching the levels of an iconic, Hall of Fame superstar—Cesar Cedeno or Raul Mondesi, let's say.

Maybe Andruw Jones is in Puig's future. Jones was brilliant early in his career, then faded as he passed thirty and became an oft traded journeyman struggling with weight issues. Don't forget Puig was twenty to thirty pounds overweight when scouts first spied him in international tournaments.

Or possibly, just maybe . . . Puig is the second coming of Willie Mays—a household name, Hall of Famer, and one of the greatest all-around players in baseball history.

For Puig, any one of these outcomes is possible. Which one will it be? Well, let's break down Yasiel Puig's tools and then try to reach a crystal ball prediction.

Throw
Puig's outfield arm is one of the strongest in modern baseball, on par with Bryce Harper, Jason Werth, and Adam Jones. His cruise missile throw to nail Andrelton Simmons of the Braves at third base in 2013 was made all the more remarkable by the fact that Puig released the ball without using a full reverse arm stroke—he simply fired the ball from his right ear, like a catcher.

Run
Several big leaguers are faster than Puig, but only Mike Trout, Carlos Gomez, and Justin Upton combine size (230 pounds) and speed as does Puig. Billy Hamilton of the Reds is probably the fastest player in the majors right now. Scouts and organizations

are notoriously reticent to reveal stopwatch times to the public, but I've caught Puig at 4.0 from home to first on a full swing when he "busts it" down the line.

Field

Puig manned right field primarily, but also, on occasion, was stationed in left field or center. He has a right fielder's arm with center field speed, so either spot is acceptable. Puig has terrific range and aggressively goes after every ball hit in his vicinity. His continent ranging catch in Toronto in 2013 as a center fielder was the finest catch I saw any outfielder make in 2013.

Power

Blessed with staggering raw power, Puig hit a series of breathtaking tape measure shots in his rookie year. He tagged 450-foot bombs at San Diego, Arizona, and Colorado, and reached at or beyond the midway point of Dodger Stadium's left field pavilion several times.

Hit

Puig's swing is a tad unusual. He releases his top hand from the bat almost instantly after contact, a move straight out of the Charley Lau hitting school of the 1970s. Puig also appears to push or drag the bat through the hitting zone instead of sweeping it through as do most big league power hitters. Technical nit picking aside, there is no denying Puig has outstanding bat speed, allowing the ball, when squared up, to rocket off his bat.

I would drop a 70–75 grade on each of Puig's individual tools, which would correspondingly give him an overall grade between 70 and 75. As previously stated, an overall plus 70 score is exceptionally rare for a position player.

None of these lofty grades answers our most pressing question: What path will Puig's career follow?

Prior to an NFL Pro Bowl game way back in the 1970s, a tacky, kitschy skills contest was held. Quarterbacks threw a football from the parking lot up the side of a tourist hotel. The winner would be the quarterback who, shall we say, reached the highest floor.

Dan Pastorini won the contest by firing a ball up to the sixth floor, thrilling giggly CBS TV cohost Phyllis George. Johnny Unitas, by then retired, was not so impressed. Sneered Unitas, "His receivers were on the second floor."

Therein lies the secret to Puig's future. He no doubt has the ability to be one of the greatest all-around players in baseball history, but he appears to be substantially more interested in making *Sports Center* highlights than in executing the proper play.

Puig is the worst base runner I have ever seen. He made a shocking number of unnecessarily aggressive and immature base running gambits in 2013.

From watching Puig play, I assume the Cuban dialect of the Spanish language does not have an equivalent form of the words, "cutoff man."

In his first month in the big leagues (June of 2013), Puig was nuclear reactor core hot with the bat. In that stretch, he kept his front shoulder tucked in, head down on the ball, and merrily drove pitches down into the right field corner.

Puig hit .437 in June of 2013. Nobody can maintain that, of course. He followed June with a respectable .287 July and an outstanding .320 August. Entering September, Puig was cruising along at .349; a dreadful .184 month caused him to plummet to .319 at season's end.

Did the league, as announcers love to say, "figure him out"? No, not really. Puig got himself out by trying to hit everything into the stratosphere, not the right field corner. Instead of staying closed with his head down on the ball and shooting it the other way, Puig's head and shoulder began to fly off the ball. He was aiming for the sixth floor instead of the second floor.

It is ridiculously easy to predict a pitcher's strategy with Puig at bat. With the fastball, pound him inside or try to get him to chase up in the zone. Throw the slider off the plate and away in a two-strike count. Puig will futilely chase that pitch and look helpless in doing so.

The key to Puig's future lies not in the stars but in himself. He must become more intelligent on the bases. He must learn to attempt the spectacular throw *only* when feasible and hit the cutoff man on all other occasions.

Like any schlub watching on TV, Puig must realize what pitchers are trying to do to him and counteract. Lay off the high fastball. Recognize the off the plate slider and let it go. Force the pitcher to throw the ball in the strike zone where he can handle it, don't get himself out on pitches out of the zone. Take a line drive single to right field and stop trying to make *Sports Center* by hitting every ball 450 feet.

My assumption is that Puig understands all these points and that Dodger instructors have discussed these issues with him repeatedly. Now it's up to him. If Puig listens and applies what is blatantly obvious and what he is being told, he'll be one of the game's all-time great superstars. If not, well . . . hello, Ruben Rivera!

•   •   •

Bryce Harper
I can't resist the feeling that Bryce Harper has a screw loose. A part missing.

Don't misunderstand me. Harper is a terrific talent and the best amateur power-hitting prospect I've ever seen. For his sake, the sake of the Washington Nationals, and the sake of Major League Baseball, I hope Harper has a long and productive career, full of highlights and flashy stats.

Yet there is something about Harper that irritates me. Perhaps it was his meltdown at the 2009 Aflac Game. Maybe it was the helmet throwing, cut eyelid incident in his rookie season of 2012. Or the home plate bat-breaking flare-up that same season. In 2014, he was benched for not hustling. A few days later he inexplicably attempted to bunt on a two-strike count. He popped to the catcher in foul territory.

The capper for me was the 2013 Home Run Derby. I was turned off by Harper's gaudy multicolored Bozo the Clown spikes and the stuck-his-hand-in-a-live-electrical-socket hairdo.

A definite source of my ambivalence toward Harper, I must confess, is not the young man himself but the ridiculous media hype surrounding him. Harper is not the "Chosen One." He is not to baseball what LeBron James is to the NBA. Harper is not now the best player in baseball and he will not be the best player ever. As a high schooler, he did not hit a ball 570 feet. And on and on.

The most egregious media offense occurred when Harper got his first big league base hit against the Dodgers in LA. Viewing the video clip, Ken Rosenthal of Fox Sports gushed, "No one in baseball can get to that pitch!" Nonsense, Rosenthal. Hitters get to that pitch every day.

Still, the overheated media blather for Harper drones on, with much of the public, sadly, in blind lockstep. Ignored is the fact that many young players are simply better than Harper: Mike Trout, Yasiel Puig, Giancarlo Stanton, Manny Machado, Carlos Gomez. It is not impossible to fathom that Wil Myers, the 2013 AL Rookie of the Year, will one day be superior to Harper. A current Minnesota Twins farmhand named Byron Buxton is a better all-around prospect *now* than Harper ever was. My guess is that you've never heard of Buxton.

A quick word to the wise: Ignore media hype on a prospect. The media has an agenda to promote and they want to jump on the bandwagon of the next "big thing." On any player, listen to what the scouts—the real pros—say. They'll praise Harper but also point out his weaknesses. The media rarely, if ever, performs the latter function.

The media hype machine also existed recently for a Baltimore Orioles pitching prospect named Dylan Bundy. I was extremely impressed by Bundy as a high schooler, but became concerned with his delivery mechanics as a minor leaguer.

Every baseball-related media outlet—*Perfect Game, Baseball America,* etc.—hailed Bundy as the greatest thing since Walter Johnson. In my discussions with pro scouts, however, we concurred that Bundy was overrated and his poor mechanics made him prone to injury. Bundy is now recovering from Tommy John surgery.

Naturally, everyone within baseball, myself included, hopes Bundy makes a full recovery and becomes an All Star. Still, the media-hype turtles have withdrawn into their shells on Bundy, at least for the time being.

Also, don't forget phenoms often fall short of expectations. A titanic amount of media hype was lavished on LPGA golfer Michelle Wie seven or eight years ago. According to the publicity avalanche at that time, by now Wie should be completely and totally dominating the LPGA tour and competing in (if not winning) men's PGA events.

How has that worked out?

Now, back to Bryce Harper. First, let's dispense with the Mickey Mantle comparison. Mantle was much, much faster than Harper is. Mantle was a vastly superior hitter, especially from his natural right-handed side. Harper has outstanding raw power, but no player in history had Mickey Mantle's raw power.

Mantle was not a great defensive outfielder but he was a better outfielder than Harper is. However, Harper does have a stronger throwing arm than Mantle had. Overall, Mantle had a clear edge in four of the five tools and from an overall standpoint was a distinctly greater player than Harper is now or will ever be.

I don't mean to rag on Harper. He has been extremely successful in baseball at a very young age. Harper loves the game, plays hard, and prepares exceptionally well. Bully for him.

Harper has a colossal throwing arm and sensational raw power. He's an above average hitter, has decent speed, and is an acceptable defender. Harper just ain't Mickey Mantle or Willie Mays, or a lot of other guys. No faulting him on that one.

Harper must be given a ton of credit for being the best Bryce Harper he can, which is pretty damn good.

Now, in 2014, Harper's story—and his future—becomes fascinating. He is only twenty-one years old at the time of this book being written. The question is this: Has Harper matured early and reached his plateau, or will he explode as he reaches his mid-twenties?

Mantle, for example, was good but not great in his first five seasons. He hit .267, .311, .295, .300, and .306. His homer totals were 13, 23, 21, 27 and 37. Not bad, but not Hall of Fame stuff.

Then, in his mid-twenties, Mantle exploded. He won the Triple Crown in 1956 by hitting .353 with 52 homers and 130 RBI. Mickey followed that with a .365 campaign in 1957 and the rest is legend.

In his first two seasons, 2012 and 2013, Harper has hit .270 and .274, with 22 and 20 home runs. Excellent totals for anyone, particularly a nineteen- to twenty-year-old. But to get into Cooperstown with a career full of those numbers, Harper will have to purchase a ticket.

Is the Bryce Harper we have seen in 2012 and '13 the Harper we will always see, or will he explode in his mid-twenties? Predicting the future is always a risky and difficult venture in any business, but I'll take a stab.

I feel Bryce Harper is that rare player who has peaked at a young age. I don't believe he will advance to the "next level" in the next few years and take off a la Mickey Mantle in 1956, Carl Yastremski in 1967, or Chris Davis in 2013.

My guess is that today's Harper will always be Harper: a .270 to .280 hitter, 20 to 30 home runs per annum.

Bryce Harper is not and will not be "God," as one baseball website once proclaimed. As it has for Michelle Wie, media frenzy over Harper should dissipate as his career proceeds, thank heavens.

My prediction is that Harper winds up being a left-handed hitting version of Rocky Colavito. Media flaks may become apoplectic at that prediction, but . . . that's still one helluva ball player.

• • •

Willie Mays

An earlier chapter in this book was dedicated to Mays, who is, in my opinion, the greatest all-around player in baseball history.

Mays is a subject matter that has been so exhaustingly and thoroughly examined that it is nearly impossible to state anything new about the "Say Hey Kid." Yet I am going to try by revealing some little known tidbits about my hero.

With the exception of his rookie year, the Giants spent every spring training period in the Phoenix, Arizona, area. During spring training batting practice, Willie would shag fly balls out in center field. Nothing unusual about that.

Except that Mays would often catch fly balls *between his legs*.

Try snagging a 350-foot fly ball between your legs—it takes skill, of course, but also a certain amount of bravado, self-confidence, and a disregard for personal safety.

A source tells me that to this day, he still receives Christmas cards from Willie—and the source was a Giants minor leaguer who never made the majors.

Several years ago, Mays did a TV beer commercial. Only Willie doesn't drink . . . or smoke. Mays tried champagne once after the New York Giants won the 1954 World Series; he threw it up.

At autograph signings well after his retirement, Mays would always politely insist that he be provided Coca Cola. No water, no Sprite, no Diet Coke; only Coke. And it had to be served in a plastic cup with crushed ice—never shaved ice, never cubed ice.

Many sports stars ignore the public at autograph signings, never engaging in conversation or even making eye contact. Willie loves to interact with fans. Once an autograph seeker pulled out his driver's license to show Mays, as his father had given him the first and middle names of Willie Mays. In glee and playfully feigned shock, Mays rose halfway out of his chair and in his familiar high-pitched voice, shrieked, "Well, what do you know about that!"

For fifty-five years, Willie has made his home in the Atherton area of Northern California near San Francisco. A friend of mine who lives in the area says that Willie can often be seen at local open air markets. Reportedly, Mays is quite an enthusiastic shopper.

Upon meeting Mays, the first thing one notices are his hands. Sasquatch doesn't have hands that size. Willie has extra long fiddler's fingers, hitch hiker's thumbs, and palms that stretch across most of Australia.

It is a distinct possibility that during the prime of his career (1954 through 1966), Mays was the strongest man in the world weighing under 200 pounds. A photo published in Robert Riger's classic baseball book, *The American Diamond*, shows a shirtless Mays smiling and chatting with reporters after the Giants beat the Dodgers in a playoff (winning two games to one) to win the 1962 NL pennant. Willie was (pick one) ripped, chiseled, cut. His build would put to shame even the most dedicated modern fitness freaks.

I began to follow Mays when I was an elementary school student in the mid-'60s. When Willie ran the bases, I could not understand why he never looked at the upcoming bag. Mays ran with his head on a swivel, constantly turning to look over one shoulder and then the other. Years later it dawned on me that Mays understood that the bases are stationary and will not move; he was looking around to see what the ball and the fielders were doing. If a bobble, misplay, or slow relay occurred, Mays would instantly accelerate and take an extra base.

In the mid-'50s, Willie blasted two home runs in a game at Ebbets Field to help the Giants beat the Brooklyn Dodgers. When Mays returned to his car in the parking lot, all four of his tires were slashed.

Mays appeared on *What's My Line?* as a celebrity mystery guest in the summer of 1954. Four blindfolded panelists, celebrities in their own right, attempted to ascertain his identity. Jack Paar was completely unable to determine if Mays was a man or a woman. Baseball and New York Giant fan Arlene Francis proudly proclaimed, "Well, sir, I think I've got you!" and eventually uncovered Willie's identity.

After his brilliant 1965 season (52 homers, NL MVP), Willie made a guest appearance on Merv Griffin's talk show, appropriately titled *The Merv Griffin Show*, which at the time was broadcast from New York. Willie was introduced, with great flourish, by Broadway star Tallulah Bankhead. After answering tepid questions from Griffin, Mays smacked plastic baseballs into the studio audience.

Let me now evaluate Mays. I'll do it anecdotally, not in a straight scouting report form.

Hit
Mays altered his stance, swing, and hitting approach as his career progressed. After a pair of phenomenal seasons in 1954 and 1955,

Willie slumped a bit in 1956 and then, from 1957 to 1960, Mays geared his offensive style toward stolen bases and a high batting average. Willie won the batting title in 1954 and finished second in batting average in 1955, '57, '58, and '60. Mays led the NL in steals in 1956, '57, '58, and '59.

As the Giants farm system produced sluggers Orlando Cepeda and Willie McCovey, San Francisco evolved into a power oriented club. Mays changed his hitting style to accommodate. Beginning in 1961, Mays concentrated on home runs, leading the NL in 1962, '64, and '65. From 1961 through 1966, Willie hit a total of 263 home runs (an average of 44 per year), but Willie never hit above .317 during that stretch.

Mays used a fascinating tactic at bat during the mid-'60s. Willie would dig a small hole in the batter's box with his right foot, creating a small mound at the back of the box. He positioned his back foot at a slight inward angle, using the mound to push off and drive his weight forward as he swung.

Power

Suffering from the aftereffects of food poisoning, Mays hit four home runs in a game in Milwaukee in 1961. Fifty years ago, Branch Rickey wrote that if a machine existed that could measure bat speed, Mays would probably generate more bat speed, swing per swing, than any other hitter in baseball.

Despite its ridiculously short foul line dimensions, the Polo Grounds in New York afforded Mays little benefit as a power hitter. From 1954 to 1957 (the Giants moved to San Francisco in 1958), Willie hit 79 home runs at home and 84 on the road. Candlestick Park in San Francisco wasn't much of a friend, either. In 1965, Willie hit 52 home runs—28 on the road and 24 at home.

In the first 100 games of the 1965 season, Mays hit 24 home runs. That pace would give him 39 for a full 162 game season. In the final 62 games that year, Mays hit 28 home runs. At that clip, he would have hit 73 homers for a full season.

Field

Mays's classic catch in the 1954 World Series is his most famous and important play, but probably not his best. Vin Scully recalls a Mays catch off of Bobby Morgan at Ebbets Field in which Willie dove head first, caught the ball, and slammed into the concrete wall, knocking himself out.

A sampling of Willie's fielding masterpieces would include his fence climbing grab against the Reds in 1970; another wall scaling impossibility at Philadelphia in 1964; All Star game catches in 1955, '62, '63, and '65, and a magician's sleight of hand theft versus the Cubs in 1960.

Throw

In Ken Burns's documentary *Baseball*, Joe DiMaggio is quoted as saying that Mays had the finest throwing arm he'd ever seen. Willie's best may have been a throw in the fifties that nailed the speedy Bill Bruton of the Braves at home from the deepest part of center field.

Bruton was out but the umpire refused to believe it. He called Bruton safe, claiming, "Nobody throws Bruton out from there!"

Run

Tim McCarver insists Mays was the best base runner he'd ever witnessed. As with any player, Willie slowed down as he got older. Even so, he was still able to swipe 23 bases in 26 attempts in 1971—at the age of forty.

My favorite aspect of scouting is asking questions of older scouts. Many of them played in the majors in the fifties and sixties and have seen every great player in the past fifty, sometimes sixty, years.

They all cite Willie Mays as the best all-around player they have ever seen.

Today, the pertinent question is: Will we ever see another Willie Mays?

Answer: Probably not.

One in a century is the most we can ask for.

• • •

Hank Aaron

On July 8, 1969, I saw Hank Aaron play in person for the first time at Dodger Stadium in Los Angeles. I was eleven years old. During batting practice, every player on both sides stopped to watch Aaron hit. Jim Lefebvre whispered to a teammate, "Look at that number 44!"

I was flabbergasted. It was impossible for me to believe that a hitter could take such an easy swing yet hit the ball so hard and far. As time passed, I came to understand: That is Hank Aaron. His playing style was so graceful and effortless it defied rationality.

Aaron never had a heroic limp, like a Mickey Mantle; he never had the flair of Willie Mays; he was never a self-promoter like Muhammad Ali; he never caught the fancy of the media and public with a record-setting single season feat, as did Joe DiMaggio and Roger Maris.

Baseball is not the only sport in which this bizarre phenomenon exists. In every ranking of heavyweight boxing champions I have ever seen, Rocky Marciano is always listed ahead of Joe Frazier, which I find baffling. Frazier weighed in at 205 pounds on March 8, 1971, the night he battered Muhammad Ali in the first of their three epic bouts.

During his reign as champion, Marciano typically weighed in at 188 pounds. If the two had squared off in the prime of their careers, Frazier would have annihilated Marciano. Joe was faster and quicker than Rocky and would have enjoyed a 17-pound weight advantage!

Jack Dempsey is another beneficiary of warped idolatry. The media and the public have long fawned over Dempsey, who, in my opinion, was the most overrated athlete in American history. Not only did Gene Tunney whip him twice, but Dempsey rarely defended his title (and fought pushovers when he did) and avoided facing black challengers.

I am certain Hank Aaron himself wonders why he has never received the proper credit for his landmark accomplishments while other athletes—some inferior to him—received more acclaim. Racism is probably not a factor, for the media and public have long adored Michael Jordan, Muhammad Ali, Willie Mays, Magic Johnson, etc. It is true that Aaron played his career far away from media centers, yet that hasn't negatively affected LeBron James today or Bill Russell in the past.

For some inexplicable reason, the media chooses to shower adulation on some athletes and withhold it from others. Unfortunately the public tends to follow the media's lead.

Both the media and the public need to wake up to the fact that Hank Aaron was the greatest right-handed hitter of all time and one of the finest all-around players in baseball history.

Contemporaries Al Kaline and Roberto Clemente were superior defensive right fielders to Aaron in both fielding and throwing. Yet Aaron was a superb outfielder, with range and a strong, accurate arm. Early in his career, Aaron played center field and acquitted himself quite well.

From 1955 to 1974, Aaron was easily the best right-handed hitter in baseball, combining to hit for power and average at a level few in baseball history have equaled. Modern Saber types may squawk that Aaron did not draw enough walks. My reply is this: Hank Aaron was born to swing a bat, not to take pitches.

In his time, Willie Davis and Lou Brock were faster than Aaron, but Hank was an outstanding base runner and base stealer. Attention naturally is paid to Hank's 3,771 hits, 2,297

RBI, and 755 home runs, but he also scored 2,174 runs and stole 240 bases, with a high of 31 steals in 1963.

Aaron's primary strength was his consistency. That may have also been the main reason he received so little acclaim until he neared Babe Ruth's record in the early seventies. Unlike Mantle, Aaron never won a triple crown. Unlike Mays, Aaron never had a 50-homer season and never seemed to make a catch anyone remembered.

In his first three seasons, Aaron hit 13, 27, and 26 homers. Fine totals, but nobody's record was in danger. Beginning in 1957 and lasting through 1973, Aaron then began to hit, it seemed, 39 to 44 homers every year.

The nation underwent epic change in the seventeen years from '57 to '73; so did baseball. It made no difference to Aaron. Beginning as a twenty-three-year-old youngster in 1957, and continuing on to the doorstep of middle age at thirty-nine in '73, Aaron kept hitting homers.

And running the bases. And hitting. And fielding his position at a near Gold Glove level. It's not Aaron's fault that so few noticed then or now how great he truly was.

In the heart of the Milwaukee era of his career (1955 to 1965), these are the grades I would give Aaron: Power: 80; Hit: 80; Throw: 65; Run: 70; Field: 65; 72 overall. A 72 ranks Aaron precisely where he should be: as one of the five best all-around players in baseball history.

· · ·

Babe Ruth

First, let's clear out the mythological stories surrounding Babe Ruth. Depending on the source, Ruth swung a bat which weighed (pick one) 42 ounces, 48 ounces, 54 ounces, 3 tons. No one can swing a bat that heavy and be successful in today's game. *No one.*

If he played today, Ruth would have to swing a bat weighing between 31 and 33 ounces. Historical romantics don't like to have their fairy tales punctured, but if Ruth tried to swing a bat weighing 40 or more ounces against today's pitching, he would be out of organized baseball in a week.

A few film clips of Ruth from Ken Burns's documentary *Baseball* show the Bambino running up in the batter's box to hit the ball. That is slow pitch softball bull pucky and would be completely impossible to accomplish in the majors today.

In the eighties, I struck up a friendship with a retired newspaper writer who was also a World War Two veteran. His father had been a ballplayer who had once faced Walter Johnson. My friend insisted that his dad claimed that Babe Ruth was a ballplayer who never made a mistake.

No offense to my late friend, but I cannot believe that claim either. Every player makes mistakes, and Babe Ruth made his share. Ruth made the last out of the 1926 World Series by foolishly trying to steal second base, getting thrown out by a considerable margin.

In every baseball interview pertaining to Ruth I have ever viewed, some baseball historian adamantly claims that Babe Ruth was the greatest baseball player of all time. That assertion is also wildly, grossly wrong.

Babe Ruth was the second most *important* player in baseball history. (Jackie Robinson was the most important player in baseball history.) Ruth definitely was *not* the best player in baseball history. I could name at least a dozen players who were better than Ruth.

Yet there is no questioning Ruth's positive impact on the game. He saved baseball from the depths of the 1919 "Black Sox" scandal. Ruth obliterated his era's home run records, transforming baseball from a speed and defense game into a power game. Along with Lou Gehrig, Ruth began the Yankee dynasty, changing a struggling ballclub into the premier dynasty in sports history.

Eighty-five to ninety years after his prime, Babe Ruth is still baseball's most famous—and popular—player.

It should also be taken into account that he was a pretty fair left-handed pitcher in his days with the Boston Red Sox.

Contemporaries of Ruth approached his feats, but didn't match or excel them. Ruth's 1927 mark of 60 home runs was challenged by Hack Wilson, who hit 56 homers in 1930, Jimmie Foxx's 58 in 1932, and Hank Greenberg's 58 in 1938.

The secret to Ruth's hitting prowess was not super-human strength but incredible visual acuity. His eyesight was freakishly good.

Columbia University researchers in the early twenties found that Ruth's vision was by far the sharpest they had ever tested. He had the ability to read a record label as it spun on an old-fashioned phonograph at any speed: 33 1/3, 45, or 78 rpm.

Now, don't fall into the trap that baseball historians and romantics fall prey to. The fantastic, surreal statistics Babe Ruth accumulated in the twenties indicate his superiority to his contemporaries. They do *not* indicate any superiority to modern players.

Ruth gained those numbers because he was a great hitter facing competition vastly inferior to modern competition. Babe faced several Hall of Fame pitchers in his day, but in general the hurlers he faced were substandard to modern hurlers. Ruth would not come remotely close to those stats facing today's pitching.

Now for the crucial question: If the Babe Ruth of 1920 to 1932 could be transported from the past into today's game, how would he fare?

Ruth would be nowhere near the best player in the game, but would be pretty darn good. Defensively, a younger Ruth could field a corner outfield spot, probably right field. His range may be ordinary, but no doubt Ruth had the arm for right field.

As he grew older, Ruth would be forced into a 1B/DH role. I believe the closest modern comparison to Ruth is David "Big Papi" Ortiz of the Red Sox. If Ruth played today, I'm convinced his numbers would closely resemble Ortiz's.

In 2014, a younger Ruth would have decent but not great speed and be an acceptable base runner; as he grew older and heavier Ruth would be a liability on the bases, necessitating a pinch runner late in close games.

As a hitter, today Ruth would be a .290 to .310 hitter with 30–40 home runs per year prior to age thirty. He would strike out 150 times a season but would be a sabermetric darling, with a high number of walks and a lofty on-base percentage, slugging percentage, and OPS. Ruth's WAR would be depressed slightly because of deficiencies in defense and speed, but would still hover around 5.0 to 7.5.

After the age of thirty, Ruth would still be productive. I'm guessing he'd hit between .275 and .290 (no leg hits), with 25 to 30 homers. His day to day role would be diminished somewhat, as he'd no longer play in the field as often, would be rested frequently, and would probably be held out of the lineup occasionally against tough left-handed starting pitchers.

Similar to a modern David Ortiz, today's Babe Ruth would be a lovable player, an enormous fan favorite, and a consistently productive, clutch hitter. There is no possibility whatsoever that Babe Ruth today would post statistics equaling the stats he put up in the twenties and thirties, but he would still be a wildly popular star player with unique charisma.

If the Babe Ruth of 1927 played in 2014, I personally would love to see him do one thing: Participate in the All Star Game Home Run Derby.

Now *that* would be a spectacle worthy of Babe Ruth.

• • •

Joe DiMaggio

In a classic episode of *Seinfeld*, Elaine walks into the diner with a new boyfriend. Her beau has a shaved head and is sporting a goatee. When he momentarily leaves the table, Jerry asks Elaine: "Is he from the future?"

In viewing seventy-five-year-old black and white newsreel footage of Joe DiMaggio from the late 1930s and early '40s, I am convinced he was history's first time traveler.

DiMaggio was the best all-around player in the first half of the twentieth century. At 6' 2" and 200 pounds, he combined modern physicality with tools that even today would rank near the top of the grading scale.

In grainy old films, DiMaggio dwarfs opposing players in both size and skill. Hank Greenberg and Ted Williams were bigger than DiMaggio, but did not possess Joe's all-around ability.

Like Muhammad Ali, Joe DiMaggio had two careers. Prior to his three-and-a-half-year exile, Ali was perhaps the best boxer in history. After his return, Ali was still a great fighter but was nowhere near his previous level.

The post–World War Two DiMaggio (1946-1951) was an outstanding player but clearly inferior to his pre-war self. Age, injury (a bothersome heel spur in particular), and tougher post-war competition depressed Joe's numbers significantly.

In his pre-war prime, from 1936 to 1941, DiMaggio was the perfect ballplayer, light years ahead of his peers and easily good enough to be a star in the modern game. It is a fascinating exercise to study DiMaggio as a hitter and then compare and contrast him to today's standards.

First off, DiMaggio is the most relaxed player I have ever watched. There is no hint of stiffness or tension in any aspect of his play. DiMaggio's famous grace and style is no fabrication invented by worshipful biographers; it jumps off the screen as one watches flickering old films.

Today, DiMaggio would offer fans a welcome respite from nervous modern hitters, who habitually wander out of the batter's box between pitches and spend an inordinate amount of time fiddling with their batting gloves and helmets.

At bat, DiMaggio used several mechanical tactics that are foreign to today's hitters. He used a spread, upright stance. No problem there. However, DiMaggio's lead (left) hip was slightly open. Staying closed with the front side before swinging is vitally important in terms of driving the ball as well as hitting pitches to the opposite field.

Modern hitters almost universally employ a "load" mechanism, which I've described in an earlier chapter. DiMaggio had no load; he began his swing from a start which was dead still. It is difficult to believe any hitter today could drive the ball consistently without some form of a pre-swing backwards weight shift.

As DiMaggio reached his "launch" position, his bat was held at a near 90 degree angle. Modern hitters, at the same point in their swing, hold the bat at a 45 degree angle. I have little doubt DiMaggio could easily make that adjustment today.

Several facets of DiMaggio's hitting mechanics are easily identifiable to modern scouts. His backswing was perfect—exceptionally short and free of unnecessary length or movement. DiMaggio had the ability to wait until the last possible instant before swinging at a pitch. That is a rare trait only the very best hitters possess.

The "Yankee Clipper" employed a compact, quiet stride, tucked his front shoulder under his chin, and drove his weight forward into the pitch as he swung. Most importantly, DiMaggio achieved separation with his hands and arms, permitting them to work freely as he swung.

To me, after viewing old films, one conclusion is clear: Joe DiMaggio had the sweetest swing in baseball history.

To complement his tools, DiMaggio possessed a supreme, quiet confidence. Legend has it that as a seventeen-year-old in 1932, he watched a Pacific Coast League game featuring his hometown San Francisco Seals from behind the plate.

"I can hit that stuff," he sniffed to himself. In 1933, as the Seals center fielder, DiMaggio hit in 61 consecutive games.

Books and songs have been written about DiMaggio's 56-game hitting streak in 1941, a major league record that still stands (and will most likely always stand). Few are aware that he came close to hitting .400 in 1939. As late as September 9 of that season, DiMaggio's average stood at .409. An eye infection severely inhibited his vision the remainder of the season, causing him to finish at .381. DiMaggio always insisted he would have topped .400 without the infection.

A tiny number of athletes from the distant past transcend time. I would cite Jim Brown in football, Oscar Robertson in basketball, and Joe DiMaggio in baseball.

Stronger pitching and tougher overall competition would serve to tamp down his stats, but there is no doubt that the Joe DiMaggio of 1936 to 1941 would be one of baseball's best players in 2014. "The Jolter" would, of course, have to adjust to the modern game.

A dead pull hitter in his day, DiMaggio would be forced to use the entire field in 2014. His miniscule strikeout totals would be impossible to maintain today. Yet, a modern DiMaggio would play in a home ballpark substantially better suited to his hitting style than the old layout of Yankee Stadium, which was death (valley) for right-handed power hitters.

From 1936 to 1941, DiMaggio hit .345. I'd guess that today's superior pitching would knock his average down to around .315 to .320. That would still make the Clipper one of the game's best hitters. In 2014, DiMaggio would average around 30 to 35 home runs per season. In contrast to the Yankee's "Murderer's

Row" style of the '30s, DiMaggio would steal many more bases today—20 to 30 per year, easily.

In addition to his offense, a modern DiMaggio would be one of baseball's premier center fielders, combining range, a rifle arm, instincts, and his uncanny fly ball "radar" to be a Gold Glove defender.

Major League Baseball has changed dramatically in the past seventy-five years. Today's players and pitchers are far superior to pre-war players and only a small percentage of pre-1947 big leaguers had the size and tools necessary to play today.

Of course, there is one notable exception to this fact:

Joe DiMaggio could play. Anytime.

21

Moneybull

IN 2002, THE Oakland A's conducted the worst draft of any ball club in Major League Baseball history.

Passionate and casual followers of baseball are instantly aware that the A's draft in 2002 was intimately detailed in Michael Lewis's *New York Times* bestselling book, *Moneyball.*

From my perspective, *Moneyball* the book is silly idol worship. As a film, I positively loved it. (Several of my scout pals were in the picture.)

If Michael Lewis—or any writer—wanted to write a book about how scouting and drafting should truly be conducted, they should study the current A's, not the 2002 version.

Billy Beane is a superlative GM and Erik Kubota has established a solid track record of success as a scouting director. The current A's scouting staff is one of the best in the business. Oakland's ability to draft and develop players stands as an industry model.

Never forget that within the baseball industry, winning is the only thing that matters. General managers or scouting directors can be singular trailblazers, but the question those within baseball *always* ask is: "Have they won anything?" (Translation: Have they won a World Series?)

Under Beane, the A's have never won a World Series. In fact, Oakland under Beane has never won an American League pennant, meaning they have never even appeared in a World Series. I can hear and see the apologists screaming as they leap to their feet in indignation.

I have this to say to them: Can it, guys. You can provide only excuses, not reasons. In 2002, the year *Moneyball* is set, the Los Angeles Angels won the World Series. The Halos that season were as far from being a sabermetric/Moneyball type organization as is humanly possible. Their '02 payroll was 16 out of 30 in the MLB at a little over 60 million, which was lower than the league average (a little under 70 million).

Yet there is no denying the A's are one of modern baseball's preeminent franchises in terms of on field results. Of the 30 Major League Baseball teams, I enjoy watching the A's pitching staff more than any other. Oakland's hurlers display simple, clean mechanics and can throw any pitch for a strike in any situation with late movement. A's pitchers work quickly, hammer the strike zone, avoid interminable 40-pitch innings, and—most importantly—don't try to miss bats; they try to miss the *center* of bats.

The train wreck that was the A's 2002 draft was presaged by a free agent signing the previous year. Paul DePodesta, then Oakland's director of research and development, identified an undrafted college pitcher named David Beck, nicknamed "The Creature."

Beck was a "soft tosser," a lefty with a puny 84 mph fastball. DePodesta's research revealed that Beck's college statistics were phenomenal and urged the A's to sign the youngster, despite his subpar velocity.

Assigned to the lowest level of organized pro ball—the Rookie level Arizona League—Beck was a dominant closer in 2001. *Moneyball* makes no mention of the fact that when moved up to higher levels in 2001 and 2002, Beck was a bust.

He left baseball after a posting a 12.15 ERA at Modesto of the Cal League in 2002.

Lewis boasts, "The Creature was the first thing to come out of Paul's computer that the A's scouting department signed. There were about to be a lot more. The 2002 draft was to be the first science experiment Billy Beane performed upon amateur players."

Chapter 5 of *Moneyball* describes the A's 2002 draft, and is titled "The Jeremy Brown Blue Plate Special."

In reading and rereading that chapter, it's clear that the A's selections are based completely on information and direction provided by DePodesta and the massive volume of stats in his trusty computer. DePodesta, after a very short stint as the Dodgers GM, is now a VP for the New York Mets.

In *Moneyball*, before the 2002 draft commenced, Lewis writes that ". . . the A's will pursue players in whom no one else has seen the greatness."

That's because there was no greatness to be seen.

Filled with hubris, armed with computer generated stats, and adding his own unique analysis, DePodesta then led the A's 2002 draft smack into organized baseball's version of an iceberg off the coast of Newfoundland.

Lewis solemnly informs us that prior to the draft, "The A's front office has a list, never formally written out, of the twenty players they would draft in a perfect world." Lewis then proceeds to formally write the list out.

These were the twenty players on that list, according to Lewis:

<u>Pitchers</u>:

Jeremy Guthrie	Ben Fritz
Joe Blanton	Robert Brownlie
Jeff Francis	Stephen Obenchain
Luke Hagerty	Bill Murphy

Not on the A's list, but available in the 2002 draft, were these pitchers:

Zack Greinke	Jon Lester
Cole Hamels	Scott Kazmir
Matt Cain	Josh Johnson

Oakland's list had twelve hitters:

Nick Swisher	Steve Stanley
Russ Adams	John Baker
Khalil Greene	Mark Kiger
John McCurdy	Brian Stavisky
Mark Teahen	Shaun Larkin
Jeremy Brown	Brant Colamarino

Oakland omitted these hitters from their list:

Prince Fielder	Denard Span
Joey Votto	B J Upton
Curtis Granderson	James Loney
Brian McCann	

Lewis makes this bold proclamation after the A's 2002 draft had concluded: "They had drafted *ballplayers*."

Is that so? Well, let's take a look at those "ballplayers.' Swisher is an obvious success and a player many teams desired prior to the 2002 draft, according to *Moneyball*.

After the slam dunk Swisher pick, Lewis lays the hokum on extra thick and adoringly writes: "Billy is now on his feet. He's got Swisher in the bag: who else can he get? There's a new thrust about him, an unabridged expression on his face. He was a bond trader who had made a killing in the morning and entered the afternoon free of fear. Feeling greedy. Certain that the fear in the market would present him with even more opportunities to exploit."

Beane's intensity is admirable; however, the A's remaining picks in the first 7 rounds in 2002 constituted a nearly complete debacle:

1st round, 24th overall: Joe Blanton, RHP. On August 13, 2013, Blanton was the proud owner of a 2-13 won-lost record and a 5.52 ERA. According to *Moneyball,* the A's firmly believed that Blanton was "the second best right-handed pitcher in the draft." Cain—taken next by the Giants with the 25th pick—was in this draft along with Greinke and Josh Johnson.

1-26: John McCurdy, SS. Quoting *Moneyball:* "Billy thought McCurdy might be the next Jeff Kent." McCurdy never played in the major leagues.

1-30: Ben Fritz, RHP. From *Moneyball:* "Third best right-handed pitcher in the draft, in the opinion of Paul DePodesta's computer." Fritz never played in the big leagues. Neither did the computer.

1-35: Jeremy Brown, C. A grand total of 5 big league games. Joey Votto was available at this point.

Chapter 5 of *Moneyball* makes Jeremy Brown into more than just a ballplayer; he is a symbol. A symbol, supposedly, of how Paul DePodesta and the A's used statistical analysis to identify skills other organizations were oblivious to. In reality, the other clubs were not unaware of those talents; they simply understood that in Brown's case—and in the case of most early 2002 A's draftees—those skills simply didn't exist.

Moneyball ends with an elaborate description of a home run hit by Brown in an Instructional League game in the fall of 2002. Brown blasts a long drive to left which clears the fence for a home run. Thinking the ball will stay in the park, Brown races toward second base and suddenly falls flat on his face—a perfect metaphor for the A's 2002 draft.

1-37: Stephen Obenchain, RHP. Never pitched in the majors.

Votto is still on the board.

1-39: Mark Teahen, 3B. Solid but not spectacular player who spent 7 years in the majors. Votto is still available, as is Granderson.

2-67: Steve Stanley, OF. Diminutive OF, never played in majors. A's still pass on Granderson.

3-98: Bill Murphy, LHP. Played tiny bits of 2 seasons in majors.

4-128: John Baker, C. Still active, a serviceable backup catcher.

5-158: Mark Kiger, SS. Two major league games.

6-188: Brain Stavisky, OF. Did not play in majors.

7-218: Brant Colamarino, 1B. Never played in majors.

Paul DePodesta is quoted in *Moneyball* stating "...Colamarino might be the best hitter in the country."

Really? The 2002 draft featured Joey Votto and Prince Fielder yet DePodesta asserts that Colamarino was the best hitter in the country?

Let us pick apart yet another ridiculous claim from *Moneyball*. Pens Lewis, "Billy's so excited he doesn't even bother to say how foolish it is to take a high school pitcher with a first round pick."

High school pitchers selected in the first round of the 2002 draft included Zack Greinke, Scott Kazmir, Cole Hamels and

Matt Cain. All have enjoyed substantially better careers than Joe Blanton. In 2006, the Dodgers picked a high school pitcher with the 7th overall choice in the first round. His name is Clayton Kershaw. Nothing foolish about that pick.

Elevating his idol worship to hilarious levels, Lewis writes: "Billy and Paul no longer think of the draft as a crapshoot. They are a pair of card counters at the blackjack tables; they think they've found a way to turn the odds inside the casino against the owner. They think they can take over the casino."

You'll need an airsickness bag for this next *Moneyball* snippet: "It was as if a signal had radiated out from the Oakland A's draft room and sought, laserlike, those guys who for their whole career had seen their accomplishments understood with an asterisk."

It gets worse. "Billy Beane was a human arsenal built, inadvertently, by professional baseball to attack its customs and rituals."

Hyped by Lewis's worshipful prose, readers of *Moneyball* were duped into believing that the A's 2002 draft was a revolutionary success. In fact, as proven in this chapter, it was a near total disaster.

Naturally, the question is: Why? The answer may be found in this quote from Paul DePodesta, buried in Chapter 5 of *Moneyball*: "You know what gets me excited about a guy? I get excited about a guy when he has something about him that causes everyone else to overlook him and I know it is something that just doesn't matter."

Dead wrong.

Tools matter. Ability matters. "Makeup" matters. The secret to determining if an amateur player will be a successful pro lies not solely in a computer, as DePodesta believed in 2002. Oakland—to their vast credit—now understands the shortcomings of the approach they took in the 2002 draft and have adjusted accordingly and successfully.

A few years ago I had a protracted discussion with a scout who is a National Crosschecker for his ballclub. His philosophy was simple and direct: In order to have a successful draft, *all* relevant information must be compiled on a prospect.

Height, weight, body type, arm strength, running speed, hitting ability, age. Medical history, vision test results, family background. Psych tests, makeup, character, computer generated statistics. All of these factors, and more, must be assembled and considered when evaluating a prospect in preparation for the draft.

The Crosschecker contended that disregarding or ignoring important facts by claiming they "just don't matter" is a woefully misguided idea. Placing singular emphasis on one information outlet, such as computer generated stats, would inevitably lead to a draft day fiasco.

A fiasco similar to the Oakland A's draft in 2002.

22

Saber-Toothed

M AJOR LEAGUE BASEBALL is currently experiencing the era of Sabermetrics.

Depending on your viewpoint, this is an era we are collectively suffering through in excruciating agony or a Golden Era to be exalted. I will say that the Sabermetric Era certainly beats the proverbial crap out of the recently completed Steroid Era, the lingering effects of which persist. (See Ryan Braun and Alex Rodriguez.)

Bill James began the Saber revolution over thirty years ago. James is a towering Rasputin-looking character who, depending on your perspective, has either re-invented baseball or ruined it. A commendably prodigious writer throughout his four decade career, James has recently published books which contain no text or prose but instead are packed with columns and columns of statistics. The excitement is bearable.

But, as much as I dread having to admit it, Bill James is a genius. Smatterings of his ideas are silly and many of his formulas are harder to decipher than the Voynich Manuscript, but none of this detracts from the fact that the majority of his insights are spot on. Even people who wish that he would stick to writing crime/mystery novels confess that James has revolutionized baseball: how we see the game, how we evaluate teams and players, how the media covers the sport.

Bill James, like every other baseball prognosticator, will occasionally be dead wrong. I recall a TV interview James did with Roy Firestone prior to the 1988 season, in which the Bill-ster ripped the Dodgers for acquiring Kirk Gibson. Gibson that season was the NL MVP, leading the Dodgers to the World Championship by clouting one of the most dramatic home runs in baseball history in Game One of that season's World Series.

Okay, so James blew that one. No problem, comes with the territory. Anyone in the prediction business will look foolish occasionally, like Fox News after the 2012 Presidential Election. To his everlasting credit, and unlike most baseball analysts, James is right five times for every time he is wrong. That's a much better percentage than most baseball pundits.

Now, I am not going into a lengthy explanation of sabermetrics. When I sat down to write this book, I pledged to myself that it would NOT be a Saber volume in any way, shape, or form. What I am going to discuss are a series of issues within baseball that arise from the current saber-obsession.

First, permit me to state my own views on this subject, from my perspective as a scout. Sabermetrics are vitally important when evaluating baseball players who are already professionals— major or minor leaguers. They are moderately helpful in evaluating players participating at the Division One college level.

At any level below the D-1 level, I feel that sabermetrics are useless. This would include D-2, D-3, NAIA, junior college, or high school baseball. In my view, sabermetrics are useless at the latter levels because the general inferiority of the competition renders the statistical sample irrelevant.

Sabermetrics should never be the primary tool for player evaluation. Observation and analysis by an experienced, trained scout should always be the foremost method of player assessment. As a secondary and supplemental evaluation tool, sabermetrics are critically important and an extremely valuable necessity.

For support of my view, I turn to none other than Branch Rickey. Not only was Rickey a visionary in baseball's integration, he paid close attention to statistics and understood their inherent value. He was far ahead of his time in this respect.

Rickey wrote an article which appeared in the August 2, 1954, issue of *Life* magazine. In that piece, Rickey pointed out distinct shortcomings in then commonly held assumptions regarding baseball statistics. In reading his piece, one may even conclude that Rickey was the father of sabermetrics, a title I am certain he would angrily scoff at if he were alive today.

Unlike many modern saber geeks, however, Rickey sagely understood the "big picture." Wrote Rickey: "Statistics, of course, cannot tell the whole story. They fall short of bridging the gap between human expectancy and fulfillment. They cannot measure such intangibles as intelligence, courage, disposition and effort."

Spurred by the colossal popularity of *Moneyball* ten years ago, the stats avalanche descended on baseball and has influenced every aspect of the pro game. With the sole exception of the advent of the amateur draft in 1965, nothing in baseball history has had a more profound impact on scouting than the saber revolution.

Ten years ago, old-school scouts despised the new wave. Many still do. I'll never forget hearing a veteran scout, loudly and profanely, blast the saber geeks: "No twelve-year-old Ivy League punk who never wore a jockstrap or played a ballgame in his life is not going to tell me how to do my job!" In 2003, that opinion was the rule—not the exception—among older scouts.

Today, both sides (traditional and saber) co-exist, sometimes uneasily. Every major league organization has an analytics guru, and several have an entire department dedicated to statistical interpretation. The open animosity present ten years ago has dissipated into a grudging, if reluctant, acceptance.

Ball clubs may tilt in one direction or the other, but every team today evaluates players utilizing a blend of traditional scouting (frame, tools, instincts, mechanics) with saber analysis (detailed study of in-game production). After a decade of often open hostility, the two camps have come to understand the importance and necessity of both approaches.

Understand that many scouts hired post-*Moneyball* would have had absolutely no chance of being hired as a scout pre-*Moneyball*. A steady stream of new scout hires have little to no experience in terms of baseball playing, scouting, or player development, but are instead eager Ivy League graduates frequently in possession of some sort of statistics or mathematics degree.

Prior to 2002, anyone who submitted such a resume would have been laughed out of baseball or had their application denied, rejected, ignored, or simply crumpled up and thrown in a trash bin. Scouting has changed drastically in the past decade and now Ivy/Saber scouts sit, stopwatch to stopwatch and radar gun to radar gun, in the crowd alongside "old-schoolers."

Not everyone is comfortable with the modern reality. A friend of mine recently inquired about an area scout job opening. He was told by the cross checker handling the hiring that the organization had decided to hire a twenty-three-year-old college grad with no baseball or scouting experience.

In recounting the conversation, my friend relayed his powerful impression that the cross checker was severely disappointed in the organization's decision and direction but was helpless to do anything.

To me, sabermetrics are like colonoscopies. Just because they are crucial, important and necessary does not mean I have to enjoy them. I find most saber stats and almost all discussions of saber stats to be as exciting as hospital Jell-O.

Approximately 27 million saber stat experts are now plying their trade on TV, publications, and the Internet, dabbling in major league analysis or fantasy league silliness. Some are legitimate, qualified experts who provide useful and important information.

Many others are crazy goofballs who remind me of this passage in the Beatle's song "Nowhere Man":

If I spoke prose you'd soon find out,
I don't know what I talk about.

However, there is one saber stat which I contend is "way cool": WAR. To the uninitiated, this acronym stands for Wins Above Replacement. I have yet to find anyone who can explain precisely how WAR is tabulated, but essentially it determines a player's overall value.

Hitters who produce flashy, Vegas-neon bright numbers but can't run, field, or throw get decimated by WAR; guys who do everything well across the board are amply rewarded.

For example, in the fifties and sixties, a brilliant all-around player such as my idol, Willie Mays, had an astronomic WAR score; a Dick Stuart, not so much.

Today, my favorite current big leaguer, Mike Trout, posts startling WAR scores; Adam Dunn does not.

Among saber dorks, WAR is the "Holy Grail," the most important factor in determining a player's true value. Keep in mind the rather amusing fact that Major League Baseball does not recognize WAR as an official statistic. Bud Selig has a hard enough time remembering what year it is; trying to explain WAR to the commissioner would be, in all probability, fruitless.

Efforts at one-upmanship are common in the arcane world of sabermetrics. Take FIP. I'm certain you are thrilled to know that this acronym stands for Fielding Independent Pitching. FIP is an attempt by sabermetricians to analyze pitchers without the interference of pesky variables like infielders or outfielders.

Not satisfied with FIP, another saber type invented XFIP. Like the newest brand of laundry detergent, XFIP proponents tout their algorithm as new, improved, and better than the original. And with a handy no-drip easy-pour spout!

According to fangraphs.com, here is the formula for XFIP:

XFIP= ((13* (flyballs* league-average HR/FB rate)) + (3* (BB+HBP))-(2*K))/IP + constant.

Simple as Pi, right? Not quite. Not satisfied with FIP or XFIP, another saber geek has invented SIERA—Skill Interactive ERA. According to its inventor, SIERA "attempts to more accurately model what makes a pitcher successful." In the human world that would usually refer to getting guys out and winning games. But, no, of course not!

Sabers love to invent new formulas. Naturally, a new formula must have a snazzy acronym. PECOTA stands for Player Empirical Comparison and Optimization Test Algorithm. Well, alrighty then. Many would assume the acronym DIPS describes sabermetricians themselves, but it actually refers to Defense Independent Pitching Statistics. Okey Dokey.

Historical reinvention is also a favorite pastime of saber nerds. As an example, let's examine the 1958 AL MVP vote. Jackie Jensen of the Red Sox beat out Mickey Mantle of the Yankees to win the award that season. Fifty-five years later, sabers are outraged.

Mantle, they point out, had more walks, a higher slugging percentage, a higher on-base percentage, and a higher OPS. The Mick's WAR in 1958 was 8.7. Jensen drove in 122 runs to Mickey's 97 (RBIs are meaningless in the saber world), but Jackie's WAR was only 4.9.

By today's standards, Mantle should have won. (He finished fifth in the voting.) By the standards of 1958, when RBIs were of primary importance and sabers stats did not exist, Jensen should have—and did—win. Sabers around the globe are outraged by this result, insisting the voters fifty-five years ago were uninformed if not insane.

Modern sabers don't understand or comprehend this fact: There was one standard in existence in 1958. In 2013, fifty-five years later, there is another standard. Fifty-five years from now, there will be yet another standard. In 2068, baseball statistics experts will reflect upon the judgments of sabers today and state, "What in the hell were these guys thinking? What a bunch of idiots!"

For all the undeniable value of sabermetrics, saber proponents can on occasion go to ridiculous, almost absurd, extremes to support their arguments. Here is a sampling of the most egregious offenses:

Recently I perused an article discussing 2013 NL and AL CY Young award candidates.

The author, an unabashed saber enthusiast, referred to a stat he named BABIP: Batting Average on Balls in Play. (Shame on those who interpret a ribald double entendre in that phrase!) The logical flip side of BABIP, I would assume, would be BABNIP— Batting Average on Balls Not In Play. I am certainly no saber stats expert, but my guess is that a hitter's Batting Average on Balls Not Put in Play will not be particularly high.

A scout who is a close friend of mine went to lunch several years ago with an acquaintance who was another organization's "stat guy." The discussion centered on Ken Griffey Jr., who had recently retired. My scout pal expressed his opinion that Griffey Jr. was one of the greatest all-around players of all time. The saber guy politely disagreed, saying, "Our saber analysis shows that Griffey Jr. was not a good defensive outfielder!"

Prior to a Justin Verlander pitching outing in 2006, several officials representing the ballclub Verlander was facing that night drove to the ballpark together. One of the officials was the team's saber stats expert. He knew Verlander's stats upside down, inside and out, but had never seen the Tiger star pitch. Asked the saber guy, ". . . Is Verlander a right-hander or a left-hander?"

Keith Law of ESPN is a baseball expert who I have a terrific amount of respect for. I refer to him as "Jimmy Neutron, Boy Genius." Law graduated from Harvard but appears to shop for clothes at the 50 percent discount table at Walmart.

Clint Frazier, a high school outfielder from Georgia, was the 5th overall pick in the 2013 draft. He was quoted saying of Law, "I don't like that guy." I find that a bit odd. Normally you have to meet Law first, then you'll decide you don't like him. Kidding!

On a cable TV panel show, Law claimed that the two recent World Series titles won by the St. Louis Cardinals (2006 and 2011) were the result of the Redbirds adherence to sabermetric principles.

True, the Cards are a saber organization and are an industry model of drafting, development, and big league results. However, they won the 2011 World Series because Ranger right fielder Nelson Cruz nonchalantly misplayed a drive by David Freese that should have been caught. With all proper deference to Law (he's the hardest working guy in the 'bidness), saber stats had nothing to do with Cruz's gaffe.

Eric Wedge, former manager of the Seattle Mariners, can tell you that Hell has no fury like saber nerds scorned. In 2013, Wedge had the audacity to criticize sabermetrics.

Dustin Ackley, a second baseman for the Mariners who had been the 2nd overall pick in the 2009 draft, was demoted to the minor leagues. The move was entirely justified, since Ackley was vastly underperforming.

Wedge reacted to the youngster's demotion by stating: "It's the new generation. It's all this sabermetrics stuff, for lack of a better term, you know what I mean? People who haven't played since they were nine years old think they have it figured out. It gets in these kids' heads."

Saber geeks from all corners of the galaxy descended on Wedge like crazed Scientologists. Blogs penned in vitriolic response were interminably long and tedious with predictable reactions. To paraphrase a few: Wedge has played and managed in professional baseball—what does he know! We sabermetricians have won the debate, we own the game! Wedge isn't a slave to sabermetrics, therefore he should be fired!

My retort to the saber mafia is this: Why should Wedge be fired? He was right!

Excessive patience by a hitter (saber approach) can often cause a player to get stuck in "pitcher's" counts, or to take pitches that are eminently hittable. Aggressiveness (traditional approach) in hyper form causes a hitter to chase balls out of the strike zone or to swing at pitches he has no reasonable chance of squaring up.

Wedge did not state his point eloquently, but he was absolutely right. *Any* approach, sabermetric or traditional, can be detrimental to a hitter if taken to an extreme.

Brian Kenny is a pleasant, earnest fellow with bushy, porcupine quill hair who hosts a saber show on the MLB Network. A joke circulating on the 2013 MLB Home Run Derby telecast insisted Kenny believes that the optimal result of any plate appearance is a walk.

Why, of course! Just think of how many iconic moments in baseball history would have been improved with a walk instead of a home run:

Babe Ruth's Called Walk. Bobby Thomson's Walk Heard 'Round the World. World Series game-winning walks by Bill Mazeroski, Carlton Fisk, Kirk Gibson, and Joe Carter.

Strike zone discipline and pitch selectivity are critical components of successful hitting, but in almost every plate appearance, the goal is to attack a pitch the batter feels is hittable. Baseball is (supposedly) an action sport. I say swing the bat, attack a hittable pitch. Walks and on-base percentage were the original foundation of sabermetrics, but I feel sabers place far too much emphasis on walks. Much more damage can be done offensively with a base hit instead of a walk, plus a hell of a lot more excitement ensues.

After the 2012 season, Kenny insisted that Miguel Cabrera's AL Triple Crown was "nonsense." His reasoning? Some gibberish about infantrymen running into artillery fire in the Civil War. Kenny preferred Mike Trout over Cabrera in his 2012 AL MVP vote, because of Trout's superior WAR rating. Kenny's view is a perfectly reasonable opinion, but Cabrera won the vote, throwing sabers nationwide into a hissy fit.

Kenny's stance on this matter, a common one in saber circles, presents a fascinating potential dilemma. This is a scenario I foresee happening in the near future, one which will likely place sabers in straightjackets: Let's assume an outfielder leads his league with a 10.5 WAR, far above his peers. His team, however, has a losing record. Let's go further and say he plays for a last place, 65-win type ballclub.

The next leading MVP candidate plays for a division winning team, in fact, let's say his club wins 98 games, best in baseball that season. This player's WAR is 5.0, less than half his main competitor.

Okay all you saber experts out there, who gets your MVP vote in this circumstance? Please explain why!

Personally, I can only watch about thirty seconds of saber blather before having to fight the urge to jump out a window. In the scant time I do watch, it seems to me that these saber enthu-siasts are oblivious to the fact that former players and managers know ten times more about real baseball than they do. I mean, it's one thing to look at a computer and make a decision, but if you've been in the batter's box or on the pitching mound, you know that stuff goes right out the window when the ump yells "Play Ball!"

Which brings up an enormously important point. There is abstract baseball knowledge (saber guys) and actual baseball knowledge (players and ex-players). I am often convinced that many saber freaks have no idea how the game is actually played, or how players think.

A few years ago, I was reading a saber discussion focusing on pitching. The author, a saber expert, claimed that wins are not a credible method of evaluating starting pitchers.

That may well be true in saber-alternate-bizarro world, but in real baseball, it's nonsense. Ask any major league starting pitcher if he would rather win a game in which he pitches poorly and surrenders five or six runs, or lose a game in which he pitches well, allowing only one or two runs.

Every single big league starter will tell you he would rather win the five to six run game than lose the one to two run game. Of course, saber types will counter, saying a hurler will not win many games in which he gives up that many runs. That's true, but completely beside the point.

A major league starting pitcher's job is to win that game on that day, no matter how it develops—low scoring, medium scoring, high scoring. What has happened in the past or what may happen in the future is of no consequence. His job is to win *today*.

I can guarantee you that any pitcher who would rather pitch well and lose than pitch poorly and win on one specific day will be traded off that ball club immediately by his general manager.

Here's another example, gleaned from a conversation I once had with a saber/fantasy league type.

Let's say a big league game is tied, 2–2, going into the top of the seventh. The leadoff hitter doubles. In almost every circumstance, the goal of the next hitter is to drive a ground ball to the right side of the diamond. If the hitter does not get a hit, he has at least "given himself up," and has moved the runner from second to third.

If the runner remains at second with one out, he can score only via a base hit. Having been advanced to third with less than two outs, the runner can score via a hit or in a variety of other ways: wild pitch, passed ball, safety squeeze, suicide squeeze, balk, error, sac fly, infield grounder, steal of home, etc.

From a saber standpoint, the hitter moving the runner along gets massacred. He has made an out and has not gotten on base. Metrics nerds prefer a walk in this situation, but a walk does not move the runner or make it easier for him to score. Also, with runners now on first and second, the chances of a rally killing double play increase drastically.

From a player's standpoint, the hitter who gives himself up and moves the runner along has made absolutely the right move and will get heartily congratulated in the dugout by his teammates.

If he has failed to move the runner along, once the hitter reaches the dugout no one will congratulate him; in all likelihood no teammate will even make eye contact.

Saber types, take note: That is how ballplayers think and how the game is actually played. Pros play to *win*. Numbers—of any type—are secondary.

The following imaginary scenario contains one of my favorite saber conundrums:

Let's postulate that in a three-year span, one specific big league hitter has been consistently productive. At the beginning of the fourth year, he is physically healthy but in a bad slump.

Saber droids will instantly pounce: he needs to draw more walks, improve his on-base percentage, increase his slugging percentage, boost his WAR. Fine.

But herein lies the dilemma: The player is not an idiot. He *knows* he is struggling. Down to the last micro numerical detail, sabers can describe how a hitter is slumping. This is of absolutely no help in solving the hitter's problems.

Every statistic in baseball is accumulated through some sort of physical action: swinging, running, throwing, fielding. A trained eye is required to recognize a physical fundamental or mechanical flaw and subsequently implement a plan to correct it.

Player development experts and scouts can detect a slight pull of the head, a hitch in the hands, a poor weight shift or an early opening of the hips or shoulder when observing a hitter at the ballpark, or by what is known in the industry as "breaking down" video.

The majority of sabers I have interacted with are clueless as to why a hitter is slumping or what physical and mechanical remedies are necessary to pull the hitter out of it. The latter fact is cheery good news for scouts and player development personnel. Despite the relentless onslaught of saber types into the profession, this guarantees that many scouting and development jobs will be safe well into the future.

In 2012 and 2013, I have gotten a perverse, giddy delight in watching sabermetricians attempt to explain the recent success of the Baltimore Orioles. Despite scoring shockingly low in many saber categories, the Birds won 93 games and qualified for the postseason in '12. The following year, Baltimore enjoyed a winning season but came up just short of qualifying for October. Number crunchers across the nation are stupefied, many turning blue in the face whilst they slap themselves silly. But . . . but . . . but . . . our data shows that the Orioles should be losers! The reason they win is . . . luck!

Wrong. A ball club can win one game by luck. Winning 93 games is not luck.

Sabermetricians are endlessly annoyed by clubs like the Orioles. Sabers delude themselves by believing their numbers explain *everything* about baseball, yet they can't completely explain Baltimore's recent success. Luck should never be a factor in mathematics or sabermetrics, correct?

Failures of saber clubs in the postseason also rattle sabermetricians. If a saber favorite loses in the postseason (like the Rays or A's, for example), sabers immediately discount the result, claiming that the postseason is a "crapshoot" and not a rejection of their ideas.

The Orioles success, as well as the failure of some saber clubs in the postseason, presents a fascinating conundrum to traditionalists and sabermetricians:

Is it possible that sabermetrics has holes, that it can't explain everything?

Hmmm. I believe so. Geometry, for example, has been around for thousands of years. Sabermetrics is a new discipline, in existence for only about thirty years. Because it is in such an embryonic state, sabermetrics is not fully formed. That means sabermetrics has holes and is far from being a finished field of study.

To sabermetricians, Ben Zobrist of the Tampa Bay Rays is a deity. In 2012, Zobrist's WAR was 5.7; in 2013, it was 4.8. The WAR posted by Adam Jones in those two years was 3.8 and 4.1; WAR posted by Bryce Harper was 5.1 and 3.5. Does anyone in their right mind truly believe that Ben Zobrist is a better player than Adam Jones or Bryce Harper? No way. My guess is, in a moment of candor, Zobrist himself would concede that he is not as good a ballplayer as Jones or Harper. For me, this is just one instance of how sabermetrics, is, let's say, "doughy."

Without hesitation, I concede the vital importance of sabermetrics in understanding and analyzing modern professional baseball. What I am unable to comprehend is why any baseball fan would cite sabermetrics as the foundation of his interest in the game, or the primary source of his love of the sport? To me, it's absolutely baffling.

Speaking for myself and I'm certain for millions of fans, baseball is not about computers, calculators, or sabermetric formulas.

For me, this is what baseball is all about: It's about the buzz of activity around the cage during batting practice. It's about watching the starting pitcher warm up and hearing the sharp echo of his fastball as it pounds the catcher's mitt. It's about eating a couple of hot dogs on a balmy summer night and singing along to the National Anthem and "Take Me Out to the Ballgame."

It's about the startling artistry of a great catch, the choreography of an expertly turned double play. It's about the player introductions at the All Star Game, a tight pennant race or the suffocating pressure of a crucial postseason game.

It's about a perfect slider on the outside corner for strike three, a long drive into the bleachers as a cluster of fans reach for the ball. It's about runners whipping around the bases and a close play at the plate—here comes the throw, it's gonna be close, he slides—is he safe or out? It's about the unbearable tension of a one run lead with two outs and the bases loaded in the bottom of the ninth.

It's about the times with my dad when I saw Sandy Koufax, Willie Mays, and Mickey Mantle play in person. As a scout, it's about the first time I laid eyes on Yasiel Puig, Adam Jones, Troy Tulowitzki, or Mike Trout.

Most importantly, it's about the glow of fond memories shared with friends and the hopeful anticipation of better times in the future.

There is not one single sabermetric number, formula, or statistic that can come remotely close to matching any of those experiences.

Acknowledgments

M̲y first acknowledgment must go to my family. All my love and thanks to all members of the Perkin and Jorgensen families, living and deceased, who are scattered about in California, Texas, and Arizona.

Deepest thanks are also extended to my friends Reka Hallgato, Susan Alger, Silke Kindle, Kim Lundy, and the incomparable Herb Fields. Also, I must express my thanks to the staff of Silverado Senior Living in Redondo Beach, California.

No living being on earth combines beauty and personality as does Gretchen, my cat; she is completely oblivious to the fact that she has helped me endure the most difficult period of my life.

This book would not have been possible without the input and assistance of my scouting pals, including Anup Sinha, Rod Fridley, the legendary George Genovese, and my scouting mentor and confidant, the remarkable Phil Pote.

Special thanks to my editor at Skyhorse Publishing, Jason Katzman, who saw potential in this manuscript that other publishing houses did not.

I must also extend my deepest thanks to the game of base-ball. A special shout out is due my biggest baseball heroes: Sandy Koufax, Willie Mays, and Mickey Mantle from days of yore, as well as my favorite players of the modern game: Mike Trout, Troy Tulowitzki, Yasiel Puig, and Adam Jones.

Finally, my deepest love and affection to one Gabriela Hallgato—the world's most wonderful little girl—to whom this book is dedicated.

About the Author

D ave Perkin is a graduate of Long Beach State University. He resides in Redondo Beach, California. Prior to entering the baseball industry, Mr. Perkin was a Paralegal and Private Investigator in Southern California.

Beginning in 2000, Mr. Perkin has worked for the Los Angeles Dodgers, the New York Mets and *Baseball America*. Currently, Dave Perkin is the Major League Baseball Draft Analyst for SI.com, the website of *Sports Illustrated* Magazine.

His articles have appeared at SI.com, in *Baseball America* and in numerous publications and websites.

In 1969, using a wood bat, Dave Perkin became the first eleven-year-old to hit a home run in the history of the Lomita Little League.

In 2008, Perkin, using a metal bat, hit a batting practice home run during an event at Dodger Stadium in Los Angeles.

Five-Plus Tools is Dave Perkin's first book.